ICBP Monograph No. 2

Cover: Siamese Fireback *Lophura diardi,* a specialist lowland forest species, assessed in this publication as threatened (painting by Kamol Komolphalin)

British Library Cataloguing in Publication Data

Round, Philip D. (Philip David)
  Resident forest birds in Thailand
  1. Thailand. Forests. Birds
  I. Title II. International Council for Bird Preservation
  598.29593

ISBN 0–946888–13–2
ISSN 1012-6201

This publication was compiled while the author was working with the Association for the Conservation of Wildlife, Thailand. Present address of author: Center for Wildlife Research, Biology Department, Faculty of Science, Mahidol University, Rama 6 Road, Bangkok 10400, Thailand

Printed and bound by S-Print, Cambridge.

The Oriental Bird Club helped with the cost of publishing this report.

INTERNATIONAL COUNCIL FOR BIRD PRESERVATION

ICBP is the longest-established worldwide conservation organisation. Its primary aim is the protection of wild birds and their habitats as a contribution to the conservation of biological diversity. Founded in 1922, it is a federation of 330 member organisations in 100 countries. These organisations represent a total of over ten million members all over the world.

Central to the successful execution of ICBP's mission is its global network of scientists and conservationists specialising in bird protection. Its ability to gather and disseminate information, identify and enact priority projects, and promote and implement conservation measures is unparalleled. Today, ICBP's Conservation Programme includes some 100 projects throughout the world.

Birds are important indicators of a country's environmental health. ICBP provides expert advice to governments on bird conservation matters, management of nature reserves, and such issues as the control of trade in endangered species. Through interventions to governments on behalf of conservation issues ICBP can mobilise and bring to bear the force of international scientific opinion at the highest levels. Conferences and symposia by its specialist groups also attract worldwide attention to the plight of endangered birds.

ICBP maintains a comprehensive databank concerning the status of all the world's threatened birds and their habitats, from which the bird Red Data Books are prepared. A series of Technical Publications gives up-to-date and in-depth treatment to major bird conservation issues. This series of Monographs (of which the present volume is the second) provides comprehensive, up-to-date information on specific or regional issues relating to bird conservation.

ICBP, 32 Cambridge Road, Girton, Cambridge CB3 0PJ, UK.

UK Charity No. 286211

Wreathed Hornbill *Rhyticeros undulatus* (male and female). Widely distributed in Thailand, but assessed in this review as Vulnerable due to forest fragmentation and hunting. *Illustration by* Kamol Komolphalin

CONTENTS

ACKNOWLEDGEMENTS

This study would not have been possible without the full cooperation of the staff of the Royal Thai Forest Department. I am especially grateful to Mr Phairot Suvanakorn, former Director of the Wildlife Conservation Division and now Deputy Director-General of the RFD who, over the past eight years, has acted to facilitate my visits to a great many protected areas. Within the Wildlife Conservation Division, I should particularly like to thank Mr Boonlerd Angsirijinda, Mrs Suvimolmanee Dobias, Mr Jira Jintanugool, Mr Seub Nakhasathien, Mr Somtob Norapuckprutikorn, Mr Wichai Panjamanont, Mr Sunthorn Rongkupatanavich and Mr Suwat Singhapant, all of whom have assisted in various ways: with access to maps or reports, explaining points of law and commenting on wildlife trade or persecution and in arranging visits to wildlife sanctuaries.

In the National Parks Division, I was greatly assisted by Mr Seri Vejaboosakorn and Mr Withya Songkakul.

In the Forest Mapping and Remote Sensing Subdivision, I should like to thank Mr Manit Nayanetra, Mr Boonchana Klankamsorn, Mr Prasobchai Namlaputhra, Mr Thongchai, Mrs Jirawan Charuppat and Mr Suchin Khantisomboon. I am also very grateful to Mr Sompon Tanhan of the National Forest Land Management Division for drawing my attention to useful references.

I am grateful to Dr Tem Smitinand of the Forest Herbarium for providing information on the utilisation of forest tree products by rural peoples.

At the National Research Council, Bangkok, Mr Suvit Vibulsreth, Director of the Remote Sensing Division, and his staff kindly allowed me to examine satellite photographs. I also thank Dr Niphan Ratanaworobhan of the Ecological Research Division, Thailand Institute of Scientific and Technological Research for permission to examine bird specimens in the National Reference Collection. I am grateful to Mr Jarujin Nabhitabhata and Mr Nivesh Nadee of TISTR for drawing my attention to many significant bird records.

Mr Virach Chantrasmi of F. E. Zuellig (Bangkok) Ltd and Dr Jarupong Boonlong of the National Environment Board provided some useful information on pesticides. Mr Pisit na Patalung of Wildlife Fund Thailand provided information on the illicit trade in wild bird species.

Much of the information on which this publication is based was extracted from the reports of both Thai and visiting overseas birdwatchers and I am very grateful to all those observers who filed their records at the Association for the Conservation of Wildlife, Bangkok. I should particularly like to record my appreciation of the work carried out by four outstanding Thai forest birdwatchers who have provided a wealth of information: Mr Kamol Komolphalin, Mr Naris Phumpakapun, Ms Pilai Poonswad and Mr Uthai Treesucon.

For their encouragement and suggestions or for their companionship on field trips, I must thank my good friends Rauf Ali, Peter Alexander-Marrack, Warren Brockelman, Bob and Jang Dobias, Surapon Duangkhae, Roland Eve, Ben King, Kamol Komolphalin, David Melville, Jelle Scharringa, Uthai Treesucon and David Wells. Craig Robson and John Parr also collected additional bird distribution data, incorporated into this report at the last minute.

Ms Pilai Poonswad, Drs Rauf Ali, Warren Brockelman, Sompoad Srikosamatara and David Wells commented extensively on a draft of this publication. I am grateful to Dr Christoph Imboden, Director, ICBP, for providing the initial encouragement to undertake this summary.

I am indebted to Dr Boonsong Lekagul at whose kind invitation I came to Thailand to study birds. He and his family have unstintingly provided support and working facilities during the past eight years and have welcomed me into their home.

I thank Mrs Suimolmanee Dobias and Mrs Dararat Sirisingkarn for kindly assisting with production of this publication and Mr Kamol Komolphalin for supplying the illustrations and helping to prepare the maps. At ICBP, I should also like to thank Irene Hughes and Gina Pfaff for carrying out the necessary word-processing, Adam Gretton and Sue Wells for proof-reading and production, and Robin Anderson of Rand Services for so generously giving his time to help with the production of camera-ready copy.

This project was originally funded by the International Council for Bird Preservation and a draft report prepared in November 1985. The incorporation of additional data and partial revision of the manuscript took place while the author was supported by the World Wide Fund for Nature (WWF International, Project 3713, Development of a Monitoring System for Species, Habitats and Protected Areas in Thailand).

I should like to dedicate this publication to the officials and staff of Thailand's many national parks and wildlife sanctuaries, whose unstinting hospitality and assistance I have enjoyed. Underpaid and often poorly equipped, they are the custodians of Thailand's remaining wild places. Society has charged them with protecting forests and wildlife but has neglected to supply them with the means and mandate to carry out this task effectively. Facing armed poachers and illegal loggers, they do a difficult and sometimes dangerous job with little prospect of reward or recognition.

SUMMARY

The status of resident bird species in Thailand is reviewed both in relation to remaining forest cover and present conservation measures. It is concluded that at least 521 of the 595 species treated are already present in existing national parks or wildlife sanctuaries. The wide geographical coverage of nature reserves, the proportion of remaining forest which is protected and the large areas of many individual sites form a promising basis for future conservation efforts. Even so, there are many severe problems and no fewer than 106 landbirds, and waterbirds associated with forest, are thought to be at risk (status endangered, threatened, vulnerable or indeterminate), while a further six species, most of which are large waterbirds, are believed already to be extinct.

While forests of the submontane slopes throughout Thailand are well represented in the nature reserve network, forests of the extreme lowlands, particularly those in proximity to major watercourses, are under-represented. Most such areas have already been cleared or settled or, in a few cases, are at risk from hydro-electric or other developments. The problem is particularly severe in the rainforest biome of Peninsular Thailand where there may be no extensive forested lowland tracts left. Urgent action to identify the few remaining areas of high lowland species diversity and to incorporate them into the reserve network is needed.

The diversity of montane birds is highest in the North and in parts of the South-west, but most such areas between 900 m and 1,800 m, both inside and outside of nature reserves, continue to be under severe threat from populations of upland shifting cultivators.

Although there is still some 'slash-and-burn' encroachment around the margins of many reserves, illegal hunting may pose the most immediate threat to many larger birds, as existing wildlife protection legislation is not rigorously enforced. Recommendations for improved protection are made.

The establishment of additional parks or sanctuaries, particularly in the Malayan rainforest zone of the extreme south and in the mountains of the far north is recommended. This would provide nominal protection for at least 22 species which appear to be absent from existing nature reserves.

The majority of nature reserves have never received any biological survey. The establishment of an integrated programme for monitoring the status of both species and habitats, inside and outside of nature reserves is recommended.

INTRODUCTION

PREAMBLE

Thailand supports an extremely diverse fauna and flora. Situated in the Indo-Chinese peninsula of the Oriental region, the country has been described as a 'zoogeographic crossroads'. The country's avifauna comprises Sino-Himalayan, Indo-Burmese, Indo-Chinese and Sundaic elements to which may be added a large number of migrant visitors from the Palearctic region. Approximately 891 bird species have so far been recorded of which roughly 638 breed or formerly bred within the country. As a consequence of this great faunal mixing, there is a low level of endemism at the species level. Only two full species of bird, the White-eyed River-Martin *Pseudochelidon sirintarae* and Deignan's Babbler *Stachyris rodolphei* are known exclusively from Thailand although there are a number of 'near-endemics' whose ranges include the border regions of adjacent countries (e.g. Gurney's Pitta *Pitta gurneyi*) and many endemic subspecies.

The great majority of resident landbirds occur in association with forests. In Thailand, as in most other tropical developing countries, large scale deforestation is a relatively recent phenomenon which has greatly modified the landscape in only one or two human generations. The country was still an estimated 70–80 percent forested at the end of World War Two (B. Lekagul pers. comm.) but by the end of 1985, total forest cover was estimated at only 29 percent of the land area (Royal Forest Department 1986). Such figures, however, obtained primarily from satellite imagery, overstate the true extent of biologically significant forest cover and include large areas of degraded, open-canopy formations, secondary growth and scrub. Invariably, deforestation has not occurred evenly across the whole gamut of wooded habitats and some biotopes (e.g. forests of the flat lowlands) have suffered disproportionately. This has important implications for wildlife conservation.

Thailand has established a large network of protected areas under the administration of the Royal Forest Department. However, such nature reserves have mostly been established in an *ad hoc* fashion. Detailed bird species inventories are unavailable for most sites and there has never been any comprehensive assessment of the likely effectiveness of the present network in furthering specific conservation needs.

AIMS

This publication examines existing bird distribution data for Thailand in order to approach the following objectives:

- To identify the chief species assemblages within different habitats and geographical regions.

- To assess the present coverage of nature reserves and remaining forest with respect to the above.

- To identify those sites which, in terms of their species richness, are key areas for forest bird conservation in Thailand.

- To make recommendations for further survey work, the establishment of additional nature reserves or other improved conservation measures.

This analysis is confined to resident bird species and to those migrant species which breed in Thailand.

Paradise Flycatcher *Terpsiphone paradisi* (Kamol Komolphalin)

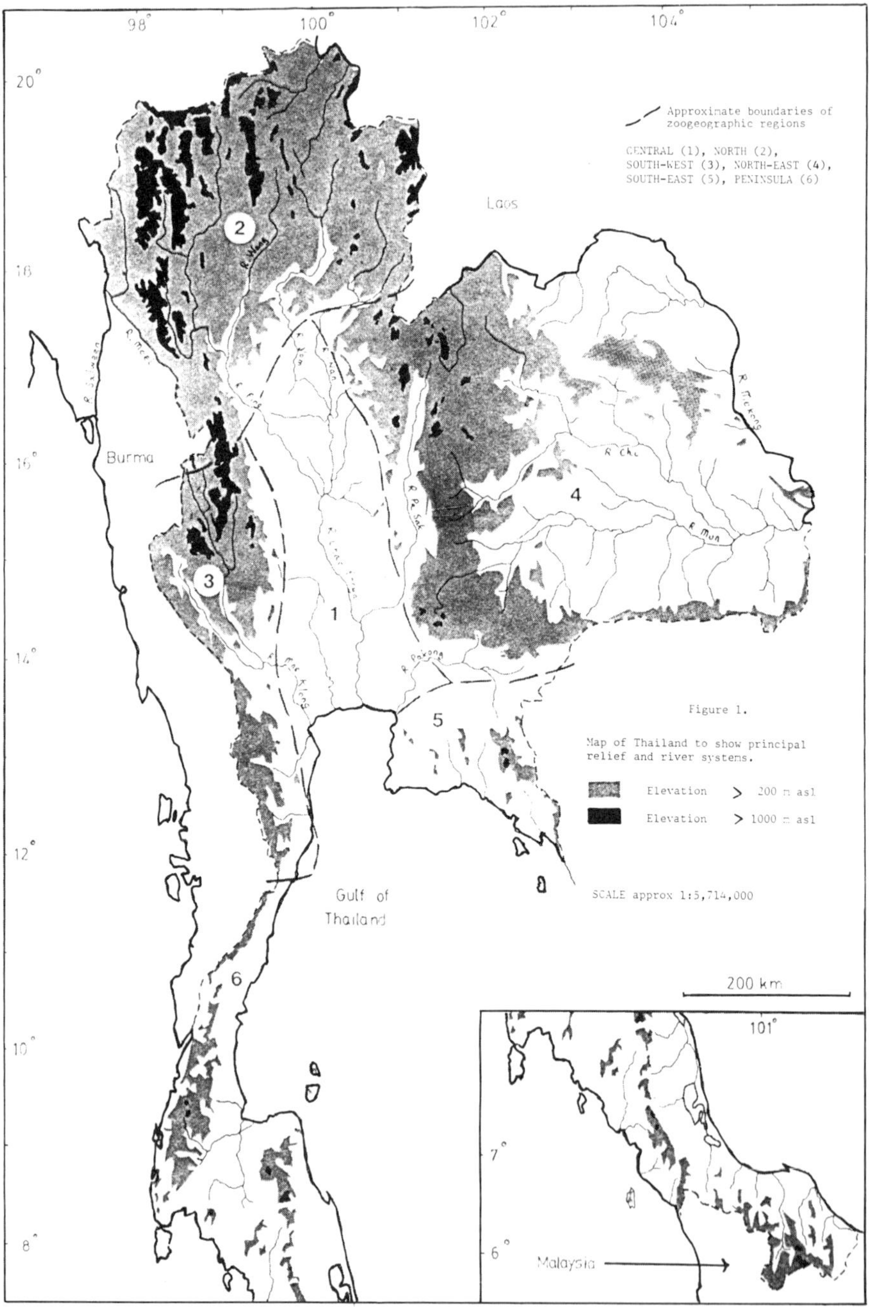

Figure 1: Map of Thailand showing principal relief and river systems.

GEOGRAPHY AND CLIMATE

PHYSIOGRAPHY

Thailand covers a land area of 513,517 sq km and extends between 5°37' and 20°30'N latitude and between 97°20' and 105°39'E longitude. The country may be divided into three geological provinces. The Central Plains, which extend to the coast around Bangkok, consist of a marshy, alluvial floodplain. The north, lying between the Mekong and Salween Rivers, is mainly mountainous and has a great many peaks over 1,500 m above sea level of which the highest, Doi Inthanon, rises to 2,590 m. The mountains and valleys are oriented north-south and the mountains extend further to form the backbone of the Malay Peninsula. Most of the north is drained by the Rivers Ping, Wang, Yom and Nan which flow south to join the Chao Phraya. Small areas of the extreme north and west are drained by the rivers Mekong and Salween respectively. The south-west is drained by the Mae Klong (Figure 1).

Almost the entire North-eastern region consists of a dry plateau (the Khorat Plateau). This is a region of poor soils derived from sands, clays and salt deposits, most of which is drained by the Mekong. The western and southern margins of the plateau are rimmed by the mountains of the Dong Phaya Yen and Phanom Dongrak ranges, which contain a number of flat-topped peaks of over 1,200 m elevation. In South-east Thailand, the isolated mountains of Khao Soi Dao rise in a westward extension of the Elephant and Cardamom Mountains of Kampuchea, to 1,670 m.

Throughout this report, the term 'Continental' has been used to describe the main body of the country, including the northern part of the peninsula. The term 'Peninsular Thailand' is used only to refer to those areas south of 12°N latitude, most of which lie within the Sunda faunal subregion.

CLIMATE

Thailand has a tropical monsoonal climate, with a pronounced dry season during November to April. Most of the rain falls from May to October, during the south-west monsoon although some parts of the Peninsula, together with the far South-east, also receive some rain during the north-east monsoon from November to January. In these regions, the average annual rainfall may exceed 3,000 mm although most of the country receives no more than 1,000–2,000 mm (Table 1).

The mean annual temperatures are relatively uniform, with the greatest fluctuation occurring in the North and North-east regions which are furthest removed from the sea and which have a generally higher elevation.

Table 1: Temperature and rainfall data for selected localities in the lowlands of Thailand, 1954–1975. (Modified from Lekagul and McNeely 1977, from data supplied by Department of Meteorology, Bangkok)

Region	Station	Annual temp. (deg. C)			Annual rainfall (mm.)			% during May-Oct.
		Max.	Min.	Mean	Max.	Min.	Mean	
North	Chiang Mai	41.5	6.0	25.8	2032	500	1268	89.1
	Nan	44.1	3.9	26.3	1997	710	1309	87.8
South-west	Kanchanaburi	43.5	5.5	27.8	1787	473	984	80.7
	Hua Hin	38.6	13.9	27.4	1792	627	1036	71.3
North-east	Udonthai	43.9	2.5	26.8	1998	929	1367	87.5
	Korat	43.4	4.9	27.1	2415	730	1197	81.8
South-east	Chanthaburi	40.8	8.9	27.2	4158	1739	3164	88.5
	Khlong Yai	36.2	13.0	26.9	6004	1938	4350	90.6
Peninsula	Ranong	38.0	13.7	26.5	5418	3471	4344	89.6
	Narathiwat	36.4	17.1	27.0	4015	1915	2644	41.2 *

* Provinces in the Malayan rainforest zone of the extreme southern Peninsula receive approximately 40 percent of their annual rainfall during the north-east monsoon, November to December.

VEGETATION

CLASSIFICATION

The great variation in topography and climate has led to the development of a complex mosaic of forest types in which the drier, more open deciduous formations in the most seasonal areas give way, with increasing rainfall, to a variety of semi-evergreen and evergreen facies, including evergreen rainforest. Mangrove forests also occur in saline, silt-rich coastal waters.

Forest types are classified in Table 2. For the most part, the various authors agree, though whereas Neal (1967) classifies the forest throughout the lowlands of Peninsular Thailand as 'tropical rainforest', Whitmore (1975) treats the forest throughout most of the Peninsula as 'semi-evergreen rainforest' and stresses the distinction between this, the Thai-Burmese floristic formation, and the Malayan floristic formation or 'evergreen rainforest' which is confined to the wettest, least seasonal areas in the extreme southernmost provinces, adjacent to Malaysia. In physical structure and appearance both forest types appear extremely similar, however, and this report follows Neal in treating all lowland forests of the Peninsula as 'rainforest'. For the ornithologist, this is the more convenient term since it serves to emphasise the distinction between the lowland forests of the Peninsula which support a relatively homogeneous Sundaic bird fauna and the semi-evergreen and dry evergreen forests of Continental Thailand where most lowland birds are of Indo-Chinese or Indo-Burmese affinity.

Evergreen forests

Tropical Rainforest. In Thailand, rainforest as defined above encompasses all the lowland terrestrial forest of the Peninsula and may be divided into two subtypes: the Thai type of rainforest, which formerly occupied most of Thailand south of 12°N latitude and the Malayan rainforest type which is confined to the provinces of Yala, Narathiwat and perhaps also southern Trang (Whitmore 1975). The distinction between these subtypes is mentioned in the Section 'Peninsular Region'. Small areas of rainforest are also recognised in the wettest areas of South-east Thailand, but these occur in a mosaic with semi-evergreen facies, with which they are included in this report.

Tropical rainforest shows pronounced stratification. A dense, continuous canopy is found at 20–25 m above the ground, above which scattered emergent trees may rise to 50–60 m in height. There is a middle storey of smaller trees and usually a further layer of yet smaller, woody saplings below this. The ground

Table 2: Classification of dry-land forest types in Thailand.

	FAO (1981)	Whitmore (1975)	Neal (1967)	Distribution		Annual rainfall (mm)	Characteristics
LOWLAND FORESTS	Open, broadleaved forest	Monsoon forest or savanna	Dry dipterocarp forest	north, west, north-east	plains-900 m	under 1,250	On shallow, lateritic soils. Deciduous; dominated by 1–2 spp. each of *Shorea*, *Dipterocarpus*. Low stature; grassy understorey.
	Decidous forest	Tropical moist deciduous	Mixed deciduous forest	north, west, north-east	plains-900 m	1,250-2,000	Richer, moister soils, mostly of plains lower hills. More species of tall trees than previous category; either *Tectona grandis* or *Lagerstroemia* sp. co-dominant. Often much bamboo; dense understorey.
	Tropical semi-evergreen	Tropical semi-evergreen (Thai-type). rainforest	Dry evergreen and semi-evergreen forest	north, west, north-east south-east	hill slopes up to 1,000 m	1,400-2,000	Some deciduous emergent trees; slightly lower stature than evergreen rainforest. Usually in moister situations than mixed deciduous, with which it often occurs in a mosaic.
			Tropical rain-forest	peninsula	plains and hill slopes to 1,000 m	over 2,000	Greater evergreen component than previous category. Thai floristic type characterised by White Meranti *Shorea* spp.
	Tropical wet evergreen	Evergreen (Malayan-type) rainforest		extreme southern peninsula only	plains-1,000 m	over 2,500	Tall (45 m+), dense forest in the least seasonal, "ever-wet" areas. Malayan floristic formation, characterised by Red Meranti group of *Shorea* species.
HILL FORESTS	Coniferous forest	Coniferous forest	Coniferous forest	north, north-east	400-1,400 m	1,000-1,500	Dominated by either *Pinus kesiya* or *P. merkusii*. Very restricted in extent and usually on drier ridges or on sandy soils. Usually in mixed stands together with dry dipterocarp or hill evergreen.
	Hill evergreen forest	Tropical lower montane forest	Hill evergreen forest	north, west, north-east, south-east, peninsula	900-2,590 m	over 2,000	Oaks, chestnuts (Fagaceae) dominate; structurally very varied, depending upon topography and elevation.

layer consists of forest floor herbs and small seedlings. The two lowest layers vary from being sparse to extremely dense, particularly where climbing palms (rattans) occur. Trees of the family Dipterocarpaceae predominate and lowland Malayan rainforest is the richest terrestrial habitat in terms of plant species diversity: 200 or more tree species per hectare have been recorded at some stations (Whitmore 1975).

Bird species diversity in rainforest is also very high; 182 species of resident birds have been found in 2 sq km of level lowlands at Pasoh, Malaysia (D. R. Wells pers. comm.) and as many as 187 in roughly the same area of forest and secondary growth at Khao Noi Chuchi, Peninsular Thailand (author's observation). However, although the majority of Sundaic lowland forest birds extend at least as far north as 10°30' latitude, there are at least six species which are apparently confined to the Malayan floristic zone of the extreme south.

Terrestrial evergreen forests occupied 14,323 sq km in Peninsular Thailand at the end of 1983 (Royal Forest Department 1986). However, in addition to lowland rainforest, this figure also includes small areas of hill evergreen forest above 1,000 m.

Semi-Evergreen Forest. Semi-evergreen forest (including the 'dry evergreen forest' of Smitinand *et al.* 1967) is the predominant lowland evergreen forest type in Continental Thailand. Throughout most of the country, semi-evergreen forest occupies the submontane slopes below 900 or 1,000 m; above this elevation it grades into hill evergreen forest while at lower elevations, it frequently occurs in a mosaic with deciduous forests and bamboo, which occupy the drier plains and foothills. In the less seasonal areas of South-east Thailand it occupies the extreme lowlands too. Like rainforest, it is dense and stratified. However, there is usually a deciduous component, particularly among the larger emergent trees. Tree species diversity is still fairly high and, as in rainforest, the family Dipterocarpaceae predominates.

Semi-evergreen forest, like rainforest, supports a great diversity of resident birds, including many pheasants, pigeons, cuckoos, owls, two species of trogon, hornbills, kingfishers, barbets, woodpeckers and representatives of many passerine families. The bird community of a particular forest area will depend upon its geographical position and altitude and will usually comprise an assemblage of Indo-Chinese, Indo-Burmese and Sino-Himalayan species.

Approximately 72 percent of the remaining evergreen forest area is occupied by semi-evergreen forest (Lekagul and McNeely 1977).

Hill Evergreen Forest. Hill evergreen forest (lower montane forest) occurs above 900 or 1,000 m and is found on the higher peaks throughout the country, with the largest areas in the north and west and much smaller areas in the South-east and Peninsula. The dominant trees are oaks and chestnuts (*Quercus* spp., *Lithocarpus* spp. and *Castanopsis* spp.) together with *Schima wallichii* Korth., *Engelhardtia spicata* Lengen. ex Bl., *Michelia champaca* Linn. and many species of the families Rosaceae, Ericaceae and Magnoliaceae. Hill evergreen forests are structurally very varied. On lower, drier ridges, the forest is more open with trees sometimes as low as 10 m in stature and with few epiphytes. Such areas are vulnerable to fires started by man and the undergrowth may consist of thorny shrubs and grasses. On moister slopes and in valleys, the forest is much taller and approaches the height of semi-evergreen forest, though is less stratified. The undergrowth is dense and the trees are frequently swathed in epiphytes. Epiphytes become more frequent in the moister conditions of upper elevations, even though the trees themselves decline in stature. On the high summit of Doi Inthanon (2,590 m), which is almost 300 m higher than any other peak in Thailand, the forest approaches an upper montane facies in both structure and species composition (Robbins and Smitinand 1966).

Hill evergreen forests support a great diversity of birds, principally species of Sino-Himalayan affinities. These include a wealth of smaller birds including minivets, bulbuls and babblers. Hill evergreen forest is of primary importance for at least two species of Phasianidae (Rufous-throated Partridge *Arborophila rufogularis* and Hume's Pheasant *Syrmaticus humiae*) and one hornbill (Rufous-throated Hornbill *Aceros nipalensis*). With increasing distance from the Sino-Himalayan region, the diversity of montane bird species rapidly decreases so that the hill evergreen forests of South-east and Peninsular Thailand are relatively species-poor. Few lowland Indo-Chinese or Sundaic forest birds occur above the lowland-montane ecotone although a number of montane species are shared by both hill evergreen forests and the lower elevation evergreen forests of the submontane slopes (e.g. Silver Pheasant, *Lophura nycthemera*).

Reliable estimates of the cover of hill evergreen forest are difficult to obtain, as upland shifting cultivators have reduced the most extensive areas in northern and western Thailand to a mosaic of grassland and successional habitats, with the most extensive forest patches remaining on the steeper slopes or above 1,800 m, the usual upper limit of cultivation. The official estimate of the cover of all categories of evergreen forest in northern Thailand is 25,568 sq km (Royal Forest Department 1986; Section 'Northern Region Habitats'). Much of this area should be within the hill evergreen forest zone but the estimate is unreliable and does not distinguish degraded and successional habitats. Lekagul and McNeely (1977) considered that hill evergreen forests covered no more than 3,500 sq km in the entire country.

Deciduous Forests

Deciduous forests are found in the lowlands of Continental Thailand where the rainfall is too seasonal to support evergreen forest. As in lowland evergreen forests, trees of the family Dipterocarpaceae are present and, in some formations, predominate but most species shed their leaves in response to water loss during the dry season. Such seasonally dry forests have been subject to modification by man, principally through the use of fire, for a long period. Many of the dominant tree species are fire-resistant and the areas covered by deciduous formations may have increased at the expense of the lowland evergreen forests over a period of millennia.

Mixed Deciduous Forest. Mixed deciduous forests occur on both alluvial plains or valley bottoms and on hill slopes, occasionally as high as 1,000 m. They are structurally quite varied, with many tall trees in the moister areas and lower stature trees on the drier ridges and have sometimes been divided into three subtypes (Neal 1967). Usually, however, two subtypes are recognised: one in which Teak *Tectona grandis* Linn. f. is dominant and one in which *Lagerstroemia calyculata* Kurz is dominant (Bunyavejchewin 1983). The largest remaining areas are of the second type, owing to the more extensive exploitation of teak.

Mixed deciduous forests are less diversified than lowland evergreen forests and usually possess three strata. More light reaches the forest floor and consequently the undergrowth is denser and often thorny. There are more grasses and herbs and there is usually much bamboo, particularly in those areas which are frequently burnt.

The bird community is fairly diverse and, in addition to the many species which are characteristic of deciduous woodlands (e.g. Black-headed Woodpecker *Picus erythropygius*, Rufous Treepie *Dendrocitta vagabunda* and Golden-fronted Leafbird *Chloropsis aurifrons*), there may also be a few species which primarily inhabit evergreen forests (e.g. Banded Broadbill *Eurylaimus javanicus* and Blue Pitta *Pitta cyanea*). In mixed deciduous forests, however, these are usually confined to the immediate vicinity of permanent streams and other sources of fresh water. Other species, such as some hornbills and the Fairy Bluebird *Irena puella* also disperse into mixed deciduous woodlands from adjoining evergreen forests in order to feed, especially during the wet season. Mixed deciduous woodlands provide a much wider range of feeding niches for small, middle storey and understorey-inhabiting birds than do dry dipterocarp forests.

The present estimate of cover of mixed deciduous forest is 33,929 sq km (Royal Forest Department 1986; Table 3). The most extensive areas are found in the North, North-east and South-west regions.

Table 3: Areas of different forest types remaining in Thailand at the end of 1983. (Source: Forest Mapping and Remote Sensing Subdivision, Royal Forest Department)

Category	Area (sq km)	Percentage of total remaining forest area
Evergreen (all categories)	67,861	43.6
Mixed Decidous	33,929	21.8
Dry Dipterocarp	48,930	31.4
Coniferous	2,162	1.4
Mangrove	2,872	1.8
TOTAL	155,754	100.0

Dry Dipterocarp Forest. Dry dipterocarp forest is the predominant forest type throughout the lowlands of Continental Thailand and it replaces mixed deciduous forest in areas of low rainfall and on the poorest and most porous soils (Neal 1967). It is a lower stature and more uniform habitat than is mixed deciduous forest and is dominated by a few species of large-leaved deciduous trees, including *Shorea obtusa* Wall., *S. siamensis* Miq., *Dipterocarpus obtusifolius* Teysm. ex Mia. and *D. tuberculatus* Roxb. The forest is usually very open, with mainly grassy undergrowth, particularly in those areas which have been subject to the most frequent burning.

Dry dipterocarp forest supports a lower bird diversity than do other forest formations as there are fewer middle storey and understorey foraging niches. Among the smaller birds, Black-faced Cuckoo-Shrike *Coracina novaehollandiae*, Black-winged Cuckoo-Shrike *C. melaschista* and Golden-fronted Leafbird frequent the canopy, while Rufescent Prinia *Prinia rufescens* and, locally, Brown Prinia *P. polychroa* inhabit the grassy understorey. At least nine species of woodpeckers, including the Great Slaty Woodpecker *Muelleripicus pulverulentus* and the White-bellied Woodpecker *Dryocopus javensis*, occur in the less disturbed areas which support larger trees as do a variety of other medium to large birds including Lineated Barbet *Megalaima lineata*, Eurasian Jay *Garrulus glandarius*, Blue Magpie *Urocissa erythrorhyncha* and Rufous Treepie.

Although dry dipterocarp forests still occupy large areas, most have been greatly modified by man, chiefly through annual, dry season burning. Present coverage is cited as 48,930 sq km (Royal Forest Department 1986; Table 3), although this undoubtedly includes large areas of degraded open savanna and scrub. Dry dipterocarp forests occur around the lowland margins of most nature reserves in Continental Thailand although the largest and least disturbed areas are found in the north and west.

Other forest types

Coniferous Forests. Conifer forests occur on drier ridges and plateaux at elevations of 400–1,400 m in the Northern and North-east regions. They are dominated by two species, *Pinus merkusii* Jungh. and de Vriese and *P. kesiya* Royle. ex Gordon, but pure stands are very limited in extent and typically, pines occur mixed in with the more open hill evergreen forests and with deciduous oaks *Quercus* spp. at the lower elevations. The local predominance of pines has probably been enhanced through the use of fire.

Coniferous forests support a low diversity of bird species. Only one species, Giant Nuthatch *Sitta magna*, appears to be restricted to pines, or more precisely to the pine – hill evergreen forest ecotone in Northern Thailand. The Great Tit *Parus major* chiefly inhabits pines in North and North-east Thailand although it frequents mangroves and coastal scrub in the Peninsula. A number of other species which are usually commoner in other forest types also occur in pines. These include Grey-headed Woodpecker *Picus canus*, Greater Yellownape *P. flavinucha*, Eurasian Jay *Garrulus glandarius* and Grey Treepie *Dendrocitta formosae*.

Coniferous forests are estimated to cover an area of 2,162 sq km (Royal Forest Department 1986; Table 3).

Bamboo. A great many bird species utilise bamboo where it occurs as a mosaic with other forest habitats. Some species which show a strong positive association with bamboo include White-browed Piculet *Sasia ochracea,* Rufous Piculet *S. abnormis,* Bamboo Woodpecker *Gecinulus viridis,* Yellow-bellied Warbler *Abroscopus superciliaris,* some parrotbills *Paradoxornis* spp. and Pintailed Parrotfinch *Erythrura prasina.*

Forest on limestone. Steep, limestone crags are a dominant feature of many parts of the country and usually occur around the margins of the major mountain massifs. Although a 'forest over limestone' formation has been described for elsewhere in Asia (Whitmore 1975), in Thailand the regional variation in rainfall is too great for the various forests found on limestone to be classified as one vegetation type. Such forests tend to have a drier, more deciduous aspect than do those of surrounding lowlands, however, and support many endemic plant species.

Only one species of forest bird, the Limestone Wren-Babbler *Napothera crispifrons* is confined to limestone habitats and this species is found in small areas of the North, South-west and at the south-west margin of the Khorat Plateau in the North-east region. Other species, though not strictly forest birds, make use of limestone crags and caves for nesting. These include the swiftlets *Aerodramus* spp., Dusky Crag Martin *Hirundo concolor,* the resident races of the Red-rumped Swallow *H. daurica* and what appears to be a hitherto unknown, resident population of the Peregrine Falcon *Falco peregrinus.* Many of the more tolerant birds of hill slope forests also occur on limestone crags, enabling such species to survive in otherwise deforested country.

Mangrove Forests. Mangroves are found in silt-rich intertidal regions, and are low to medium stature forests which have a much lower plant species diversity than do terrestrial evergreen forests. Mangrove forest is usually dominated by trees of the family Rhizophoraceae although on the landward edge of the mangrove, there may be a transition to a floristically more diverse, terrestrial forest formation.

Two bird species, the Brown-winged Kingfisher *Pelargopsis amauroptera* and the Mangrove Pitta *Pitta megarhyncha* are, in Thailand, wholly confined to the mangroves of the west coast while the resident population of the Ruddy Kingfisher *Halcyon coromanda* also appears to be mainly confined to mangroves. The Flyeater *Gerygone sulphurea,* Mangrove Whistler *Pachycephala cinerea* and Copper-throated Sunbird *Nectarinia calcostetha* occur mostly in mangroves and coastal scrub while there are a number of other small landbirds which are shared between mangrove and semi-open country and man-made habitats. Mangroves are also of great importance in providing nesting and roosting areas for large colonial waterbirds. Many areas still support colonies of egrets, while this habitat may still support the Great-billed Heron *Ardea sumatrana* and perhaps Lesser Adjutant *Leptoptilos javanicus.* The Brahminy Kite *Haliastur indus* is also mainly associated with mangroves.

Mangrove forests are found in the Gulf of Thailand and along both Peninsular coasts, reaching their greatest development along the west coast which supports 63 percent of the total mangrove area of 2,872 sq km (Royal Forest Department 1986; Table 3). However, almost all remaining areas of mangrove have been cut over for fuelwood, charcoal production and for construction materials while huge areas have been cleared in order to establish fish or shrimp ponds.

Freshwater Swamp Forest. Large areas of this habitat were formerly found in inland depressions and along rivers but most have been destroyed. Some small areas of secondary, scrub forest, dominated by *Melaleuca cajuputi* Powell remain in Peninsular Thailand. There is, in addition, a small remnant of tall, species rich primary peat swamp forest remaining in the Pa Phru Non-Hunting Area of Narathiwat Province, in the far south (Santisuk and Niyomdham 1985).

No species of birds are entirely restricted to swamp forests, although such areas may formerly have been important for nesting colonies of herons or storks, and may also have supported the White-winged Duck *Cairina scutulata*. Many arboreal forest birds which are apparently restricted to the level lowlands (e.g. Cinnamon-headed Pigeon *Treron fulvicollis*, Large Green Pigeon *T. capellei*, Red-crowned Barbet *Megalaima rafflesii*, Fluffy-backed Tit-Babbler *Macronous ptilosus*) utilise freshwater swamp forest as well as terrestrial rainforests (Medway and Wells 1976, U. Treesucon pers. comm.).

AREAS OF DIFFERENT FOREST TYPES

A detailed assessment of forest cover is given later for each separate region (Section 'Regional Analysis'). However, the approximate areas of different types are presented in Table 3, above. Available statistics do not differentiate between the various categories of evergreen forest. Approximately half of all remaining forest is deciduous.

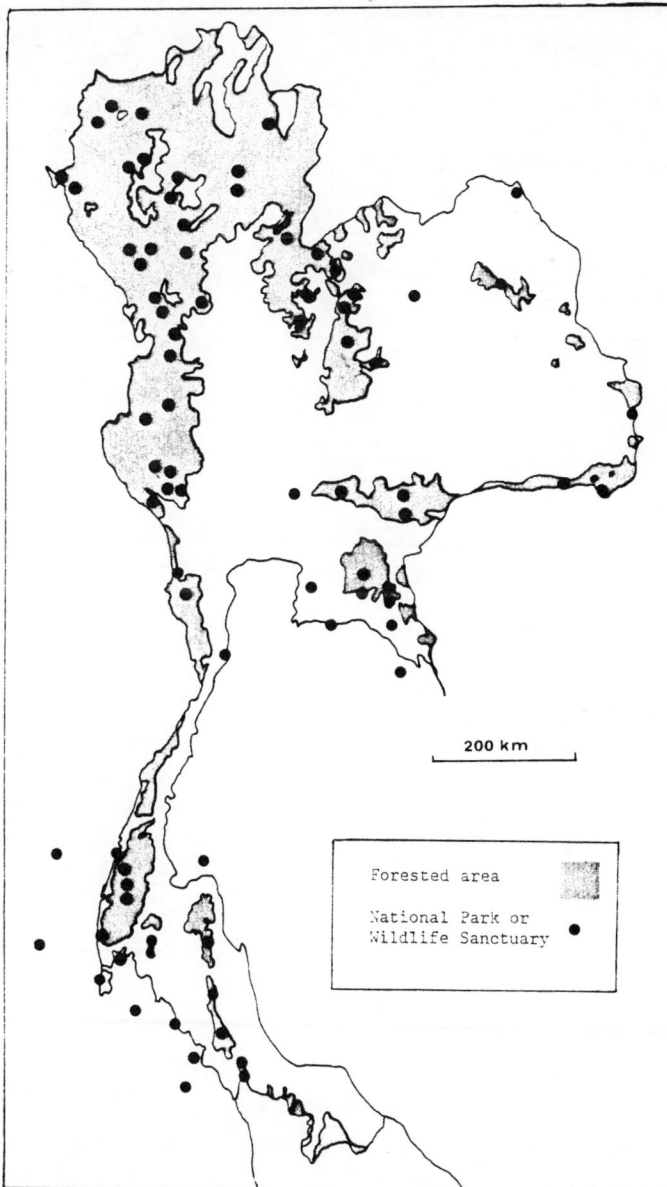

Figure 2: Map of Thailand showing approximate cover of remaining forest in relation to distribution of national parks and wildlife sanctuaries.

CONSERVATION MEASURES

LEGISLATION

Laws for the conservation of terrestrial ecosystems are administered by the Royal Forest Department of the Ministry of Agriculture and Cooperatives. The laws offer two basic approaches: protection of forest habitats and direct species protection through controls on hunting or trade. Laws relating to National Parks are enforced by the National Parks Division while other conservation legislation is enforced by the Wildlife Conservation Division. Both of these bodies are divisions of the Royal Forest Department. Officers of these divisions may be assisted in the enforcement of legislation by the police. In addition, Provincial Forestry Officers, most of whose activities revolve around administration of concessions, replanting schemes and so on, are also, in theory, expected to enforce conservation legislation in the areas under their jurisdiction.

A brief resume of conservation legislation is presented below. Such information is presented more fully in the IUCN Policy Guidelines for Nature Conservation in Thailand (1979), in Sayer (1981) and Anon. (1987).

Laws protecting habitats

The National Parks Act (1961); The Wild Animals Reservation and Protection Act (1960).

The various categories of protected areas, established under the above laws, are set out as follows.

National Parks. National Parks are totally protected in law from any act which modifies the environment, including burning, cutting or damming of watercourses. No hunting or capture of any wild animal or collecting of vegetation is permitted. National Parks are important in education and recreation. While the majority of National Parks are high grade nature conservation sites, there has been a recent tendency to include areas which are more of value for their scenic beauty or recreational potential, such as many coastal sites and islands. A total of 52 National Parks had been established up to April 1986, ranging in size from 44 sq km to 2,500 sq km and covering a total area of 26,576 sq km, or a land area of 22,852 sq km (Anon. 1987).

Wildlife Sanctuaries. Wildlife Sanctuaries are established under the jurisdiction of the Wild Animals Reservation and Protection Act. Wildlife Sanctuaries are equivalent to National Parks in both their size and their completely protected status. As in National Parks, modification of the environment is forbidden.

However, the collecting of animals and plants is permitted for scientific purposes, subject to the issuance of permits. In contrast to National Parks, recreational use of Wildlife Sanctuaries, though permissible, is not actively encouraged.

A total of 28 Wildlife Sanctuaries had been established by 1 March 1986. These range in size from 95 sq km to 3,200 sq km and cover an area of 21,638.5 sq km (Anon. 1987). Many of the most important wildlife conservation sites in the country have Wildlife Sanctuary status.

Settlements, other than those of administrative personnel, are not legally permitted in either National Parks or Wildlife Sanctuaries. When some such areas were established, villagers were actively moved out. However, there are many parks and sanctuaries in the north and west of the country in which ethnically distinct minorities (hill tribes) are present. In most cases, such peoples have been allowed to remain.

The establishment, extension or declassification of a National Park or Wildlife Sanctuary can only be accomplished through Royal Decree. Though no existing park or sanctuary has ever been declassified, there are a few instances where such a decree has been invoked in order to carry out large scale development, such as hydro-electric dams or roads, within park boundaries.

The term 'nature reserve' or 'protected area' is used in this report to refer only to National Parks or Wildlife Sanctuaries, since these form the basic network of sites upon which the conservation of forest wildlife is based. The location of all 80 National Parks and Wildlife Sanctuaries in relation to remaining forest cover is shown in Figure 2 above. Larger scale maps giving the boundaries of protected areas may be found in Appendix IV. Other categories of nature reserve are usually much smaller in area and often have human populations living within them. These are listed below but only those sites of particular significance for forest bird conservation are dealt with in this report.

Non-Hunting Areas. These are areas in which there is no restriction upon any activity other than hunting. In practice, however, the presence of officials often means that forest legislation (see below) may be applied more effectively than would otherwise be the case, thereby giving some measure of habitat protection. Non-Hunting Areas include many wetland sites, colonies of nesting waterbirds, caves etc. as well as a few small areas of forest. Some of the more significant sites for forest birds are mentioned as 'Additional Sites' in the Section 'Regional Analysis', usually with the recommendation that these be upgraded to Wildlife Sanctuary Status. A total of 41 Non-Hunting Areas had been established up to 1986 (Anon. 1987).

Forest Parks. These are areas which are administered by the National Parks Division or by Regional and Provincial Forest offices for their recreational potential. These are generally much smaller than National Parks; ranging in size from only one hectare to 236 sq km. Fifty such sites have been established.

Biosphere Reserves. Thailand has also established three Biosphere Reserves under the Man and Biosphere Programme: Sakaerat (81.05 sq km), Huai Thak (47 sq km) and Mae Sa-Kok Ma (142 sq km).

Species protection legislation

The Wild Animals Reservation and Protection Act (1960 and subsequent amendments).

This legislation aims to protect wildlife through the imposition of controls upon trade and hunting. Almost all bird species are fully protected by law. Legal protection even extends to the vast majority of small, insectivorous and granivorous species as well as to the larger, more vulnerable birds (Royal Forest Department 1983b). Where species are not listed, this is usually due to bureaucratic oversight rather than deliberate policy. The law is, at present, under review in order to rectify such omissions.

There is a provision, however, which allows the live capture of any bird species subject to the issue of a permit. Only 61 species of birds may be killed for sport or food, again, only under permit. In practice, very few permits are issued. In addition, hunting is forbidden within any protected area.

Trade, for both domestic and export markets, is permitted in only 39 species of birds for which annual quotas are set (Table 4). For most species, the annual quota per dealer does not exceed 30 individuals. 199 export permits for wildlife and wildlife products were issued in 1984 (B. Angsirijinda pers. comm.).

In practice, however, wildlife protection laws are very poorly enforced. Other than in a few instances where minor traders have been prosecuted, wildlife protection legislation has never been invoked in regard to any bird species outside of any national park or wildlife sanctuary. Most of the hunting and live capture of birds is carried out by rural people who are entirely ignorant of the law, while most firearms are unlicensed.

In addition, the law itself has many inconsistencies which render it extremely difficult to enforce. Any person may own two individuals of any bird species without a permit, even though a permit would be legally required for that species' capture or sale. This applies equally to rare or endangered species and to common species. The burden of proof of illegal sale or capture therefore falls upon the Wildlife Conservation Division.

The threats posed by both hunting and trade are discussed further (see Section 'Threats').

Forestry legislation

The Forest Act (1941); Forest Act (1960); The National Forest Reserve Act (1964).

Under these acts a system of National Reserve Forests was established. Such areas have been set aside primarily for timber exploitation and secondarily for watershed protection. Almost all areas of forest which are not listed in any of the previously mentioned categories constitute National Reserve Forest and in

Table 4: Bird species live trade quotas for 1987. (Source: Wildlife Conservation
Division, Royal Forest Department)

Species	Number of individuals allowed per trader
Francolinus pintadeanus	10
Amaurornis phoenicurus	20
Gallicrax cinerea	50
Gallinula chloropus	30
Porphyrio porphyrio	40
Gallinago (four species)	20
Treron curvirostra	30
Streptopelia chinensis	20
Geopelia striata	50
Psittacula (three species, excluding P. eupatria)	60
Loriculus (two species)	20
Eudynamys scolopacea	10
Pycnonotus jocosus	50
Garrulax (ten species)	20
Copsychus malabaricus	10
Acridotheres tristis	60
A. javanicus	60
Gracula religiosa	30
Erythrura prasina	50
Lonchura (five species)	50

law, may only be cut under licence. Official government policy, stressed in
successive Five-Year Plans, is that at least 40 percent of the land area of the
country should be maintained as forest. In December 1985, the Thai Cabinet
approved a Draft National Forest Policy which reaffirmed this, and divided forests
into two categories. Protected Forest, which should account for 15 percent of
the nation's land area, encompasses all those areas set aside for nature
conservation, watershed protection, research and recreation, including national
parks and wildlife sanctuaries. The second category, accounting for the remainder
of all forest lands, is Productive Forest which is to be utilised for the
exploitation of timber and forest products.

In reality, the distinctions between these areas are blurred since many of
Thailand's parks and sanctuaries had already been logged before they were
established. In addition, the government is still allowing timber concessions in
primary forests, even though, by the most optimistic estimates, forest cover has
already been reduced to 29 percent. In practice, productive forestry usually
implies the eventual clear felling and subsequent replacement of natural forests
with monocultures of both native and exotic tree species. Even if an area is not
completely denuded by concessionaires, settlers usually enter along the logging
roads in order to clear the land for agriculture in flagrant violation of the law.
Thus the areas of National Reserve Forest which are of value for wildlife
conservation are rapidly declining. The total remaining area is estimated at
102,282 sq km (Table 5), much of which is already logged or secondary forest.

Table 5: Legislative classification for forest areas in Thailand.

Category	Present Area (sq km)	Projected Area * (sq km)
National Parks	23,674 +	24,493 +
Wildlife Sanctuaries	21,596	20,480
Forest Parks	1,501	1,264
National Reserve Forests	102,282 ++	160,800
Total Forest Area	149,053 (29.05% of the country's land area)	205,280 (40% of the country's land area)

* Source: The Fifth National Economic and Social Development Plan, National Economic and Social Development Board, Office of the Prime Minister, Bangkok.

+   Land Area only; includes some areas of non-forested country.

++   Calculated from total forest area, minus the various categories of protected area. Royal Forest Department (1986) lists coverage of National Reserve Forest as 218,155.48 sq km. However, this includes huge tracts of deforested land and farmland as well as small areas of recently established plantation.

OTHER CONSERVATION MEASURES

Reafforestation

A total of only 5,400.81 sq km has been reafforested by both government and private sectors in Thailand since the inception of reafforestation schemes over 40 years ago. This compares with an average annual forest loss of 5,191 sq km during the period 1961–1985 (Royal Forest Department 1986). Such a small area of plantation is unlikely to have any more than minor local impact upon wildlife conservation. In addition, the predominant species planted is teak *Tectona grandis*. Although this is native to Thailand, monocultures of teak which lack any understorey support a highly impoverished bird community and are of minimal conservation value. Small areas of another native species, *Pinus kesiya*, have also been planted but most plantations are comprised of exotics such as *Acacia* spp., *Casuarina* spp. and *Eucalyptus* spp.

Highland Agriculture Project

The principal aim of the Highland Agriculture Project is to encourage hill tribes to cease growing opium in favour of alternative cash crops such as fruits, flowers and vegetables. Because this should lead to an eventual cessation of pioneer shifting cultivation, in which primary forest is destroyed, in favour of stable agriculture on already deforested areas, the Highland Agriculture Project has considerable potential to aid wildlife conservation. A total of 28 project sites has been established in Chiang Mai Province and two of these are in National Parks (Doi Inthanon and Doi Suthep-Pui).

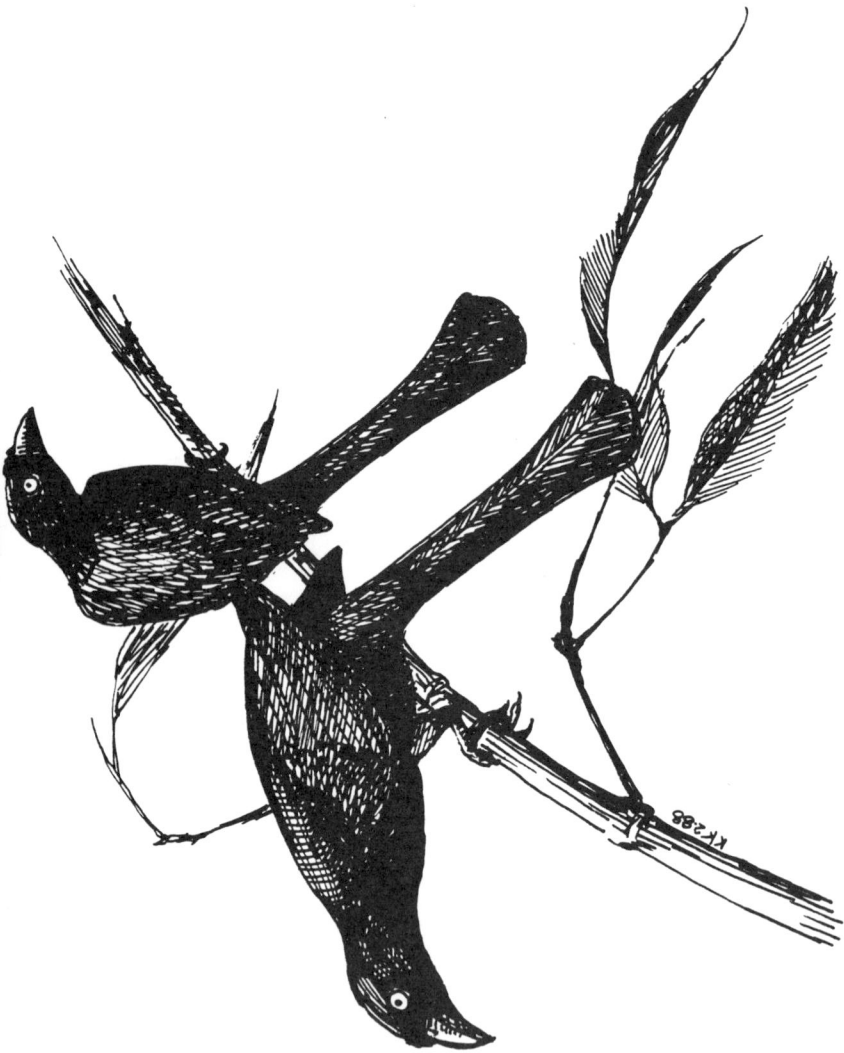

Racket-tailed Treepie *Crypsirina remia* (Kamol Komolphalin)

THREATS

DEFORESTATION

The most serious global threat facing wildlife is the destruction of natural habitat which is a consequence of the rapid, exponential increase of human populations (IUCN 1980). While man's activities, principally through shifting cultivation and the use of fire, have slowly modified the drier, more seasonal South-east Asian forests over a period of millennia (Whitmore 1975), the actual proportion of forested land in the region remained high until recently. Even at the close of World War Two, Thailand was probably still 70–80 percent forested (B. Lekagul pers. comm.).

Present forest cover is estimated at 149,053 sq km (29.05 percent of the land area of Thailand), based on data from satellite imagery, supported by ground checks (Royal Forest Department 1986). As will be mentioned (Section 'Regional Analysis, Methods and Interpretation'), this is certainly an overestimate of actual cover which may result from difficulties over interpretation. The decline of Thailand's forest cover can be attributed both to government sanctioned logging and to illegal encroachment.

Logging

Early logging in Thailand was aimed mostly at the extraction of teak, which is found primarily in the lowlands of the north. Most remaining areas of teak forest have now been greatly depleted, however, so that teak constituted only 1.94 percent of the total volume of timber produced in 1985. Trees of the family Dipterocarpaceae are now the principal source of timber (Royal Forest Department 1986). Whereas formerly forests were usually selectively logged, current forestry policy is either to clear fell or to remove at least 50 percent of natural tree cover and to replace areas of natural forest with monocultures of exotic species.

Logging is permitted through the administration of limited concessions in areas of National Reserve Forest. In theory, no logging is allowed within boundaries of national parks or wildlife sanctuaries. In many cases, however, such nature reserves have been established on former concession areas which have already been selectively logged, while a few national parks are threatened by logging concessions which have not yet expired and which are still being allowed to operate within their boundaries. No allowance has been made for the establishment of 'buffer zones' around nature reserves so that logging concessions usually extend to the very boundaries of parks and sanctuaries.

Although legalised timber extraction does not directly threaten forests inside most existing nature reserves it will, through the removal of intervening forest areas, cause many parks and sanctuaries to become increasingly isolated from each other. Continued logging will further reduce the options for any possible future additions to the nature reserve network.

Illegal Encroachment

Unregulated incursions by settlers and illegal loggers has been the major factor in the decline of Thailand's forest cover. In the First National Development Plan (1961–1965), forest cover was to be maintained at 50 percent of the land area of the country, which is well in excess of present actual cover. During the period 1973–1982 alone, the decrease in forest area varied from 10.8 percent of the total in relatively prosperous, fertile, high rainfall areas of the Peninsula to as much as 48.9 percent in the dry, poor and densely-populated North-east region (Klankamsorn and Charuppat 1984).

Much of the initial impact was centred upon the extreme lowlands. The most fertile areas which could support stable agriculture, along major waterways and lowland valley bottoms, were cleared first. Many areas which had been selectively logged were subsequently encroached and cleared as landless farmers and illegal loggers used logging roads to gain access. With further pressure on land, the suboptimal hill slopes, often of marginal value for agriculture, were encroached upon. Shifting 'slash-and-burn' agriculture using maize, hill rice or tapioca as the chief crops is usually practised in such areas. This has led to a high level of encroachment into most remaining forests and around the low-lying margins of many national parks and wildlife sanctuaries. In Khao Yai National Park, 92.4 sq km (4.3 percent of the total park area) have been encroached since the park's creation in 1962 (Royal Forest Department 1985). However the actual area of forest which has been degraded through selective timber poaching is probably much greater, through not detectable through the use of satellite imagery. Small scale timber poaching and encroachment is continuing around the margins of nature reserves throughout the country and this places particular pressure upon the few remaining areas of extreme lowland forest habitat.

The uplands of north and west Thailand are inhabited by ethnically distinct peoples of Tibeto-Burman or Chinese stock, known collectively as 'hill tribes'. With the exception of groups such as the Karen, who practise stable agriculture and grow rice on terraces, these peoples are mostly pioneer swidden cultivators (Kunstadter et al. 1978) who clear large areas of primary forest in order to cultivate opium as a cash crop. Their activities are centred in the cooler, more humid, hill evergreen forest zone between c.900–1,800 m and as a result, most mountains in Northern Thailand have been converted into a patchwork of successional habitats. The least disturbed hill evergreen forests remain on the taller mountains, above the usual upper limit of cultivation, between 1,800–2,590 m. The hill tribes are the only groups of people who are permitted to maintain settlements within National Parks or Wildlife Sanctuaries. Previously, small populations of Thai or Laotian villagers were found on some of the flat-topped mountains of the Dong Phaya Yen or Phanem Dongrak of North-east Thailand. However, such peoples have been moved out of those areas which have been declared as nature reserves. The hill evergreen forests of South-west, South-east and Peninsular Thailand are much less disturbed. A few cardamom or ginger fields remain in the mountains of South-east Thailand (Brockelman 1977a).

Burning

Large areas of standing forest, both outside and inside nature reserves are deliberately burnt every year by rural people. Flames sweep through the forest undergrowth, consuming the previous year's leaf litter and in addition kill or damage a small proportion of mature standing trees. Such fires are most prevalent in areas of deciduous forest in which an estimated 80–100 percent of the total forest area is burnt annually. In hill evergreen forests and semi-evergreen forests, the burning is mostly confined to drier ridges and forest margins (Round 1984).

The reasons for this practice are not altogether clear. Burning certainly serves to keep trails open, improves visibility and thus facilitates the poaching of game animals. Many rural people also entertain a distinct antipathy towards dense forest, which is regarded as being a refuge for dangerous wild animals as well as harbouring evil spirits. In already deforested areas, fire is used to clear old growth and encourage the appearance of new grass shoots, thereby improving the opportunities for domestic grazing animals.

Quantative data on the effects of fire upon vegetation and upon bird communities are lacking. It is self evident that repeated annual burning will lead to a gradual reduction in total forest area and to the replacement of lush, dense evergreen forest by drier, more open formations with a predominantly grassy understorey and ground layer (Wharton 1969). Fire may prevent the regeneration of some broadleaved evergreen trees and lead to their replacement with fire-resistant species such as teak, pines or bamboo. Within the past 15 years, the repeated use of fire in Doi Suthep-Pui National Park has reduced the areas of moist, dense understorey and some species of forest birds have become much scarcer or have disappeared (Round 1984). Most burning takes place during the late dry season when most forest birds are nesting (Round 1982) and as a result, many nests and fledglings almost certainly perish.

The very great scale of annual forest burning in Thailand is not generally appreciated but because such fires are equally prevalent both inside and outside protected areas, their impact upon the continuing degradation and fragmentation of Thailand's forest cover requires study.

Development

Although logging concessions are not usually granted within national parks or wildlife sanctuaries, other developments which have been initiated by government agencies, such as major highways or hydro-electric dams, have been allowed to damage the integrity of such sites. In many cases, the areas required for construction or inundation are logged beforehand.

Major new highways have recently been constructed in two national parks, Nam Nao and Khao Yai. In addition to their direct effects in damaging forest, both through the initial cutting of trees and through subsequent soil erosion, such roads may facilitate forest encroachment or the motorised poaching of wildlife. Where a wide highway entirely bisects a forest block, it may possibly even act as a barrier to the dispersal of the more sensitive or sedentary forest birds, thereby fragmenting large, interbreeding populations into smaller, isolated ones.

A more serious threat is posed by hydro-electric projects. A total of 17 major hydro dams have already been completed or are under construction on major lowland waterways in Thailand (Tuntawiroon and Samootsakorn 1986) of which at least four have inundated important lowland valley bottom habitats within previously existing nature reserves. A further hydro dam has been proposed within Thung Yai Wildlife Sanctuary which encompasses some of the largest areas of little-disturbed lowland habitats anywhere in the country. The proponents of dam schemes have usually argued that such projects flood only a small percentage of the total nature reserve area and have suggested that such habitat loss could be offset by the adoption of improved protection measures in other parts of the reserve. This fails to take account of the fact that lowland riverine habitats usually support many bird species, together with many other plants and animals, which are absent from the drier hill slopes. Owing to the disproportionate pressure on lowlands, very few undisturbed valley bottom forests remain.

HUNTING

Even the remotest areas within nature reserves in Thailand are visited fairly regularly by rural people who collect a variety of forest products (Brockelman 1987). These include fragrant wood (used for making incense) from the trees *Aquilaria crassna* Pierre. ex H. Lec. and *A. malaccensis* Lamk., beans and seeds from tall forest trees such as *Parkia* spp. and *Archidendron jiringa* Nielsen, the latex-like sap of the tree *Garcinia hanburyi* Hook. f., resin from some *Dipterocarpus* spp. and a variety of rattans and bamboos (T. Smitinand pers. comm.). Groups of men typically camp out in the forest and routinely shoot or trap birds and mammals for food. The principal species taken include pheasants, pigeons, hornbills, gibbons *Hylobates* spp. and leaf-monkeys *Presbytis* spp. In addition, villagers who live around the margin of nature reserves also practise subsistence hunting and this has certainly resulted in the local depletion of the larger birds and mammals. While most bird species are hunted for immediate consumption, a few (e.g. pheasants and the larger pigeons) are also sold for meat in local markets.

The effects of hunting are most evident in Northern Thailand where there is a high population density of hill tribes. Even where significant areas of forest still remain, some larger birds have been extirpated. Only the smallest and most ecologically tolerant species of hornbill, *Anthracoceros albirostris* was recorded in over 130 days observation in Chiang Mai Province (Round 1984). Pheasants, pigeons and many smaller species of forest birds had also been greatly reduced. While the more secretive ground dwellers (e.g. *Lophura* pheasants) may be less vulnerable to shooting, they are nevertheless widely caught in noose traps (Figure 3).

To summarise, National Parks and Wildlife Sanctuaries offer no more than partial protection from hunting. This activity is so frequent and widespread that a species' occurrence in a number of protected areas does not necessarily guarantee its security.

TRADE

A detailed review of the trade in live wild birds is outside the scope of this report. However some general comments may be made. Large numbers of wild birds are trapped by rural people and a very significant proportion of these are taken from within National Parks or Wildlife Sanctuaries. Unlike in India, there appear to be no groups of people for whom the live capture of birds represents a traditional or principal activity and birds appear to be trapped on a more casual or opportunistic basis. Nevertheless, villagers regard the live capture and sale of birds as an important means of supplementing their income. Birds are caught mainly by using baited or decoyed nooses or spring traps, mist nets and, to a lesser extent, 'bird lime'. Large numbers of young birds are also taken from the nest, particularly in the case of hole-nesting species such as parakeets, hornbills, barbets and mynas.

There has not been any systematic review of the bird trade since observations were made at the Bangkok Weekend Market during 1966–1969 (McClure and Chaiyaphun 1971). At that time, open country species such as Red-whiskered Bulbuls *Pycnonotus jocosus* and wintering wagtails and buntings were the most numerous species. Among the great variety of forest birds which were traded, two parakeets, *Psittacula alexandri* and *P. roseata*, the Hill Myna *Gracula religiosa* and the Pin-tailed Parrotfinch *Erythrura prasina* predominated. The overall proportion of these principal species has probably not changed significantly to the present day although certain other, rarer species such as the Red-naped Trogon *Harpactes kasumba*, Diard's Trogon *H. diardii*, Wrinkled Hornbill *Rhyticeros corrugatus* and Gurney's Pitta *Pitta gurneyi* are today much less frequent or are absent. This may reflect a decrease in abundance caused primarily by habitat destruction. The Bangkok Weekend Market is only one of a series of major outlets for the sale of wildlife, which supply both a domestic and an international market and trade in the more valuable species, such as pheasants, hornbills and the scarcer pittas takes place behind closed doors. In most cases, bird trappers sell their captives to middlemen who supply the major animal trading companies which are based in Bangkok and in other major centres.

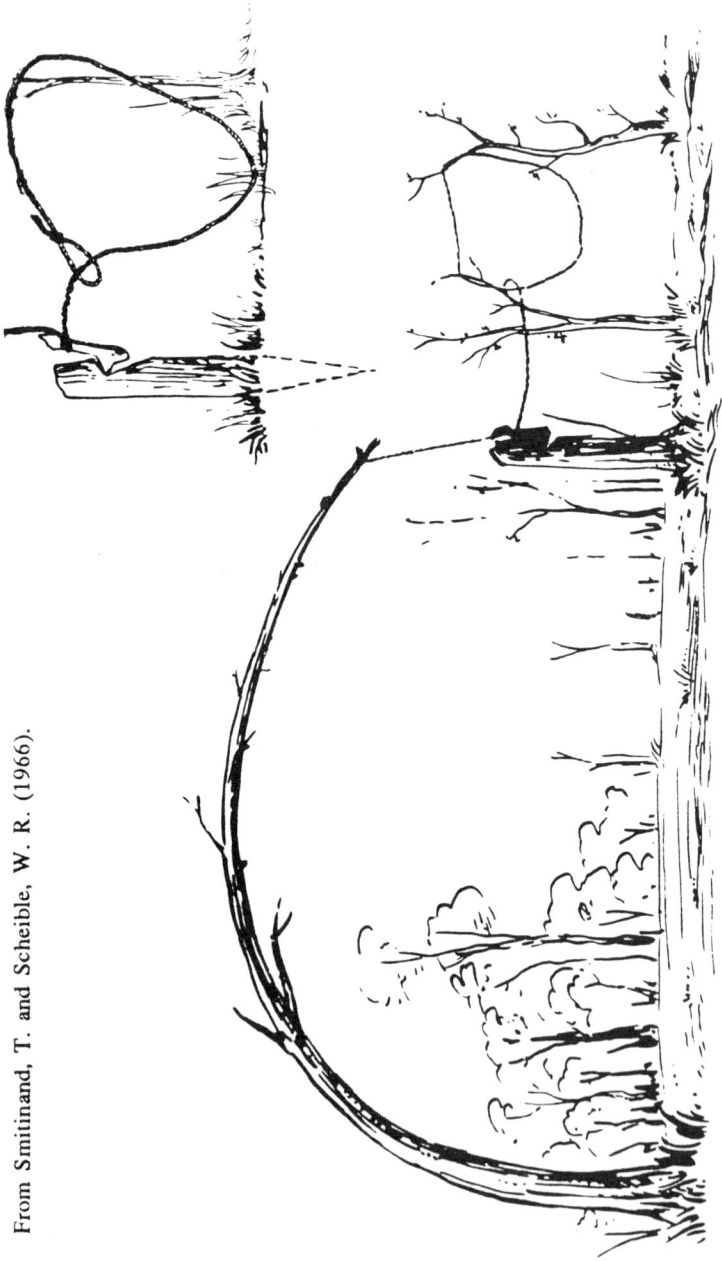

Figure 3: Noose trap used for catching small animals. For catching ground-living birds, nooses are set close to the ground. Long hurdles serve to direct birds towards the noose traps.

From Smitinand, T. and Scheible, W. R. (1966).

By far the greater proportion of all such trade, both domestic and international, is illegal under Thai law. As mentioned elsewhere (see Section 'Species Protection Legislation'), trade is legally permitted in relatively few species and trade quotas are very small. In practice, however, there is very little active enforcement. The Wildlife Conservation Division maintains a station at the Weekend Market and yet pheasants, hornbills and other protected bird species (together with protected mammals such as gibbons and 'spotted' cats) are offered for sale almost every week.

The greater proportion of the trade is aimed at the domestic market as there are a great many aviculturists in Bangkok. Live capture certainly has an impact upon populations of scarcer and more sought after species, such as pheasants. A race of Silver Pheasant *Lophura nycthemera lewisi* is endemic to the mountains of South-east Thailand and South-west Kampuchea. In 1981, only three captive individuals of this subspecies were known in Bangkok (S. Norapuckprutikorn pers. comm.). However, with increased interest among pheasant keepers there was a sudden and massive demand for this distinctive subspecies. Many aviculturists sought out illegal bird trappers living around the margins of Khao Soi Dao Wildlife Sanctuary and the prices paid for undamaged birds spiralled. As a result, the trapping pressure increased and local people now claim that the population within the sanctuary has been depleted. *Lewisi* Silver Pheasants are still being procured, but most are now reported to come from Kampuchea.

International trade also appears to be unhindered, notwithstanding the fact that Thailand ratified CITES in 1982. No more than two officials are assigned to monitor wildlife shipments through the Bangkok International Airport. In addition, the upgrading to international status of the airports at Phuket and Hat Yai, Peninsular Thailand, without the corresponding provision of wildlife shipment monitoring, has greatly facilitated the illegal export of wildlife (P. Na Patalung pers. comm.).

PESTICIDES

The impact of pesticides upon wildlife populations in Thailand has never been assessed in spite of the fact that extremely large quantities are imported (Table 6). It is generally assumed that the impact of persistent pesticides is minimal in forest areas, since most pesticides use takes place in open country and on agricultural land. However, much DDT is still used for malaria control (about 3/4 of that imported in 1981 was used for this purpose) and since much of this would be applied around the margins of forested areas, there would be some possibility of the contamination of forest ecosystems. Persistent organochlorines may have been implicated in the spectacular decline of large waterbirds, Black Kites and vultures. However, these chemicals have mostly been superseded in rice growing areas by non-persistent, organo-phosphorus compounds and carbamates, though small quantities are still used for dryland crops, such as maize, cotton and tapioca. Endrin, BHC and some other persistent pesticides have now been banned while DDT is now only permitted for malaria control.

Table 6: Quantities of selected pesticides imported into Thailand during 1981.
(Source: Agricultural Regulatory Division, 1982)

Product	Quantity (kg)
Aldrin	33,800
DDT *	405,817
Dichlorvos	95,815
Dieldrin	41,150
Endrin *	20,569
Gamma BHC/Lindane *	9,400
Heptachlor	54,432
Malathion	150,080
Toxaphene *	319,729

(* Import for use in agriculture subsequently banned).

Malayan Night Heron *Gorsachius melanolophus* (Kamol Komolphalin)

REGIONAL ANALYSIS

METHODS AND INTERPRETATION

Six zoogeographic regions for Thailand are usually adopted (Deignan 1963, Kloss 1915) and are followed in this report: Central, Northern (north-west), South-west (western), North-east (eastern), South-east and Peninsular (Figure 1). However, further taxonomic and distributional studies could lead to some future refinements of this system. For example, because of the similarity of its montane fauna, the extreme north-western part of the North-east is sometimes included in the North (Deignan 1945, King *et al.* 1975). Likewise, the position of the boundary between the North and the South-west may need further examination. Central Thailand is omitted from detailed consideration in this report, since it is entirely given over to intensive cultivation and no significant forest cover remains.

The avifauna, status of forest cover and the representation of nature reserves in each region are reviewed. Information on forest cover and forest types was supplied by the Forest Mapping and Remote Sensing Section of the Royal Forest Department. The data was extracted from 1982 maps of forest cover (scale 1:250,000 and 1:500,000) which had been compiled from data from LANDSAT 1, 2 and 3, supplemented by aerial photographs and ground checks. Figures for the total forest area in each region have since been updated to 1985, with data obtained from LANDSAT 4 and 5 (Royal Forest Department 1986). Approximate cover of the different forest types for each region, dating from 1982, is also given, although the Forest Department Regions for which this information is available do not coincide precisely with the zoogeographic regions used in this report. Detailed forest type maps are not available for individual parks and sanctuaries, although the predominant vegetation types are listed for those sites which have been visited.

There are some difficulties involved in the interpretation of forest cover data in that they certainly overstate the actual areas of forest which are of significance for wildlife conservation. The satellite data was analysed by commercial foresters rather than by biologists. Although the forest maps give a good indication of areas which have been clear-cut, they do not differentiate between primary forests and areas which have been selectively logged or otherwise degraded. The forest cover data is least precise for the Northern region which still appears mainly forested (Appendix IV, Maps 1, 2, 3) but which in reality is covered by a mosaic of successional habitats and degraded scrub as well as by some primary forest. In the Peninsula (Maps 11, 12, 13), where the climax forest is evergreen, there is a much clearer gradation between remaining forests and cleared areas. Even there, however, the data is no longer completely accurate. The spread of continuing slash-and-burn encroachment in the worst affected areas is such that forest cover maps are often already outdated by the time they are produced.

The locations of all national parks and wildlife sanctuaries established up to the end of 1983 were examined in relation to existing forest cover and the largest contiguous forest block remaining in each region was measured. Particular attention was paid to forested areas outside of nature reserves which encompassed such features as lowland valley bottoms and major waterways as well as higher mountains. The term 'key site' was used to indicate those areas which were judged to be of particular importance. A key site fulfils at least two of the following criteria.

- It has a total area of forest of over 1,000 sq km or is part of a contiguous nature reserve block of over 1,000 sq km.
- It contains important, extreme lowland or montane habitat.
- It supports one or more threatened or endangered bird species.
- It supports any species or endemic Thai subspecies of forest bird which is not represented in any other nature reserve or which is known from fewer than three discrete sites.

All national parks and wildlife sanctuaries for each region are listed and described and each is identified by a code number, which corresponds to that used in Appendices I, II and IV. Within each region, sites are generally numbered sequentially from north to south and from west to east. National parks are numbered before wildlife sanctuaries.

Faunistic interpretations for the various regions are primarily based upon Deignan (1963) or Medway and Wells (1976). Most recent information on bird distribution is compiled from the author's own observations and from those of reliable observers who filed their records at the Association for the Conservation of Wildlife or at the Center for Wildlife Research (CWR). In the context of this report, the term 'recent' applies to sightings made from 1978 onwards. Previous authors have been drawn upon as there are many older records from areas which have been subsequently established as nature reserves. Such records are included only if the habitat is thought still to be sufficiently intact to support the species under consideration. The chief sources for such information are Deignan (1945), Dickinson and Chaiyaphun (1968–1973), King (1966) and Riley (1938). As well as listing those species which are thought to be at risk in each region, a few of the more noteworthy species which occur in the better known nature reserves are mentioned. The conservation status of resident birds is reviewed more thoroughly in the Section 'Species Status Review' while detailed habitat and distributional information for all resident landbirds is presented in Appendix I.

NORTHERN REGION

Land area (sq km)	Forest area (sq km)	Area of nature reserve
113,425	61,374 54.1% of land area	11,369 10.0% of land area 18.5% of forest area

Geography

This region is bounded by the Rivers Salween and Moei to the west, the Mekong River to the north and east and by the Central Plains to the south. It comprises the largest area of uplands in the country and includes six peaks of over 2,000 m elevation. The plains areas lie mostly above 200 m and are highest in the north and west of the region. The major valleys and mountain ranges are oriented north-south. The climate is highly seasonal with a pronounced cool season and average annual rainfall is 1,200–1,300 m in the lowlands (Table 1).

Habitats

Forest type	Evergreen (all categories)	Mixed deciduous	Dry dipterocarp	Coniferous
Area (sq km)	25,568	25,006	34,318	2,018
Percentage of total	29.4%	28.8%	39.5%	2.3%

(Note: Areas of different forest types are approximate only, since the boundaries of the region for which this information is available do not coincide with the boundaries of the Northern Region as defined in this publication).

Most areas of the foothills are dominated by dry dipterocarp woodlands with areas of mixed deciduous forest being found in some areas of richer soil, close to watercourses and on the alluvial plains. There is a greater evergreen component in the lowlands of the north and east of the region than in the west. Stands of pines occur at moderate elevation, often delimiting the dry dipterocarp forests of the foothills from the hill evergreen forests of the uplands.

Although forest cover is apparently higher than for any other region, the present estimate does not give a reliable indication of areas occupied by primary forest. Most of the lowlands are covered with degraded, scrub formations with relatively few large trees. The most extensive and least disturbed lowland forests are found in the west of the region. Most of the evergreen forest cover is of hill evergreen formations, above 1,000 m. Huge tracts of hill evergreen forest have been cleared by shifting cultivators (hill tribes) so that most of the uplands are covered by a patchwork of successional habitats in which relict forest stands alternate with small clearings. The least disturbed hill evergreen forests are found on the highest mountains, above 1,800 m elevation. Such areas are usually above the upper margin of cultivation.

Forest cover in Northern Thailand declined by 22.75 percent during the years 1973–1982 (Klankamsorn and Charuppat 1984).

Bird Fauna

Lowlands. The lowland bird fauna is almost entirely shared with that of the other regions of Continental Thailand. Only five resident lowland species, *Gecinulus grantia, Riparia paludicola, Enicurus immaculatus, Saxicola jerdoni* and *Passer domesticus* are restricted to Northern Thailand. The Khun Tan mountain range is regarded as an important zoogeographical boundary and many subspecies of lowland bird which occur in the drier forests to the west are of Indo-Burmese affinity (Deignan 1945, Smythies 1953). Many of these species and subspecies extend also into South-western Thailand. The lowlands to the east of the Khun Tan range have more Indo-Chinese affinities and evergreen forests in this region support species such as *Lophura diardi* and *Carpococcyx renauldi* which are widespread in North-east and South-east Thailand.

Among the lowland birds, those species which inhabit the larger forested streams and rivers are most at risk, both from habitat destruction and from hunting. These would include *Cairina scutulata, Sarkidiornis melanotos, Icthyophaga humilis* and *I. ichthyaetus, Aegypius calvus, Pavo muticus, Heliopais personata* and *Megaceryle lugubris*. Most lowland valley bottoms have been cleared and settled while previously remote forested stretches of the Ping and Nan rivers have been inundated by hydro-electric dams.

Montane. Northern Thailand is of primary importance for the large number of Sino-Himalayan species which occur in association with hill evergreen forests or successional habitats; 58 species of breeding birds are apparently restricted to this region. Some species, such as *Saxicola torquata*, appear to be recent colonists which have moved into deforested areas. Other montane species are shared with the uplands of the South-west or the North-east while a few also extend into the mountains of the South-east or the Peninsula.

While the majority of montane species are widespread on many mountains of Northern Thailand, between 1,000–1,800 m, there are a small number of 'upper montane' birds which may only occur on those few mountains of over 2,000 m elevation. These are *Columba pulchricollis, Sylviparus modestus, Minla strigula, Brachypteryx montana, Rhipidura hypoxantha* and *Dicaeum melanoxanthum*. Two more 'upper montane' species, *Phylloscopus maculipennis* and *Aethopyga nipalensis* are only found around the summit of Thailand's highest mountain, Doi Inthanon.

The mountains of the extreme north of Chiang Mai Province, and those further east in the northern part of the Khun Tan Range and in Chiang Rai and Nan Provinces support a few species of montane bird which are absent from Doi Inthanon and other mountains to the south and west. These include all those species listed in Table 8, together with *Picoides cathpharius*, and *Tesia cyaniventer*, listed in Table 7. In addition, these areas support more Yunnanese or Laotian races of birds than do the areas to the west, where the bird fauna is

Table 7: Species which are present or probably still present in Northern Thailand and which are thought to be at risk. (See Section 'Discussion and Recommendations')

(R = restricted to Northern Region, U = unrepresented in any nature reserve in Thailand).

Anatidae:	*Cairina scutulata, Sarkidiornis melanotos* (U)
Accipitridae:	*Milvus migrans* (U), *Icthyophaga humilis, I. ichthyaetus* (U), *Gyps bengalensis* (U), *Aegypius calvus*
Phasianidae:	*Arborophila rufogularis, A. brunneopectus, Lophura leucomelana, L. nycthemera, L. diardi, Syrmaticus humiae* (R), *Polyplectron bicalcaratum, Pavo muticus*
Heliornithidae:	*Heliopais personata*
Columbidae:	*Treron pompadora, T. phoenicoptera, Ducula aenea, Columba pulchricollis* (R)
Psittacidae:	*Psittacula eupatria*
Alcedinidae:	*Megaceryle lugubris*
Bucerotidae:	*Ptilolaemus tickelli, Aceros nipalensis, Rhyticeros undulatus, Buceros bicornis*
Picidae:	*Gecinulus grantia* (RU), *Dryocopus javensis, Picoides cathpharius* (RU), *P. mahrattensis* (U)
Sittidae:	*Sitta magna* (R), *S. formosa* (RU)
Certhiidae:	*Certhia discolor* (R)
Cinclidae:	*Cinclus pallasii* (R)
Timaliidae:	*Alcippe rufogularis*
Turdidae:	*Cochoa purpurea* (R), *Saxicola jerdoni* (RU)
Sylviidae:	*Abroscopus albogularis* (R), *Tesia cyaniventer* (RU)

Table 8: Bird species which, though not thought to be at risk, are restricted to the Northern Region and appear to be absent from existing nature reserves.

Phasianidae:	*Bambusicola fytchii*
Columbidae:	*Treron seimundi*
Hirundinidae:	*Riparia paludicola, Hirundo rustica*
Pycnonotidae:	*Pycnonotus xanthorrhous*
Aegithalidae:	*Aegithalos concinnus*
Timaliidae:	*Garrulax merulinus, G. sannio, G. milnei, Liocichla phoenicea, Yuhina flavicollis*
Panuridae:	*Paradoxornis guttaticollis, P. atrosuperciliaris*
Turdidae:	*Cinclidium frontale, Saxicola torquata*
Sylviidae:	*Bradypterus luteoventris*

closely similar to that found on Mount Muleyit in South-east Burma (Deignan 1945, Smythies 1953). Thus based on differences in both the lowland and montane bird communities, Northern Thailand can be further subdivided.
- The Salween and Ping Drainage. This includes the mountains of Doi Inthanon, Doi Suthep-Pui and Doi Chiang Dao, together with the areas to the west.
- The Drainage of the Mekong and Rivers Wang, Yom and Nan. This includes the mountains of Doi Pha Hom Pok, Doi Langka – Doi Mae Tho and other peaks of the northern Khun Tan Range and the mountains of Nan Province, close to the Laotian border, including Doi Phu Kha.

These regions will be mentioned further when the representation of nature reserves is examined.

The pressures on montane birds are much greater in this region than in any other, owing to the presence of large numbers of hill tribes who live in close proximity to the forest. Many birds of prey, partridges *Arborophila* spp., pheasants, the larger pigeons and hornbills have been greatly reduced. The most critically endangered montane species is *Syrmaticus humiae* which is listed in the IUCN/ICBP Red Data Book. This species has certainly disappeared from areas where it was previously known on Doi Suthep, though it may still be present on Doi Chiang Dao and has also been reported from Doi Langka (Young 1967), which has not been recently surveyed. The larger hornbills are thought to be close to extinction in Northern Thailand (Round 1984). The situation is especially severe for *Aceros nipalensis* which has a relatively restricted range in Thailand, being shared only with the South-west.

The impact of deforestation upon smaller montane birds is more difficult to judge. Selective cutting, combined with repeated burning continues to degrade most remaining areas of hill evergreen forest. Although many recently deforested mountains still support populations of smaller understorey birds in relict forest patches along streamsides and on steeper mountain slopes, it is not clear whether such populations will be self-supporting in the long term. While a great many babblers and bulbuls are relatively ecologically tolerant and inhabit forest edge and secondary growth, other species which depend upon large, mature trees or lush, moist understorey may be more vulnerable. Four species of small, montane bird (*Sitta magna*, *Certhia discolor*, *Garrulax erythrocephalus* and *Niltava grandis*) could not be relocated in Doi Suthep-Pui National Park during intensive surveys in 1978–1984 even though these species were apparently fairly common there 50 years previously (Round 1984).

List of sites

PING AND SALWEEN DRAINAGE

The remoter north and west of this region includes large areas of lowland deciduous woodlands, some of which are in the immediate vicinity of larger streams and rivers. This region also includes three of Thailand's highest mountains, Doi Inthanon (2,590 m), Doi Chiang Dao (2,175 m), and Khao Kha Khaeng (2,152 m).

Existing nature reserves

LUM NAM PAI WS 1,194 sq km, maximum elevation 1,955 m (Map 1; code no. 13).

Habitat: Dominated by dry dipterocarp woodlands in the lowlands, with small areas of mixed deciduous forest and semi-evergreen forest along valleys. Much of the area is secondary or logged. The most important lowland, riverine habitat lies along the southern boundary of the reserve. Includes extensive areas of hill evergreen forest. The sanctuary encompasses both hill tribe and lowland Thai villages and is suffering encroachment. It is transected by a highway.

Bird community: Preliminary species inventory, mostly confined to lower elevations (Eve and Guigue 1984). Possesses rich deciduous woodland bird fauna and may still support *Pavo muticus*. Evergreen forest still supports *Buceros bicornis* while *Sitta magna* is present in upland pinewoods.

Assessment: KEY SITE. Boundary should be extended to cover both banks of the Lum Nam Pai waterway, which at present forms the southern margin.

NAMTOK SURIN NP 397 sq km; maximum elevation 1,752 m. (Map 1; code no. 01).

Habitat: Smaller areas of extreme lowland habitat and of upland than in Lum Nam Pai. Most of area is of low, rolling hills. Not surveyed in detail.

Bird community: No species inventory exists, but probably supports fewer species than Lum Nam Pai.

SALAWIN WS 875 sq km; maximum elevation 1,130 m. (Map 1; code no. 12).

Habitat: Not surveyed in detail, but mostly comprises rolling hills of low to moderate elevation covered with mixed deciduous and dry dipterocarp woodland, situated in a loop of the Salween River, which forms the western boundary of the sanctuary (and also the Thai-Burmese border). The entire area has been logged. Lowland riverine areas are occupied by Karen hill tribes.

Bird community: Not surveyed. Unlikely to be of importance for montane birds, but probably supports a rich lowland forest fauna. Riverine valley bottom areas may possibly support *Sarkidiornis melanotos* and *Pavo muticus*.

Assessment: Highly disturbed, but lowland fauna may still be fairly diverse.

MAE PING NP, MAE TUEN WS and OM KOI WS 3,400 sq km, maximum elevation 1,847 m. Three separate nature reserves which are contiguous and are best treated as a single block. (Map 1; code nos. 05, 17, 18).

Habitat: Extensive areas of lowland mixed deciduous and dry dipterocarp forests, hill evergreen forest and successional habitats. The Ping River flows through the nature reserve area, though the important riverine habitats have been inundated by the construction of the Bhumipol Reservoir. Many hill tribe villages are located within the reserve area.

Bird community: Preliminary survey. Lowland areas support a wealth of deciduous forest species. Unconfirmed reports of the continued presence of *Sarkidiornis melanotos* have been received. The hill evergreen forest community

includes species which are at risk, such as *Arborophila rufogularis*, hornbills (possibly including the threatened *Aceros nipalensis*) and *Cochoa purpurea*. *Yuhina humilis*, so far recorded nowhere else in Thailand, is present (Round 1983a).
Assessment: KEY SITE.

TAKSIN MAHARAT NP and LANSANG NP   254 sq km; maximum elevation 1,177 m. (Map 2; code nos. 09, 10).
Habitat: Not surveyed in detail. Mostly dry, secondary lowland woodland. No significant lowland stream valleys. Transected by highway.
Bird community: Not surveyed.

KHLONG LARN NP   300 sq km, maximum elevation 1,439 m. (Map 2; code no. 11).
Habitat: Not surveyed, extreme lowland valley bottom habitats are present on boundary only.
Bird community: Not surveyed.

DOI CHIANG DAO WS   521 sq km, maximum elevation 2,175 m. (Map 1; code no. 14).
Habitat: A steep, limestone massif which, on its eastern slopes, contains some of the most intact semi-evergreen forest in the northern region. Hill evergreen forest of higher elevations is partly depleted due to shifting cultivation, but is still extensive on steeper slopes.
Bird community: A fairly detailed recent inventory exists for the semi-evergreen forests of lower elevation and there has also been some coverage of the higher elevations; 239 bird species are known. An endemic species, *Stachyris rodolphei* is apparently restricted to this mountain (Deignan 1939), while *Syrmaticus humiae* may still occur. *Sitta magna* is still present.
Assessment: KEY SITE, supporting fairly diverse lowland and montane faunas.

DOI SUTHEP-PUI NP   262 sq km; maximum elevation 1,685 m. (Map 1; code no. 02).
Habitat: Dry dipterocarp woodlands on lower slopes grade into disturbed hill evergreen forests and successional habitats above 1,000 m. Both hill tribe and Thai settlements are present on the mountain.
Bird community: Detailed survey; 326 species of resident and migrant birds known or formerly known from the mountain (Round 1984). Larger species, such as hornbills (5 species) have been extirpated and populations of many other species have been reduced by hunting and habitat destruction. Montane bird fauna still diverse, but lacks the few higher elevation species which are found on other peaks such as Doi Inthanon and Doi Pha Hom Pok.
Assessment: Relatively rich bird fauna in spite of high disturbance level. The most extensive submontane forests on the eastern slopes are threatened by a proposed cable-car project.

DOI INTHANON NP 482 sq km; maximum elevation 2,590 m. (Map 1; code no. 03).
Habitat: Dry dipterocarp woodlands dominate the lower slopes. Hill evergreen forest remains above 1,500 m and is least disturbed from 1,800–2,590 m. In the vicinity of the summit, the forest approaches an upper montane facies which is unique in Thailand (Robbins and Smitinand 1966). The moderate elevations (1,000–1,600 m) are almost entirely deforested due to the activities of shifting cultivators. A number of hill tribe and Thai villages are located on the mountain and a metalled road leads to the summit.
Bird community: Detailed inventory; at least 344 resident and migrant species are so far known although some species, including *Cairina scutulata* and hornbills have been extirpated. Of overwhelming importance for montane forest birds, supporting Thailand's only population of *Phylloscopus maculipennis* together with an endemic race of the Green-tailed Sunbird, *Aethopyga nipalensis angkanensis*. The only site where *Monticola rufiventris* and *Dicaeum melanoxanthum* are known to over-summer and probably breed.
Assessment: KEY SITE. Integrity of site in jeopardy due to continued deforestation and hunting pressure from hill tribes, combined with uncoordinated development activities (including road construction, the Highland Agricultural Project, tourism and military presence).

Additional sites

YUAM RIVER. The Yuam River, upstream from its confluence with the R. Moei, to Khun Yuam (18°51'N, 97°58'E). Approximately 150 km. (Map 1).
Site certainly much disturbed and degraded, with a major highway running along the southern part of the valley, and many settlements. A lowland river valley, still with some remaining evergreen and deciduous forests. May possibly still support *Pavo muticus*.

SALWEEN and MOEI RIVERS. The Salween River, downstream of the southern boundary of the Salawin Wildlife Sanctuary to its confluence with the Moei River, and upstream along the Moei to Ban Tha Song Yang (17° 33'N, 97°55'E). Approximately 125 km. (Maps 1, 2).
Two large, lowland rivers. Many Thai and Karen settlements along their banks, with extensive cleared areas. However, some lowland forest remains. These rivers form the Thai-Burmese border. Reputed to still hold *Pavo muticus* and may support other large, lowland birds, possibly including *Icthyophaga* spp.

KHAO KHA KHAENG (16°10'N, 99°03'E). Elevation 2,152 m. (Map 2).
Khao Kha Khaeng is Thailand's fourth highest mountain and is the highest mountain anywhere in the country to the south of Doi Inthanon. At present, it is biologically unexplored but it could encompass the southernmost extremity of the Thai range of a number of montane forms. Forest cover below 1,800 m is believed to have been greatly reduced, but the extreme high elevations could be of great conservation importance.

Additional sites established as nature reserves during 1984-1986 for which no data is available:

Mae Yuam Fang Khwa WS 292 sq km

MEKONG DRAINAGE, WANG-YOM-NAN DRAINAGE

The highest montane areas within this subregion are all outside the boundaries of existing nature reserves and support many of the species listed in Table 8.

Existing nature reserves

DOI KHUN TAN NP 255 sq km; maximum elevation 1,373 m. (Map 1; code no. 04).
Habitat: Dry dipterocarp and hill evergreen forest. Most of the area of moderate elevation, lacking extreme lowland valley bottoms and with only small upland areas.
Bird community: Fairly detailed inventory of 192 species compiled from old records (Deignan 1945, Riley 1938), and one recent visit. Formerly supported *Arborophila brunneopectus*, *Lophura nycthemera* and three species of hornbill, but is now subject to a high level of hunting pressure and most larger birds probably much reduced. *Sitta magna* is present (R. Eve pers. comm.).

DOI PHA MUANG WS 583 sq km; maximum elevation 1,313 m. (Map 1; code no. 16).
Habitat: Chiefly mixed deciduous woodland; much cut-over. Partial inventory; 60 species recorded but very few large birds remain due to the high level of illegal hunting.

WIANG KOSAI NP 410 sq km; maximum elevation 1,267 m. (Map 1; code no. 06).
Habitat: Logged semi-evergreen forest with much bamboo which is burnt-over in the dry season.
Bird community: Partial inventory; 79 species known.

SRISACHANALAI NP 213 sq km; maximum elevation 1,285 m. (Map 1; code no. 07).
Habitat: Not surveyed in detail; most of park comprises hills of low to moderate elevation, lacking both extreme valley bottoms and any major uplands.
Bird community: Not surveyed; probably fairly restricted.

RAMKHAMHAENG NP 341 sq km; maximum elevation 1,185 m. (Map 2; code no. 08).
Habitat: A steep, isolated mountain which supports both deciduous and evergreen forests (Dobias 1982). No areas of extreme lowland habitat.
Bird community: Preliminary inventory; 56 species so far recorded. *Muelleripicus pulverulentus* present.

DOI PHA CHANG WS 577 sq km; maximum elevation 1,614 m. (Map 3; code no. 15).
Habitat: Most of the area lies at elevations 500–1,000 m; only very small areas of uplands above 1,400 m. No extreme lowland habitats.
Bird community: Not surveyed. One record of *Carpococcyx renauldi* (P Voravan pers. comm.).

Additional sites

DOI PHA HOM POK (20°04'N, 99°09'E). Elevation 2,285 m. (Map 1).
Habitat: Bamboo on lower slopes; good hill evergreen forest above 1,700 m. Middle elevations mostly deforested. Supports a large population of hill tribes.
Bird community: Detailed recent bird inventory; 291 species known. Supports most of the higher montane species known from Doi Inthanon and in addition, holds *Bambusicola fytchii, Picoides cathpharius, Pycnonotus xanthorrhous, Garrulax sannio, G. milnei, Yuhina flavicollis, Paradoxornis guttaticollis* and *P. atrosuperciliaris*. It is the only site in Thailand for *Aegithalos concinnus, Sitta formosa, Garrulax merulinus* and *Cinclidium frontale*. Supports other species at risk, including *Arborophila rufogularis, Lophura nycthemera, Columba pulchricollis* and *Buceros bicornis* (Deignan 1945, King 1966; CWR).
Assessment: KEY SITE. Deserves nature reserve status.

DOI LANGKA-DOI MAE THO (19°00'N, 99°24'E). Elevation 2,031 m. (Map 1).
Habitat: Hill evergreen forest; current status of forest cover unclear, but believed to be little disturbed above 1,800 m.
Bird community: No recent surveys; known to have supported a similarly diverse fauna to Doi Pha Hom Pok, including such local species as *Garrulax milnei* (Deignan 1945). Reported to have held many *Syrmaticus humiae* (Young 1967).
Assessment: POSSIBLE KEY SITE. A full survey is required in order to determine suitability for nature reserve status.

DOI PHU KHA and adjacent peaks (19°05'N, 101°01'E). Elevation 1,980 m. (Map 3).
Habitat: Current cover of hill evergreen forest is unclear, though has been much reduced by hill tribes.
Bird community: No recent surveys, but known to have supported a rich montane fauna (Deignan 1945). The only known site for *Tesia cyaniventer*. Supports a possibly endemic race of laughing thrush, *Garrulax erythrocephalus subconnectens* (Deignan 1963).
Assessment: KEY SITE. A full survey is required in order to determine the area's suitability for nature reserve status.

NAN RIVER. From Ban Khaem (18°30'N) downstream to Ban Phak Li (18°00'N). Approximately 75 km. (Map 3).

This river section lies mainly at 100–200 m elevation and the banks appear to be mainly wooded. It may still support some lowland riverine forest birds.

Additional sites established as nature reserves during 1984–1986 for which no data is available:

Mae Yom NP 455 sq km
Doi Luang WS 97 sq km
Khao Sanam Phriang WS 101 sq km

Regional Assessment

Nature reserves account for only 18 percent of the available forest area, a lower proportion than for any other region. An expansion of the nature reserve network in Northern Thailand would therefore be desirable. One difficulty in identifying potential sites, however, is· that existing forest cover maps fail to adequately differentiate between primary forests and significantly degraded areas. The Mae Ping-Om Koi Mae Tuen nature reserve block may already contain some of the best remaining lowland deciduous woodlands. Recommendations are made below for surveys of three additional lowland riverine areas (the Salween-Moei, the Yuam River and the Nan River) and there may also be other, as yet unidentified, lowland sites which continue to support a moderately high bird diversity.

In order to ensure that a representative selection of montane sites is protected, the present nature reserve network should be expanded to include the higher peaks in the north and north-east of the region, such as Doi Pha Hom Pok, Doi Langka-Doi Mae Tho and Doi Phu Kha.

The level of encroachment into nature reserves in Northern Thailand is far worse than for most other regions, particularly in the upland areas. The declaration of these areas as nature reserves has so far done little to halt illegal forest clearance so that the integrity of sites such as Doi Inthanon cannot be maintained without greatly improved protection measures.

Recommendations

Nature reserve establishment. Doi Pha Hom Pok should be established as a Wildlife Sanctuary or National Park. This would provide nominal protection for 14 of the 26 species listed in Tables 7 and 8 which are not represented in any existing nature reserve.

Surveys in areas which lack protected status. Detailed surveys of the status of both forest cover and bird species are needed in the following areas: Salween and Moei Rivers, Yuam River, Nan River, Khao Kha Khaeng, Doi Langka-Doi Mae Tho, Doi Phu Kha.

Surveys in existing nature reserves. Of the 22 national parks and wildlife sanctuaries in the region, only two (Doi Inthanon and Doi Suthep-Pui) have received adequate, recent bird surveys. Of the remaining sites, the following should be accorded priority for such surveys: Mae Ping NP, Mae Tuen WS, Om

Koi WS, Lum Nam Pai WS, Salawin WS, Doi Chiang Dao WS, Doi Pha Chang WS.

Boundary changes to existing reserves. The southern boundary of Lum Nam Pai WS should be extended to encompass both banks of the Pai River.

Species surveys. Lowland open forests, particularly those areas close to major waterways, should be searched for Ciconiiformes, *Cairina scutulata*, *Sarkidiornis melanotos*, *Icthyophaga humilis*, *I. icthyaetus*, *Aegypius calvus*, *Pavo muticus*. Evergreen forests of the mountains and hill slopes should be searched for *Syrmaticus humiae* and for populations of the large hornbills, particularly *Aceros nipalensis*.

SOUTH-WESTERN REGION

Land area (sq km)	Forest area (sq km)	Area of nature reserve
75,365	33,041	12,777
	43.8%	17.0% of land area
		38.7% of forest area

Largest contiguous forest block 17,910 sq km, of which 8,775 sq km is nature reserve. (Encompasses Srinagarind NP, Chaloem Rattanakosin NP, Erawan NP, Huai Kha Khaeng WS, Thung Yai WS, Salak Phra WS: Map 4).

Geography

The main mountain ranges of the North-west extend south through this region, which is taken to include the northern part of the Peninsula as far as 12°N latitude. The mountains are, on average, lower than those of the northern region with the highest peak rising to 1,811 m. Though predominantly hilly, this region nevertheless includes some significant areas of lowland valley bottoms of which the most extensive and important are along the River Khwae (Kwai) and its tributaries. This region is bounded to the east by the Central Plains. South-west Thailand is a seasonally hot, dry region with temperatures which range from 5.5° to 43.5°C and an average annual rainfall of approximately 1,000 mm (Table 1).

Habitats

Forest type	Evergreen (all categories)	Mixed deciduous	Dry dipterocarp
Area (sq km)	12,449	5,192	540
Percentage of total	68.4%	28.6%	3.0%

(Note: Sample area only, boundaries of South-west Region as defined above do not coincide precisely with boundaries of Royal Forest Department

Region. Proportions and total areas occupied by mixed deciduous and dry dipterocarp formations are greater than shown).

The seasonally dry conditions have favoured the development of a predominantly mixed deciduous forest in the lowlands, which grades into semi-evergreen forest above 400–600 m and along the major watercourses. In the extreme south of this region, which receives more rain, semi-evergreen forest predominates. Extensive areas of bamboo are found, particularly among those mixed deciduous forests where the impact of fire has been marked. Smaller areas of dry dipterocarp woodland are found in the driest areas, mostly in the north-eastern part of the region. Although the total extent of mixed deciduous forest is smaller than for the Northern Region, most areas of this habitat in South-west Thailand are much less degraded and constitute the most intact and least disturbed valley bottom, riverine habitats remaining anywhere in the country.

Large areas of hill evergreen forest are found above 1,000 m and these, too, are less disturbed than are the hill evergreen forests of the north as there are many fewer hill tribes.

Forest cover in this region declined by 22.75 percent during 1973–1982 (Klankamsorn and Charuppat 1984).

Bird Fauna

South-west Thailand is notable as a region in which a Sino-Himalayan montane fauna, which extends along the Dawna Range of Tenasserim, merges with a lowland, Indo-Burmese fauna.

Lowlands. Only one species of resident bird, *Bubo coromandus*, appears to be restricted to this region. However, since this species has been recorded in Malaysia, it might also be expected to occur in Peninsular Thailand. *Rhyticeros subruficollis* may also be restricted, today, to the South-west although there is at least one former record from the Peninsula (Medway and Wells 1976). Two further species, *Criniger flaveolus* and *Hysipetes viridescens*, though restricted to the extreme western fringe of Thailand, are shared with the Northern Region. The great majority of other lowland birds are more widely distributed although a number of these are represented by races which are endemic to the North Tenasserim region of the Thai-Burmese border. Lowland Indo-chinese species, exemplified by *Lophura diardi* and *Carpococcyx renauldi*, are absent. The extreme southern boundary of this region is marked by the northernmost extension of the ranges of many Sundaic species, such as *Argusianus argus*. Only a very few Sundaic species, such as *Rhizothera longirostris* and *Nyctyornis amictus*, extend appreciably into South-west Thailand.

This region is of particular conservation importance because it continues to support populations of larger, more sensitive birds which inhabit forests or successional habitats along undisturbed lowland waterways, such as *Cairina scutulata, Icthyophaga humilis* and *Pavo muticus* (Table 9).

Table 9: Bird species which are present or possibly still present in South-west Thailand and which are believed to be at risk.

(U = unrepresented in any nature reserve in Thailand, M = status uncertain, possibly represented only by migrant, non-breeding individuals, N = reported, but continued presence as yet unconfirmed)

Pelecanidae:	*Pelecanus philippensis* (UM)
Ciconiidae:	*Mycteria leucocephala* (UM), *Leptoptilos dubius* (M)
Anatidae:	*Cairina scutulata*
Accipitridae:	*Icthyophaga humilis, I. ichthyaetus* (UN), *Gyps bengalensis* (U), *Aegypius calvus*
Phasianidae:	*Rhizothera longirostris* (UN), *Arborophila rufogularis, A. brunneopectus, Rollulus rouloul* (UN), *Lophura leucomelana, Polyplectron bicalcaratum, Pavo muticus*
Heliornithidae:	*Heliopais personata*
Columbidae:	*Treron pompadora, T. phoenicoptera, Ducula aenea*
Psittacidae:	*Psittacula eupatria*
Strigidae:	*Bubo coromandus*
Alcedinidae:	*Megaceryle lugubris*
Bucerotidae:	*Ptilolaemus tickelli, Aceros nipalensis, Rhyticeros undulatus, R. subruficollis, Buceros bicornis*
Picidae:	*Picus xanthopygaeus* (U), *Dryocopus javensis*
Eurylaimidae:	*Cymbirhynchus macrorhynchos*

Montane. The montane bird fauna of this region is similar to that of Northern Thailand, although fewer species are represented in this region and the number of montane species declines further with progression southwards. Because the hill evergreen forests have been less disturbed by hill tribes than have those in the north, South-west Thailand is of particular importance for such vulnerable or threatened species as *Arborophila rufogularis, Polyplectron bicalcaratum* and *Aceros nipalensis* (Table 9).

List of sites

Existing nature reserves

THUNG YAI WS 3,200 sq km; maximum elevation 1,811 m. (Map 4; code no. 08).
Habitat: Extensive, relatively level areas of 500–600 m elevation, with a preponderance of semi-evergreen and mixed deciduous forest and bamboo. Bisected by the River Khwae, the sanctuary contains the largest and least disturbed riverine forest in Thailand, though at slightly higher elevation than that found in Huai Kha Khaeng WS. Larger upland areas than in Huai Kha Khaeng WS.
Bird community: Partial inventory; at least 245 resident and migrant bird species (Phumpakapun and Kutintara 1983, N. Phumpakapun pers. comm.). Supports large population of *Lophura leucomelana, Polyplectron bicalcaratum,*

though *Pavo muticus* less numerous than in Huai Kha Khaeng WS. Probably six species of hornbill, including *Aceros nipalensis, Rhyticeros subruficollis*. The only site in Thailand where *Megaceryle lugubris* is still present. Both *Cairina scutulata* and *Heliopais personata* present.

Assessment: KEY SITE for both lowland and montane species. Integrity threatened by proposed Nam Choan hydro dam, which would inundate the important riverine forest habitat. Hmong tribes have deforested some areas of upland which are contiguous with Huai Kha Khaeng WS to the east, while some lowland areas are occupied by Karen tribes.

HUAI KHA KHAENG WS   2,575 sq km; maximum elevation 1,554 m. (Map 4; code no. 07).

Habitat: Dominated by a mosaic of dry dipterocarp and mixed deciduous forest in lowlands, with semi-evergreen forest and hill evergreen forest on the hill slopes. Little-disturbed riverine forest and natural clearings along the Huai Kha Khaeng waterway, a tributary of the Khwae Yai, which bisects the sanctuary.

Bird community: Detailed inventory (CWR; Phumpakapun, Kutintara and Naksatit 1986). At least 318 species of resident and migrant birds recorded. Lowland areas in the vicinity of the main river support Thailand's largest population of *Pavo muticus* and other endangered or threatened species, including *Cairina scutulata, Icthyophaga humilis, Aegypius calvus*. One recent record of *Leptoptilos dubius*. Evergreen forests support three species of *Arborophila, Lophura leucomelana, Polyplectron bicalcaratum* and six species of hornbills, including *Aceros nipalensis* and *Rhyticeros subruficollis*.

Assessment: KEY SITE for both lowland and montane species. Integrity threatened by timber operations and by uncontrolled settlement adjacent to the eastern margins of the site. There is a high level of poaching activity. Hmong tribes, formerly resident in the sanctuary, have been evicted. The eastern and southern boundaries of the sanctuary have recently been extended in order to enclose additional areas of the Khao Manorom mountain massif and the lower Huai Kha Khaeng, listed under 'Additional Sites'. A buffer zone should also be established in the logged lowlands to the east.

SRINAGARIND NP   1,532 sq km; maximum elevation 1,072 m. (Map 4; code no. 01).

Habitat: Mosaic of deciduous and semi-evergreen forest on hills of low to moderate elevation, around the Srinagarind Reservoir, formed by the damming of the lower Khwae Yai.

Bird community: Not yet surveyed, but certain to be much less diverse than in either Huai Kha Khaeng WS or Thung Yai WS.

Assessment: Forms a contiguous block with Erawan NP, Chaloem Rattanakosin NP and Salak Phra WS to the south.

CHALOEM RATTANAKOSIN NP   59 sq km; maximum elevation 1,257 m. (Map 4; code no. 02).

Habitat: Dry hill slopes; habitat similar to Salak Phra WS, with which contiguous.
Bird community: Not surveyed.

SALAK PHRA WS 859 sq km; maximum elevation 1,130 m. (Map 4; code no. 09).
Habitat: Hill slopes of low to moderate elevation, covered in degraded mixed deciduous forests in which bamboos predominate (Wiles 1980).
Bird community: Partial inventory; 173 species of migrant and resident birds known. Still supports *Lophura leucomelana* and at least three species of hornbill (CWR; Wiles 1980). *Aegypius calvus* may still occur. Reports of the presence of *Pavo muticus* are unconfirmed and the species has probably been extirpated.

ERAWAN NP 550 sq km; maximum elevation 996 m. (Map 4; code no. 04).
Habitat: Dominated by mixed deciduous forest and bamboo, with small areas of semi-evergreen forest (Dobias 1982). No significant valley bottom, riverine forest areas.
Bird community: Preliminary survey only; limestone areas may support *Napothera crispifrons*.
Assessment: Contiguous with Srinagarind NP to the north; isolated from Salak Phra WS to the east by deforested and settled areas along the River Khwae Yai.

SAI YOK NP 500 sq km; maximum elevation 1,327 m. (Map 4; code no. 03).
Habitat: Dominated by mixed deciduous woodlands with much bamboo in the lowlands, and by semi-evergreen and hill evergreen forests. Many areas within the boundary are already significantly encroached upon and degraded. Encloses small areas of lowland streamside habitat. Much limestone.
Bird community: Preliminary inventory. Supports *Lophura leucomelana* and probably *Polyplectron bicalcaratum*; continued presence of small numbers of *Pavo muticus* also reported. One recent sighting of *Psittacula eupatria* (U. Treesucon pers. comm.). *Napothera crispifrons* is fairly common among the limestone crags.

MAE NAM PHACHI WS 489 sq km; maximum elevation 1,068 m. (Map 5; code no. 10).
Habitat: Not surveyed; probably mainly mixed deciduous woodland and deforested country on dry hills of low to moderate elevation. No extensive lowland riverine habitats.
Bird community: Not surveyed.

KAENG KRACHAN NP 2,915 sq km; maximum elevation 1,513 sq km. (Map 5; code no. 05).
Habitat: Dominated by semi-evergreen forests, with hill evergreen forest above 1,000 m. The lower reaches of two major streams have been dammed and are

mostly deforested, but the upper reaches may still contain some moist, valley bottom forest at low elevation. Parts of the area have been logged.
Bird community: Partial inventory; 149 species so far recorded. More remote areas are certain to support *Arborophila brunneopectus*, *Lophura leucomelana* and *Polyplectron bicalcaratum*, however, and possibly also *Rhizothera longirostris*. Of the hornbills, two species of *Rhyticeros* may be present, in addition to *Buceros bicornis*.
Assessment: POSSIBLE KEY SITE. Needs a detailed survey.

KHAO SAM ROI YOT NP 98 sq km; maximum elevation 605 m. (Map 5; code no. 06).
Habitat: A coastal site, with freshwater marsh and saltmarsh. Also supports an isolated outcrop of rugged hills, covered in a dry, stunted forest.
Bird community: Partial inventory. Area previously supported both *Lophura leucomelana* and *Heliopais personata* (Riley 1938), but these species have almost certainly disappeared with deforestation of surrounding lowlands. Resident diurnal raptors include *Haliaeetus leucogaster*, *Spilornis cheela* and *Falco peregrinus*. *Bubo coromandus* is also present (G. Clark *in litt.*). The freshwater marsh is important for wintering *Aquila clanga*, for harriers *Circus* spp. and for passage or wintering Ciconiiformes.

Additional sites

KHAO MANOROM (15°24'N, 99°21'E). Elevation 1,554 m. (Map 4).
Habitat: Hill evergreen and semi-evergreen forest. Forms the eastern boundary of Huai Kha Khaeng WS and comprises the largest peak within the sanctuary. However, sanctuary boundary follows the summit ridge of Khao Manorom, thereby excluding valuable habitat on east-facing slopes.
Bird community: Supports populations of threatened or vulnerable birds, including *Polyplectron bicalcaratum* (six territories located in approximately 3 sq km; author's observation) and *Aceros nipalensis*.
Assessment: Bird populations threatened by illegal hunters and possibly by burning of the hill evergreen forest habitat. The entire mountain should be included within Huai Kha Khaeng WS.

LOWER HUAI KHA KHAENG The lower reaches of the Huai Kha Khaeng, from the southern boundary of the Huai Kha Khaeng Sanctuary downstream to the confluence with the River Khwae Yai. (Approximately 20 km). (Map 4).
Habitat: Open mixed deciduous forest, bamboo and man-made clearings. Valley bottom significantly flatter and lower elevation than areas further upstream. Area formerly supported a few Karen villages.
Bird community: Unknown; probably supports *Aegypius calvus*, *Pavo muticus*; *Sarkidiornis melanotos*, *Icthyophaga ichthyaetus* could possibly also be present.
Assessment: POSSIBLE KEY SITE. Should be surveyed to determine its suitability for inclusion in Huai Kha Khaeng WS.

Regional Assessment

The total nature reserve area (12,777 sq km) represents 38.7 percent of all remaining forest cover in the region. Representative areas of all terrestrial forest habitats in the region occur in existing nature reserves. These include the only extensive, little-disturbed, lowland riverine habitats remaining anywhere in Continental Thailand, in the Thung Yai and Huai Kha Khaeng Wildlife Sanctuaries. The hill evergreen forests enclosed within these reserves are also better preserved than are those in Northern Thailand so that the South-west region is of key importance for the future of wildlife conservation in Thailand.

Threats to the integrity of these areas are posed not only by the gradual encroachment of rural people which is prevalent throughout the country, but also by the proposed Nam Choan Hydro-Electric Project (Tuntawiroon and Samootsakorn 1986). This would not only inundate all the lowland riverine forest in Thung Yai Wildlife Sanctuary but would also divide the large, contiguous block of nature reserve of 5,775 sq km into smaller, isolated forest patches. The Thai Government has suspended the project, but no decision has been taken on its future.

Recommendations

Surveys in existing nature reserves. Of the ten parks and sanctuaries in South-west Thailand, only two (Huai Kha Khaeng WS and Khao Sam Roi Yot NP) have received near-adequate coverage. Priority for future bird surveys should be accorded to Thung Yai WS, Sai Yok NP and to Kaeng Krachan NP, as well as to the areas along the lower Huai Kha Khaeng, recently added to the sanctuary.

Boundary changes to existing nature reserves. The eastern boundary of Huai Kha Khaeng WS should be extended in order to encompass the entire Khao Manorom massif.

Consideration should also be given to extending the southern boundary of Thung Yai WS. This would link this site with other parks and sanctuaries to the south, creating a contiguous nature reserve block of over 8,000 sq km.

Species surveys. Surveys should be concentrated upon lowland, riverine habitats in order to establish the present status of Ciconiiformes, *Cairina scutulata, Icthyophaga ichthyaetus, Aegypius calvus, Pavo muticus* and *Heliopais personata.* The status of the little known *Rhyticeros subruficollis* should also be investigated, as it may be restricted to lowland habitats.

Upland habitats should be surveyed to determine the present status of *Arborophila rufogularis, Aceros nipalensis* and other montane species.

NORTH-EASTERN REGION

Land area (sq km)	Forest area (sq km)	Area of nature reserve
216,194	34,543	13,239
	16.0% of land area	6.1% of land area
		38.3% of forest area

Forest cover maps show largest contiguous forest area as 4,030 sq km of which 2,898 sq km is nature reserve. (Encompasses Phu Kradeung NP, Nam Nao NP and Phu Khieo WS). In actual fact, Phu Kradeung now appears to be isolated by deforestation while Nam Nao is transected by a major highway. Much of remaining forest outside of aforementioned protected areas is now significantly degraded. (Map 6).

Geography

The North-east consists of a huge, dry plateau (the Khorat Plateau), most of which lies above 100 m elevation. The highest peaks (usually 1,200–1,500 m) lie in the Dong Phaya Yen mountain range along the western boundary of the plateau. The lower peaks of the Phanom Dongrak range, which mainly lie at 400–600 m, form the southern boundary of the plateau although in the south-west corner, in Khao Yai National Park, they rise to 1,371 m. To the north and east, the plateau is bounded by the Mekong River which forms the Thai border.

The climate is more markedly continental than in other regions and the North-east shows the greatest annual fluctuation in temperature. It is also subject to a very long dry season. Although the wettest areas around the plateau margins may receive 1,400–2,000 mm rainfall per year, the driest areas in the centre of the region receive less than 1,000 mm (Table 1).

Habitats

Forest type	Evergreen (all categories)	Mixed deciduous	Dry dipterocarp	Coniferous
Area (sq km)	10,937	3,731	14,072	144
Percentage of total	37.9%	12.9%	48.7%	0.5%

(Note: Sample area only; boundaries of North-east Region as defined in this report do not coincide precisely with boundaries of Royal Forest Department Region).

Due to the low rainfall and generally rather poor soils, the lowlands of North-east Thailand mainly support dry dipterocarp forest. Semi-evergreen forests are found on the moister hill slopes and along some river valleys, but below approximately 600 m, most semi-evergreen forest occurs only very patchily. On the southern slopes of the plateau, which merges with the moister Central Plains and the South-east Region, low elevation semi-evergreen forest is more extensive.

The higher hill slopes also support semi-evergreen forest, which grades into hill evergreen formations at 900–1,000 m. Typically, along the Dong Phaya Yen mountains, which encompass many nature reserves, the densest forest is found on the hill slopes. The flat-topped mountains of this region support a fire climax vegetation in which open, pine-studded grasslands alternate with relict patches of evergreen forest. Many such areas formerly supported villages, which have since been relocated. Otherwise, upland habitats are generally much less disturbed than in the Northern Region, as hill tribes are absent.

North-east Thailand has a very high human population density, which is exceeded only by that in the more fertile Central Plains. As a result, low to moderate elevation forests have been very greatly reduced, and forest cover declined by 48.9 percent during the years 1973–1982 alone (Klankamsorn and Charuppat 1984). At present, a lower proportion of the total area is forested than in any other region.

Bird Fauna

Lowlands. No species of resident lowland bird is restricted to the North-east Region. While the majority of species in the dry, lowland forests are shared with Northern Thailand, the races of many species differ in having Indo-Chinese affinities. Approximately 11 endemic Thai races of birds occur in this region. Because of the uniformity of the lowland dry dipterocarp woodland habitat, bird species diversity is low throughout most of the region. Species which are characteristic of lowland semi-evergreen forest, such as *Gorsachius melanolophus*, *Lophura diardi* and *Carpococcyx renauldi*, are much more patchily distributed in the North-east than in the moister South-east where semi-evergreen forest predominates in the level lowlands as well as on the hill slopes. *Lophura diardi*, for example, is especially at risk because it is restricted to the fragmented patches of semi-evergreen forest above the upper limit of lowland cultivation but below approximately 750 m, its upper altitudinal limit. Bird species diversity is highest along the southern and western margins of the plateau, where the largest areas of semi-evergreen forest occur.

Large waterbirds such as *Ciconia episcopus* and *Leptoptilos dubius* which formerly occurred in open woodlands and along river valleys have been extirpated or, if still present, are found only as passage migrants. Although a few unconfirmed reports of *Pavo muticus* have been received, it is doubtful that any undisturbed riverine areas which are sufficiently large to support a viable population remain.

Montane. On present evidence, only two species of hill birds, *Treron sieboldii* and *Paradoxornis davidianus* are restricted to this region. However, it might be expected that both of these species would occur also in the mountains of the Wang, Yom and Nan Drainage of the northern region. The bird community shows a progressive reduction in species diversity southward along the Dong Phaya Yen mountain range. Whereas Phu Luang, in the north of the region, possesses most of the montane birds that are found at equivalent elevation in Northern Thailand,

Khao Yai NP at the south-west corner of the Khorat Plateau has a much more impoverished montane bird fauna.

Owing to the absence of hill tribes, hunting pressure in areas of higher elevation forest is much less intense than in the north. Gamebirds such as *Arborophila* spp., *Lophura nycthemera* and *Polyplectron bicalcaratum*, large birds of prey such as *Ictinaetus malayensis* and hornbills (*Ptilolaemus tickelli, Rhyticeros undulatus, Anthracoceros albirostris* and *Buceros bicornis*) are much more numerous than in the Northern Region. Overall, however, the montane bird community is less diverse than in the north, and some of the more threatened species, such as *Syrmaticus humiae* and *Aceros nipalensis*, are absent from the North-east. Species that survive in the North-east but which are at risk are listed in Table 10.

Table 10: Species which are still present in North-east Thailand and which are believed to be at risk.

(U = unrepresented in any nature reserve in Thailand, M = probably occurs only as a non-breeding visitor)

Pelecanidae:	*Pelecanus philippensis* (UM)
Ciconiidae:	*Mycteria leucocephala* (UM), *Leptoptilos dubius* (M)
Anatidae:	*Sarkidiornis melanotos* (U), *Cairina scutulata*
Accipitridae:	*Milvus migrans* (UM), *Gyps bengalensis* (U)
Phasianidae:	*Arborophila rufogularis, A. brunneopectus, Lophura nycthemera, L. diardi, Polyplectron bicalcaratum, Pavo muticus*
Columbidae:	*Treron pompadora, T. phoenicoptera, Ducula aenea*
Psittacidae:	*Psittacula eupatria*
Bucerotidae:	*Ptilolaemus tickelli, Rhyticeros undulatus, Buceros bicornis*
Picidae:	*Picus xanthopygaeus* (U), *Dryocopus javensis, Picoides mahrattensis* (U).
Eurylaimidae:	*Cymbirhynchus macrorhynchos*
Timaliidae:	*Alcippe rufogularis*

List of sites

PHU MIANG-PHU THONG WS   545 sq km; maximum elevation 1,564 m. (Map 6; code no. 12).

Habitat: Not surveyed. May comprise significant areas of semi-evergreen forest at low elevation. Eastern boundary is formed by the Nam Phak river at 300–400 m elevation.

Bird community: Not surveyed.

Assessment: POSSIBLE KEY SITE for lowland species though needs survey to determine the present status of habitats along eastern boundary.

PHU RUA NP   120 sq km; maximum elevation 1,365 m. (Map 6; code no. 01).

Habitat: Mountainous, no lowland valley bottom areas. Mostly semi-evergreen and hill evergreen forest. Isolated from nearby, much larger Phu Luang WS.
Bird community: Not surveyed.

PHU LUANG WS   848 sq km; maximum elevation 1,571 m. (Map 6; code no. 13).
Habitat: A steep sided plateau, almost bisected by a now largely deforested lowland river valley. Deciduous and semi-evergreen forests at lower elevations; hill evergreen forest and fire-climax vegetation on plateau.
Bird community: Partial inventory; 137 species of resident and migrant birds so far known. Higher elevations support *Arborophila rufogularis, Lophura nycthemera, Polyplectron bicalcaratum*, and many smaller montane birds hitherto unrecorded from this region (e.g. *Megalaima franklinii, Paradoxornis nipalensis*; K. Komolphalin and U. Treesucon pers. comm.).
Assessment: KEY SITE. Needs further survey work to determine present status of lower elevation semi-evergreen habitats. Isolated from large, contiguous nature reserves (Nam Nao NP and Phu Khieo WS) to the south.

PHU KRADEUNG NP   348 sq km; maximum elevation 1,316 m. (Map 6; code no. 02).
Habitat: A flat-topped mountain with dense, semi-evergreen forest on hill slopes. Summit plateau open, with scattered pines. Lowland stream valley at 300–400 m forms southern boundary.
Bird community: Partial inventory (Dickinson and Chaiyaphun 1973, J. Nabhitabhata pers. comm.); 135 species of resident and migrant birds known.
Assessment: Relatively small and now isolated from larger Phu Luang WS to the west and Nam Nao NP to the south.

NAM NAO NP   962 sq km; maximum elevation 1,271 m. (Map 6; code no. 03).
Habitat: An area of rolling hills with smaller areas of upland than Phu Luang WS. Mostly dry dipterocarp forest, with smaller areas of semi-evergreen, pine and hill evergreen. Most extensive lowland areas in south of reserve flooded by the Chulabhorn hydro dam. Transected by a major highway.
Bird community: Detailed inventory; 185 species of resident and migrant birds known. *Lophura nycthemera* is common. Not known whether there are sufficient areas of semi-evergreen forest at a low enough elevation to support *L. diardi*. At least three species of hornbills present.
Assessment: KEY SITE. Together with the contiguous Phu Khieo WS to the south, forms a contiguous block of nature reserve of 2,550 m.

PHU KHIEO WS   1,560 sq km; maximum elevation 1,310 m. (Map 6; code no. 15).
Habitat: Most of area is a huge, steep-sided plateau approximately 800 m elevation, with small areas of lowland of 500–600 m. Dominated by mixed deciduous and smaller areas of semi-evergreen forest in lowlands, with hill

evergreen forests and semi-natural clearings at higher elevations. The lowlands of the Nam Phrom basin, which lies between Phu Khieo and Nam Nao, are partly flooded by the Chulabhorn hydro dam.

Bird community: Partial inventory; 102 bird species so far recorded. Supports *Lophura diardi, L. nycthemera* and *Polyplectron bicalcaratum*. Probably also four species of hornbill. A single *Cairina scutulata* was found dead in November 1986 (O. Kopkate pers. comm.).

Assessment: KEY SITE for both lowland and montane species.

THUNG SALAENG LUANG NP   1,262 sq km; maximum elevation 1,003 m. (Map 6; code no. 04).

Habitat: Predominantly dry dipterocarp forest, with smaller areas of semi-evergreen forest on low, rolling hills. Most of park area lies at 500–800 m. Valley bottom areas, some of which are as low as 100 m, are now encroached and deforested. Approximately 70 percent of park area is still forested.

Bird community: Preliminary inventory; known to have formerly supported such species of low elevation semi-evergreen forest as *Gorsachius melanolophus, Lophura diardi, Carpococcyx renauldi, Ptilolaemus tickelli, Alcippe rufogularis. Paradoxornis davidianus* also recorded here in grassland (Dickinson and Chaiyaphun 1970).

Assessment: POSSIBLE KEY SITE. Needs survey to determine present status of habitats and species.

TAT TON NP   217 sq km; maximum elevation 943 m. (Map 6; code no. 05).

Habitat: Not surveyed. Plateau, mostly 500–800 m elevation.

Bird community: Not surveyed.

PHU WUA WS   187 sq km; maximum elevation 449 m. (Map 8; code no. 14).

Habitat: Low hills, approximately 6 km from the River Mekong. Present status of vegetation cover unknown.

Bird community: Not surveyed.

PHUPHAN NP   665 sq km; maximum elevation 550 m. (Map 8; code no. 06).

Habitat: Three forest types: mixed deciduous (101 sq km); dry dipterocarp (270 sq km) and dry evergreen (113 sq km). Lower elevation boundary at c.250 m. Transected by three roads (Srikosamatara and Doungkhae 1982).

Bird community: Not surveyed; may support *Lophura diardi* and *Carpococcyx renauldi*, but hunting pressure intense and populations of many larger birds probably reduced.

KAENG TANA NP   80 sq km; maximum elevation 556 m. (Map 9; code no. 07).

Habitat: Low hills and plains, bordered on two sides by River Mekong and River Mun. Vegetation not surveyed.

Bird community: Not surveyed.

YOT DOM WS   203 sq km; maximum elevation 693 m. (Map 9; code no. 16).
Habitat: Southern edge of the Khorat Plateau. Most of sanctuary at 300–600 m. Mosaic of dry dipterocarp, semi-evergreen forests, pines and clearings. Bounded by a major river valley, the Lam Dom Yai, along its eastern margin.
Bird community: Reported to support *Cairina scutulata* and *Pavo muticus*.
Assessment: KEY SITE. Not surveyed due to presence of armed Khmer Rouge insurgents. Boundary should be extended eastwards in order to cover both banks of the Lam Dom Yai watercourse.

PHANOM DONGRAK WS   316 sq km; maximum elevation 671 m. (Map 9; code no. 17).
Habitat: Southern edge of the Khorat Plateau. Most of sanctuary 400–600 m. Semi-evergreen forest, clearings. Secondary forest at lower elevations is mostly deciduous in character, following removal of original evergreen (Enderlein 1976).
Bird community: Not surveyed. Previous reports of *Rhyticeros undulatus*, *Buceros bicornis*. May have once supported *Pavo muticus*, but continued presence is unlikely.

TAB LAN NP, PANG SIDA NP   3,084 sq km; maximum elevation 992 m. (Map 7; code nos. 9, 10).
Habitat: Large areas of semi-evergreen forest, with small areas of deciduous forest types around margins. Contains considerable areas of lowland at 100–400 m.
Bird community: Not surveyed. Markedly lower elevation than most of Khao Yai NP and should therefore be valuable for conservation of key lowland species, such as *Lophura diardi* and *Treron pompadora*.
Assessment: KEY SITE. One of the largest contiguous blocks of nature reserve in the country. Probably badly encroached upon and needs detailed habitat survey.

KHAO YAI NP   2,169 sq km; maximum elevation 1,351 m. (Map 7; code no. 08).
Habitat: Extreme south-west corner of the Khorat Plateau. Much of the area lies above 700 m, with lower elevation habitats reaching down to 250 m around the park margins. Most of area covered with primary semi-evergreen forest; small areas of mixed deciduous forest along northern margin. Hill evergreen forest occurs above 1,000 m (Smitinand 1968). Completely traversed by metalled road.
Bird community: Detailed inventory; at least 300 species of resident and migrant birds recorded (Dickinson and Chaiyaphun 1970, McClure 1974; CWR). Larger birds include *Gorsachius melanolophus*, *Ictinaetus malayensis*, *Spizaetus cirrhatus*, *Lophura diardi*, *L. nycthemera*, *Carpococcyx renauldi* and four species of hornbills.
Assessment: KEY SITE. Some encroachment by villagers into lower lying park margins, especially in the east.

SAM LAN NP 44 sq km; maximum elevation 312 m. (Map 7; code no. 11).
Habitat: Secondary, deciduous woodland and scrub on low hills.
Bird community: Detailed inventory; 82 species recorded. Few large birds other
than *Spilornis cheela*. No hornbills present.

Additional sites established as nature reserves during 1984–1986 for which no
data is available:

> Phu Hin Rong Kla NP 307 sq km
> Phu Kao-Phu Phan Kham NP 322 sq km

Regional Assessment

The present coverage of nature reserves represents 38.5 percent of remaining
forest cover. Because most remaining forests outside of national parks and
wildlife sanctuaries are already degraded or do not encompass any additional
significant areas of lowland valley bottom or higher montane habitat,
opportunities for establishing any additional forest nature reserves within the
region are very limited.

As already indicated, the species which are most at risk are those which are
limited to the lower elevation, semi-evergreen forests. Species which inhabit
semi-evergreen forests of the upper hill slopes and hill evergreen forests, such as
Lophura nycthemera and the region's four species of hornbill are well represented
in existing parks and sanctuaries. Other than the larger species such as *Pavo
muticus*, which have probably been extirpated by hunting, most other
inhabitants of lowland deciduous woodlands may still be represented within the
large areas of these habitats in Nam Nao NP and Phu Khieo WS.

The dry, inhospitable environment of the deforested parts of the North-eastern
Region, combined with a high population density, has reduced many rural people
to conditions of extreme poverty. As a consequence, 'slash and burn'
encroachment and subsistence hunting in all remaining forests (including nature
reserves) is a very major problem.

Recommendations

Surveys in existing nature reserves. Of the 17 parks and sanctuaries in North-east
Thailand only three, Nam Nao NP, Khao Yai NP and Sam Lan NP have been
subjected to detailed bird surveys. It is recommended that priority for future
surveys be given to Thung Salaeng Luang NP, Tab Lan NP, Pang Sida NP, Phu
Khieo WS, Yot Dom WS and Phu Miang-Phu Thong WS.

Boundary changes to existing nature reserves. Subject to the continued presence
of lowland, valley bottom forest, the eastern boundary of Phu Miang-Phu Thong
WS should be extended to encompass the hills to the east of the Nam Phak
River.

The boundaries of Nam Nao NP and Phu Khieo WS should be extended to
encompass the Nam Phrom basin which lies between them. The boundary of Yot

Dom WS should be extended to incorporate additional forests to the east of the Lam Dom Yai.

Species surveys. Remaining areas of lowland woodland in the vicinity of major reservoirs and along the River Mekong should be searched for large Ciconiiformes, *Sarkidiornis melanotos*, vultures and possibly for *Icthyophaga ichthyaetus*. The Nam Phrom Basin and other areas in and around Phu Khieo WS, as well as in Yot Dom WS and elsewhere along the Thai-Kampuchean border, should be searched for *Cairina scutulata*.

SOUTH-EASTERN REGION

Land area (sq km)	Forest area (sq km)	Area of nature reserve *
22,423	4,578 20.4% of land area	1,473 6.6% of land area 32.2% of forest area

(* Excludes areas of coastal water lying within national parks)

RFD (1983a) gives largest contiguous forest block as 2,165 sq km (encompassing Khao Ang Ru Nai WS and Khao Soi Dao WS). However, this is no longer accurate as much of area has been selectively logged and has been subject to devastating encroachment by illegal settlers and loggers. Possibly less than 1,000 sq km remains.

Geography

South-eastern Thailand is bounded by the Gulf of Thailand to the south and west, the deforested lowlands along the Bang Pakong River to the north and by the Kampuchean border to the east (Figure 1). Most of the area consists of lowlands apart from the mountains of Khao Soi Dao which rise to 1,670 m. A number of islets are found offshore of which the largest is Ko Chang (192 sq km). This is one of the least seasonal areas of the country, with temperatures ranging from 8.9°C to 40.8°C and a very high rainfall, averaging 3,000–4,000 mm per year in the wettest areas (Table 1).

Habitats

The high rainfall has favoured the development of a predominantly semi-evergreen facies throughout the lowlands, which grades into a true rainforest in the wettest areas (Whitmore 1975). All such areas are classified as 'semi-evergreen' for the purposes of this analysis, however. Above 900–1,000 m, areas of hill evergreen forest are found.

The largest areas of forest remain in the eastern parts of the region. Most of the areas further west, closer to the main centres of population, have been almost completely deforested. During 1973–1982, forest cover in South-east

Forest type	Semi-evergreen	Hill evergreen *	Mixed deciduous +	Mangrove
Area (sq km)	3,380	40	746	418
Percentage of total	73.7%	0.9%	16.3%	9.1%

* Hill evergreen forest area calculated by measuring areas of uplands above 1,000 m, assuming all such areas to be forested.

\+ Deciduous forest almost certainly all secondary facies, resulting from the degradation of the original semi-evergreen caused by repeated burning.

Thailand declined by 46.8 percent (Klankamson and Charuppat 1984) and this rate of loss has been sustained to the present time. Above the level of the contiguous lowland deforestation, some small clearings are also found on the forested, submontane slopes where shifting cultivators have grown cardamom *Amomum krevanh* Pierre (Brockelman 1977b). The semi-evergreen forests of higher elevation and the relatively small areas of hill evergreen forest are not thought to have been significantly disturbed by shifting cultivation.

The few remaining areas of coastal mangrove have been very significantly degraded.

Bird Fauna

Lowlands. The bird fauna of this region shows a strong affinity with South Indo-China, with which it shares many subspecies of birds. In addition, eight subspecies of lowland or submontane forest bird are thought to be endemic to this region of Thailand. South-eastern Thailand shares many of the bird species that inhabit the semi-evergreen forests of the North-east though one species, *Pitta elliotti* (so far known only from market-purchased specimens) is believed to be restricted to the region.

Many lowland species are at great risk from continued deforestation, particularly those such as *Cymbirhynchus macrorhynchos* which is confined to forests below 300 m in the immediate vicinity of waterways. *Pitta elliotti* is thought to be mainly confined to forests of the lowlands below 400 m (Delacour 1929, F. G. Rozendaal *in litt.*), and would be particularly threatened since the topography is fairly steep in most existing nature reserves. Even though *Lophura diardi* is still fairly common in logged lowland forest in this region, it is acutely threatened both by the speed of continuing destruction and by hunting and live capture. *Ciconia episcopus*, which has been extirpated elsewhere in the country, is still present in the last extensive piece of lowland forest in this region.

Montane. The Thai range of four species of montane or submontane bird (*Arborophila cambodiana*, *Pitta soror*, *Cissa thalassina* and *Alcippe peracensis*) is almost entirely restricted to the major uplands of Khao Soi Dao WS and its major outlier, Khao Sabap NP. (*Cissa thalassina* and possibly *Alcippe peracensis* also occur on the smaller, more isolated mountain of Khao Chamao NP; Appendix I). The subspecies *A. cambodiana diversa* and *A peracensis eremita* are thought to be endemic to Thailand. A number of Sino-Himalayan montane species also occur in this region. The populations of some (e.g. *Cochoa viridis*) have apparently not differentiated from those elsewhere in their range while others (e.g. *Lophura nycthemera lewisi* and *Cinclidium leucurum cambodianum*) have distinct, South Indo-Chinese subspecies which are shared between the mountains of South-east Thailand and South-west Kampuchea. A few other taxa of montane bird (e.g. *Garrulax strepitans ferrarius*), formerly listed for Thailand (Deignan 1963), are apparently not known west of Khao Kuap, the coordinates of which (12°25'N, 102°50'E) actually place the site in Kampuchea.

Populations of smaller montane and submontane species are probably not at risk because the areas of habitat, though small, are little-disturbed and lie entirely within existing nature reserves. The primary threats to populations of the larger species, particularly gamebirds, are hunting and live capture for trade. The population of *Lophura nycthemera lewisi* is thought to have been greatly reduced in recent years as a great many have been trapped to supply pheasant keepers in Bangkok.

Mangroves, offshore islands. No mangrove species are restricted to this region and the mangrove bird fauna comprises fewer species than does that of the west coast of Peninsular Thailand. Mangroves of the mainland coast and of the offshore islands may be of importance in the conservation of two species listed in Table 11, *Ardea sumatrana* and *Heliopais personata*. Terrestrial island forests are of importance for the conservation of *Ducula aenea*.

Table 11: Species which are present in South-east Thailand and which are believed to be at risk.

(U = unrepresented in any nature reserve in Thailand)

Ardeidae:	*Ardea sumatrana*
Ciconiidae:	*Ciconia episcopus*
Phasianidae:	*Arborophila cambodiana, Lophura diardi, L. nycthemera*
Heliornithidae:	*Heliopais personata*
Columbidae:	*Treron pompadora, Ducula aenea*
Bucerotidae:	*Rhyticeros undulatus, Buceros bicornis*
Eurylaimidae:	*Cymbirhynchus macrorhynchos*
Pittidae:	*Pitta elliotti* (U)
Timaliidae:	*Alcippe rufogularis*

List of sites (Map 10)

Existing nature reserves

KHAO ANG RU NAI WS 108 sq km; maximum elevation 777 m. (Code no. 07).

Habitat: Much of area consists of selectively-logged, semi-evergreen forest on level ground and in the vicinity of larger streams at 100–200 m elevation. Some steep hill slopes.
Bird community: Partial inventory; 156 species known. Supports a high density of *Lophura diardi*, together with *Treron pompadora*, *Carpococcyx renauldi*, *Rhyticeros undulatus* and *Buceros bicornis*. It is the only remaining site in the country for *Ciconia episcopus*.
Assessment: KEY SITE. Khao Ang Ru Nai is the only nature reserve in Southeast Thailand to comprise extensive areas of forest in level lowlands. It is part of the largest contiguous forest block in the region extending across the low, rolling hills of the Chachoengsao-Chanthaburi Watershed.

KHAO SOI DAO WS   745 sq km; maximum elevation 1,670 m. (Code no. 08).
Habitat: Most of area consists of semi-evergreen forest on hill slopes; small areas of lowland valley bottom habitat along streamsides, close to the sanctuary margins. Contains the only significant montane areas with hill evergreen forest in South-east Thailand (Brockelman 1977a,b).
Bird community: Detailed inventory; at least 216 species of resident and migrant birds so far known (King 1966; CWR). Larger birds include *Gorsachius melanolophus*, *Ictinaetus malayensis*, *Hieraaetus kienerii*, *Spizaetus cirrhatus*, *Arborophila cambodiana*, *Lophura diardi*, *L. nycthemera*, *Rhyticeros undulatus* and *Buceros bicornis*. All of the bird species now restricted to the South-east, with the possible exception of *Ciconia episcopus* and *Pitta elliotti*, occur in the sanctuary.
Assessment: KEY SITE for both lowland and montane species though threatened by both small scale encroachment and hunting. The sanctuary may still be connected by secondary growth to the largest contiguous block of forest remaining in South-east Thailand.

KHAO KITCHAKUT NP   59 sq km; maximum elevation 1,083 m. (Code no. 03).
Habitat: Semi-evergreen and small areas of hill evergreen forest on steep hill slopes.
Bird community: Preliminary inventory only; 59 species so far recorded.
Assessment: Contiguous with Khao Soi Dao WS to the north.

KHAO SABAP NP   134 sq km; maximum elevation 924 m. (Code no. 04).
Habitat: Selectively logged, semi-evergreen forest on hill slopes. Isolated from any other forest areas.
Bird community: Partial inventory based largely on old records (Riley 1938); 95 species known. Probably still supports *Arborophila cambodiana*, *Lophura nycthemera*.

KHAO CHAMAO NP   84 sq km; maximum elevation 1,028 m. (Code no. 02).
Habitat: Steep mountain slopes, covered in semi-evergreen forest. Now almost completely isolated from the large forest block to the north.

Bird community: Partial inventory; 53 species known. Supports *Lophura nycthemera, Rhyticeros undulatus* and *Buceros bicornis* (Brockelman and Sophasan 1979).

KHAO KHIEO WS 145 sq km; maximum elevation 798 m. (Code no. 06).
Habitat: Steep mountain slopes, covered with selectively logged semi-evergreen forest. Lower slopes support small areas of secondary deciduous formations (Maxwell 1980).
Bird community: Partial inventory; 79 species known. Supports small populations of *Spizaetus cirrhatus, Rhyticeros undulatus, Buceros bicornis* (04,45).

KO SAMET NP 131 sq km, of which 123 sq km is marine; maximum elevation 125 m. (Code no. 01).
Habitat: Offshore island and adjacent rocky headland on the mainland. Deforested.
Bird community: Partial inventory. Of no conservation significance for forest birds. Still supports *Haliaeetus leucogaster*.

MU KO CHANG NP 650 sq km including marine area of 458 sq km; maximum elevation 743 m. (Code no. 05).
Habitat: Offshore island. Still mainly forested.
Bird community: Partial inventory based on old records; at least 40 species known (Riley 1938). Supported *Rhyticeros undulatus, Buceros bicornis*.

Additional sites

CHACHOENGSAO – CHANTHABURI WATERSHED AREA (13°18'N, 101°57'E).
Habitat: Low, rolling topography. Semi-evergreen forest in the vicinity of major streams below 200 m elevation. Area approximately 300 sq km.
Bird community: Not surveyed; may be important for extreme lowland species.
Assessment: KEY SITE, extending east and south of Khao Ang Ru Nai WS and perhaps still linked by secondary growth with Khao Soi Dao WS. Area probably encroached upon and needs a ground survey to determine the present status of the habitat. Insurgents may still be present.

KHAO SAM NGAM and surrounding area (12°48'N, 102°22'E); maximum elevation 727 m.
Habitat: Low mountain, surrounded by forested lowlands containing major streams at 200–300 m elevation. Area c.386 sq km.
Bird community: Not surveyed.
Assessment: No recent ground checks to confirm status of habitat. Extends eastward to the Kampuchean border and is therefore a militarily 'sensitive area'.

KHLONG PUN PIAK and surroundings (12°24'N, 102°44'E).
Habitat: An area of level, forested lowlands adjacent to a major stream, elevation 100–200 m. Area c.130 sq km.
Bird community: Not surveyed.
Assessment: Part of an extensive tongue of forest, extending along the hills of the Thai-Kampuchean border. In military terms, a 'sensitive area'.

COASTAL MANGROVE INLETS. Located between the towns of Chanthaburi and Trat, 12°35'N, 102°00'E to 12°10'N, 102°41'E.
Habitat: Three major mangrove inlets close to major regional population centres. Areas of mangrove alternate with coastal fish ponds and cultivation.
Bird community: No recent surveys. Previously supported *Heliopais personata* (King 1966). Probably supports such mangrove species as *Treron vernans*, *Gerygona sulphurea*, *Pachycephala cinerea* and *Nectarinia calcostetha*.

Regional Assessment

Even though almost one third of the remaining forest in South-east Thailand lies within nature reserves, the proportional representation of different habitat types is uneven. One hundred percent of the montane forest, above 1,000 m, is already protected. This mostly lies within the largest reserve, the contiguous Khao Soi Dao-Khao Kitchakut block, which is a steep mountain massif with only relatively small areas of forested lowlands and foothill habitat remaining. Forests of the level lowlands are rather poorly represented: even though a single block of approximately 1,000 sq km of lowland forest remains in the Chachoengsao-Chanthaburi watershed area, no more than 108 sq km of logged forest is protected as the Khao Ang Ru Nai Wildlife Sanctuary. The boundary of this site should be extended to encompass additional areas of lowland forest, logged forest and secondary growth extending to the south and east in order to ensure the survival of viable populations of larger birds and to protect the lowland forest community as a whole.

Hunting and live capture probably present the most immediate threats to the larger montane species. Indeed, both lowland and montane birds face severe hunting pressure and this can partly be attributed to the relatively small size and hence large perimeter to area ratio of most nature reserves in the region. An assessment of the status of the species most at risk (*Ciconia episcopus*, *Lophura diardi*, *Cymbirhynchus macrorhynchos* and *Pitta elliotti* in the lowlands and *Arborophila cambodiana* and *Lophura nycthemera lewisi* in the uplands) is required.

PENINSULAR REGION

Land area (sq km)	Forest area (sq km)	Area of nature reserve*
70,715	15,485	6,412
	21.9% of land area	9.1% of land area
		41.4% of forest area

(* Excludes areas of coastal waters lying within national parks)

Largest contiguous block = 4,426 sq km (encompasses Khao Sok NP, Khlong Nakha WS and Khlong Saeng WS). This now includes some selectively logged and degraded forest areas.

Geography

Peninsular Thailand is taken to include that part of the country which lies south of 12°N latitude, extending to the Malaysian border. The Tenasserim Range, which flanks western Thailand, extends south to form the steeply mountainous backbone of the region. The mountains rise to their highest elevation at Khao Luang, 1,835 m, though very few other peaks exceed 1,300 m. The most extensive lowland areas lie along the east flank of the peninsular mountain spine and along a corridor which extends south-west between Surat Thani and Krabi. The western coastline is highly crenellated with many mangrove inlets and offshore islands (Figure 1).

The Peninsula is much less seasonal than are most areas of Continental Thailand with temperatures ranging from 13.7°C to 38.0°C and an annual rainfall of 1,500–4,000 mm (Table 1). The seasonal distribution of rainfall, however, varies markedly throughout the region: some parts, particularly along the eastern seaboard and in the far south, receive rain from both monsoons so that the dry season is of no more than 2–3 months duration. Along the west coast, from 8° to 10°N latitude, while total rainfall may be even higher, around 3,000–4,000 mm, roughly 80 percent of precipitation occurs during the south-west monsoon, from May to October so that the duration of the dry season is about six months.

Habitats

Forest type	Hill evergreen *	Rainforest	Mangrove
Area (sq km)	376	13,925	2,141
Percentage of total	2.3%	84.7%	13.0%

* Hill evergreen forest area estimated by measuring areas of uplands above 1,000 m, assuming all such areas to be forested.

The high rainfall in Peninsular Thailand has contributed to the development of a lowland rainforest biome which supports a flora and fauna of Sundaic affinities. Under a progressively more seasonal climate, the rainforest is replaced by 'dry evergreen' or semi-evergreen forest, the ecotone being placed by Smitinand *et al.* (1967) at around 10°40'N latitude. This limits the northward dispersal of the Sundaic lowland bird fauna. For the purposes of this report, however, the northern limit of the Peninsular Region is placed at 12°N latitude. The best position for the boundary between the Peninsular and South-west Regions is now largely an academic point, however, since very little forest remains between 11° and 12°N latitude.

A second boundary runs south-west between 6° and 7°N latitude and this is the ecotone between the 'Thai-type' or semi-evergreen rainforest which occupies the more seasonal areas and the 'Malayan-type' or evergreen rainforest in the least seasonal areas (Whitmore 1975). These rainforest subtypes may be distinguished by differences in their floristic communities. At least five bird species appear to be restricted to the Malayan rainforest zone so that, in terms of both vegetation and lowland bird fauna, Peninsular Thailand may be further subdivided.

- *The Thai-type rainforest zone.* The world range of one species of bird, *Pitta gurneyi*, is entirely restricted to this vegetational zone in Peninsular Thailand and in adjacent South Burma. *Rhinomyias olivacea*, which is absent from Malaysia but which reappears in the Greater Sundas, also occurs here. Many subspecies of birds in the Thai-type rainforest zone differ from those in Malaysia and nine are apparently endemic. All of the existing nature reserves in Peninsular Thailand are situated in this subregion.

- *The Malayan-type rainforest zone.* This encompasses the forest in the southernmost provinces of Pattani, Yala and Narathiwat. Five to seven species of bird (*Eurostopodus temminckii, Pitta granatina, Hemipus hirundinaceus, Criniger finschii, Trichastoma sepiarium* and probably also *Buceros rhinoceros* and *Rhinomyias umbratilis*) may be restricted to this zone. One further species, *Loriculus galgulus*, is apparently shared between this zone and the far south of the Thai-type rainforest zone. No national parks or wildlife sanctuaries have yet been established in this subregion.

The level lowlands in Peninsular Thailand have been almost entirely cleared for agriculture and settlement. No more than 4.7 percent of the estimated original rainforest cover, below 200 m elevation, now remains, even by the most optimistic estimate, while approximately one-third of the area of hill slope forests below 600 m elevation has also now been cleared (from data supplied by Royal Forest Department and analysed by Center for Wildlife Research). Hill slopes clearance has been exceptionally severe in the Malayan-type rainforest zone of the extreme southern provinces where the mountain topography is less steep. Existing forest cover maps for the Peninsula probably give a better indication of those areas which are of significance for wildlife conservation than do those in other regions, because of sharper gradation between the remaining evergreen forests and the drier, degraded areas. Even so, many selectively logged and degraded areas, and in a few cases even oil-palm and rubber plantations, are still classified as forest. The present estimates of the cover of mangrove are also believed to be highly unreliable. An aerial survey of the entire west coast of the

Peninsula in 1984 revealed that very little tall primary mangrove remained (Starks 1985).

Bird Fauna

Lowlands. The lowland bird fauna of the Peninsular Thailand is principally of Sundaic origin and there are approximately 137 species of birds whose Thai range is confined to the region. At least five species, *Rhizothera longirostris*, *Rollulus rouloul*, *Nyctyornis amictus*, *Indicator archipelagicus* and *Arachnothera affinis* extend into South-west Thailand while three more, *Cuculus vagans*, *Malacopteron cinereum* and *Zosterops everetti*, though apparently absent from the South-west, reappear in South-east Thailand. (*M. cinereum* even extends into the extreme south of the North-eastern Region.) The bird fauna of the entire Malay Peninsula has been studied in great detail and fewer Sundaic species occur with northward progression along the Peninsula, most reaching their northern limit in the Isthmus of Kra, between 10°30'N and 11°00'N latitude (Medway and Wells 1976). On the wetter, Burmese side of the peninsular mountain spine, many species extend further north still and, even in Thailand, the exact northern limit for some species is unknown since the Kra zoogeographical boundary has received little attention in recent years

Many Sundaic bird species are mainly restricted to the forests of the level lowlands (Table 12). Such species either do not occur above the hill-foot boundary or, where they do, populations may not be self-supporting in those areas which lack adjoining flat land forest (Wells 1985, D. R. Wells *in litt.*). This 'diversity attenuation phenomenon' is a very severe conservation problem in Thailand where almost all areas of level lowlands have been cleared (Figure 4). Most nature reserves comprise forests of the submontane slopes, above 100 m elevation and have no more than small fragments of lowland habitats around their margins. In addition, it appears that more lowland Sundaic birds are either more altitudinally restricted or are more patchily distributed in Thailand than in Malaysia and are more liable to be confined to the level lowlands (Table 12). The Dark-throated Oriole *Oriolus xanthonotus* and the Rufous-crowned Babbler *Malacopteron magnum*, for example, neither of which is regarded as a lowland specialist by Wells (1985) have been found to be abundant in fragments of level lowland forest, even at the northern extremity of their Thai ranges, yet both species are either extremely scarce or are absent on hill slopes. The trogon, *Harpactes diardii*, has been found up to 900 m in Malaysia, but in Thailand, apart from one record at 300 m, there have been no sightings away from the lowlands and foothills (author's observations). The reduction in bird species diversity with increasing elevation is presumed to be correlated with a decline in overall biotic diversity, which may in turn be related to topography and exposure. The more rapid attenuation of the lowland bird fauna in Peninsular Thailand than in Malaysia may be correlated with the smaller area and much steeper topography of the Thai mountains, combined with the destruction of all the extensive flat land forests which would formerly have surrounded them.

Table 12: Forest bird species resident in Peninsular Thailand which are thought to be at risk due to destruction of extreme lowland forests.

Column 1: Species which are entirely or almost entirely restricted to areas below the hill-foot boundary (D. R. Wells *in litt.*) or which are listed as 'lowland specialists' (Wells 1985).

Column 2: Species not listed as lowland specialists by Wells (1985) but which are apparently more altitudinally restricted in Thailand than in Malaysia.

(R = species restricted to the Peninsula; U = apparently unrepresented in existing nature reserves in Thailand; * species endemic to Peninsular Thailand and S Burma)

Column 1	Column 2
Ciconia stormi (R)	*Macheirhamphus alcinus* (R)
Icthyophaga ichthyaetus (U)	*Rhizothera longirostris* (U)
Spizaetus nanus (R)	*Rollulus rouloul* (U)
Arborophila charltonii (RU)	*Harpactes kasumba* (R)
Lophura ignita (R)	*H. diardii* (R)
Polyplectron malacense (RU)	*H. duvaucelii* (R)
Heliopais personata	*Pitta caerulea* (R)
Treron fulvicollis (RU)	*P. gurneyi* (RU) *
T. olax (R)	*Hemipus hirundinaceus* (RU)
T. capellei (RU)	*Pycnonotus zeylanicus* (RU)
Ducula aenea	*P. eutilotus* (R)
Psittinus cyanurus (R)	*Oriolus xanthonotus* (R)
Otus sagittatus (R)	*Malacopteron magnum* (R)
O. rufescens (RU)	*Stachyris maculata* (RU)
Batrachostomus auritus (RU)	*S. leucotis* (R)
B. stellatus (RU)	*S. nigricollis* (RU)
Harpactes orrhophaeus (R)	
Rhyticeros corrugatus (R)	
R. subruficollis	
Anthracoceros malayanus (R)	
Megalaima rafflesii (R)	
Dryocopus javensis	
Pitta granatina (RU)	
Coracina striata (R)	
Platysmurus leucopterus (R)	
Trichastoma rostratum (R)	
T. bicolor (R)	
Malacopteron affine (RU)	
Kenopia striata (R)	
Napothera macrodactyla (R)	
Macronous ptilosus (RU)	

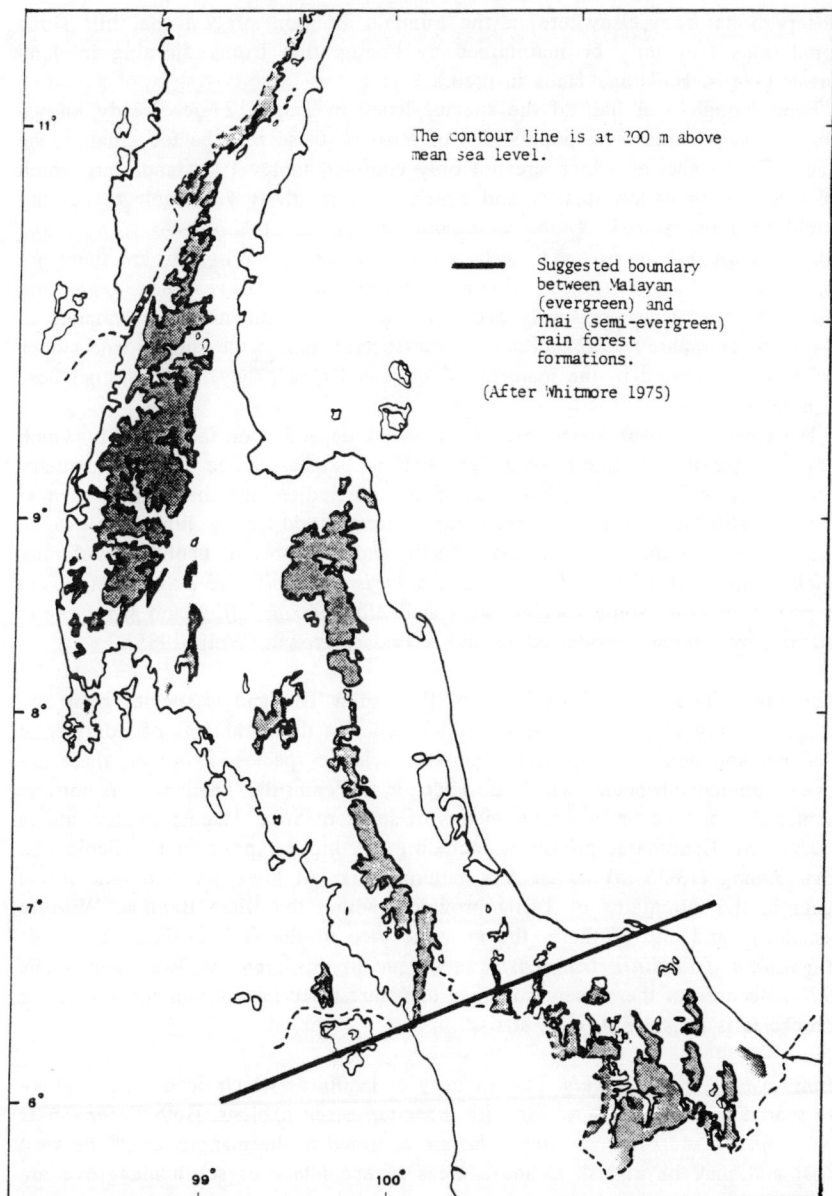

The contour line is at 200 m above mean sea level.

——— Suggested boundary between Malayan (evergreen) and Thai (semi-evergreen) rain forest formations.

(After Whitmore 1975)

Figure 4: Map of Peninsular Thailand to show approximate cover of remaining forest in relation to elevation.

Observations from elsewhere in the Sunda subregion suggest that hill slope populations may only be maintained by immigration from adjoining lowland forests (Wells, Hails and Hails in prep.).

Even though over half of the species listed in Table 12 are already known from protected areas, the populations of most of these may be too small to be viable. Those species which are not only confined to level lowlands but which are large, occur at low density and which are particularly vulnerable to hunting would be most at risk. *Ciconia stormi*, the pheasants *Lophura ignita* and *Polyplectron malacense* and the hornbill *Rhyticeros corrugatus* are therefore considered to be endangered. Although species such as *Argusianus argus* and *Rhinoplax vigil* have previously been considered to be threatened or endangered (Bain and Humphrey 1982), because these species inhabit the submontane slopes and are still present in the majority of protected areas, they may be much less vulnerable.

The conservation of many smaller birds may depend upon the extent to which they can survive in small, secondary habitat patches, since so little primary forest remains in the level lowlands. There are indications that *Pitta gurneyi* may be able to survive in secondary growth and scrub jungle, close to watercourses (Round and Treesucon 1986b) and a number of babblers, including *Trichastoma rostratum*, *T. bicolor* and *Stachyris nigricollis* have also been found in such situations. Some species, such as *Malacopteron affine* and *Macronous ptilosus*, may actually prefer edges and secondary growth (Wells 1985).

Montane. The montane bird fauna of Peninsular Thailand is species poor and comprises only 27 of those species which occur in the mountains of Continental Thailand and none of the Sunda montane endemic species. However, there are seven montane subspecies which are endemic to Peninsular Thailand. All but one montane species occur in the mountains of southern Surat Thani province and in Nakhon Si Thammarat province, including the highest peak in the Peninsula, Khao Luang (1,835 m) which is a national park. At least nine montane forms occur in the mountains of Trang province, within the Khao Banthad Wildlife Sanctuary, and one of these, the endemic race of the Golden-throated Barbet *Megalaima franklinii trangensis*, is unique to this area (Medway and Wells 1976). Because of the present coverage of nature reserves, no montane species or subspecies is considered to be at risk.

Mangrove, offshore islands. The majority of landbirds which occur in mangrove are shared with coastal scrub or with other terrestrial habitats. Both *Pelargopsis amauroptera* and *Pitta megarhyncha* are confined to the mangroves of the west coast and may be at risk as more areas of secondary or scrub mangrove are converted to fish ponds. *Halcyon coromanda*, which breeds in mangroves, may also be at risk although this species breeds in adjacent coastal vegetation (Medway and Wells 1976). The loss of large stature mangrove trees is almost certainly implicated in the decline of larger waterbirds which have been deprived of secure nesting areas. The present status of *Ardea sumatrana* is not reliably known although it still occurs on some offshore islands. *Leptoptilos javanicus* has declined severely and may no longer nest in Thailand.

Island forests support far fewer bird species than do those on the mainland and this probably reflects post isolation selective pressures, chance extinctions and habitat differences. Island forests are, however, the key habitats for certain species such as the pigeons *Ducula bicolor* and *Caloenas nicobarica*. *C. nicobarica* is entirely restricted to islands while both *Ducula bicolor* and *D. aenea* are much commoner on islands than on the mainland. The seasonal status of *Columba punicea* is somewhat unclear as most records are from the winter months. However, there have been unconfirmed reports of it breeding in the Tarutao National Park. Undisturbed island forests which support all these species are found in this and some other island national parks.

Table 13: Additional bird species which are present in Peninsular Thailand and which are thought to be at risk, other than those in Table 12.

(R = range in Thailand restricted to the Peninsula, U = unrepresented in any nature reserve)

Ardeidae:	*Ardea sumatrana*
Ciconiidae:	*Mycteria leucocephala* (U), *Ephippiorhynchus asiaticus* (U), *Leptoptilos javanicus* (U)
Accipitridae:	*Icthyophaga humilis*, *Gyps bengalensis* (U)
Phasianidae:	*Argusianus argus* (R)
Columbidae:	*Caloenas nicobarica* (R)
Alcedinidae:	*Pelargopsis amauroptera* (R), *Halcyon coromanda*
Bucerotidae:	*Berenicornis comatus* (R), *Anorrhinus galeritus* (R), *Rhyticeros undulatus*, *Buceros rhinoceros* (RU), *B. bicornis*, *Rhinoplax vigil* (R)
Eurylaimidae:	*Cymbirhynchus macrorhynchos*
Pittidae:	*Pitta megarhyncha* (R)

List of sites

Existing nature reserves (Map 12).

KHLONG NAKHA WS, KHLONG SAENG WS and KHAO SOK NP 2,280 sq km; maximum elevation 1,395 m. (Code nos. 15, 16, 04). Three separate but contiguous administrative units which are best treated as a single nature reserve block.

Habitat: Steep, forested slopes with small areas of lowland habitat below 100–200 m remaining and with some areas of limestone crags. Some parts of the area have been selectively logged. The most significant lowland forested areas, 165 sq km below 100 m elevation, along the Khlong Phrasaeng and its tributaries, were flooded during 1986–1987 by the Chiew Larn hydro-electric dam.

Bird community: Partial inventory. Supports many vulnerable or endangered bird species, including *Ciconia stormi* (Nakhasathien 1987), *Lophura ignita*,

Argusianus argus, Heliopais personata, Harpactes orrhophaeus and at least six species of hornbills. *Dinopium rafflesii* is also present.

Assessment: KEY SITE. The largest contiguous nature reserve area in Peninsular Thailand.

KHAO LUANG NP 570 sq km; maximum elevation 1,835 m. (Code no. 05).

Habitat: Rainforest on lower slopes, with areas of elfin, low stature hill evergreen forest at high elevation. Reserve boundary mostly follows the 300 m contour so that there is very little extreme lowland habitat remaining. The park is now transected by a highway.

Bird community: Partial inventory (King 1966; J. Nabhitabhata pers. comm.). Still supports *Argusianus argus* and *Berenicornis comatus*. The high elevations support a number of endemic races of small montane birds, including *Aethopyga nipalensis australis*.

Assessment: KEY SITE for montane species and subspecies. Part of a contiguous forest block of ca. 1,000 sq km.

KHLONG PHRAYA WS 95 sq km; maximum elevation 502 m. (Code no. 17).

Habitat: Rainforest on steep mountain slopes. The approximately 23 sq km of the sanctuary area in the level lowlands has been mainly cleared and planted with oil palm and other crops, although at least one key lowland patch of 5 sq km remains.

Bird community: Partial survey; at least 168 species known, including many key lowland species: *Macheirhamphus alcinus, Treron olax, Harpactes kasumba, H. diardii, Rhyticeros corrugatus, Napothera macrodactyla* and *Macronous ptilosus*. One territory of *Pitta gurneyi* has been located immediately outside the sanctuary boundary (J. Parr pers. comm.).

Assessment: KEY SITE, which has been greatly damaged by illegal logging and by the encroachment of villagers within the past five years. Much better protection is needed and in addition, the boundary should be extended in order to encompass lowland secondary growth around the margins and additional areas of hill slope forest to the east and south, thereby linking the site with the adjacent Khao Phanom Bencha National Park.

KHAO PHANOM BENCHA NP 50 sq km; maximum elevation 1,350 m. (Code no. 10).

Habitat: Rainforest on slopes of a steep, 8 km wide mountain range. Small areas of hill evergreen forest.

Bird community: Partial survey; 151 species of bird known, including *Argusianus argus, Berenicornis comatus, Rhinoplax vigil* and *Kenopia striata*. Three territories of *Pitta gurneyi* have been found in lowland forest/secondary growth patches outside the eastern boundary of the site (J. Parr pers. comm.).

Assessment: KEY SITE which has been subject to illegal logging and a high level of hunting pressure. Much improved protection, including the construction of additional guard stations, is needed. The boundary should be extended in order to encompass secondary growth and logged forest patches outside the park margins.

KHAO PU NP 694 sq km; maximum elevation 810 m. (Code no. 11).
Habitat: Rainforest on steep slopes. The park boundary is highly convoluted, mostly following the 100 m contour and habitats at the lower elevations are probably much encroached. The park area includes some isolated mountain outcrops which are separated from the main body of the park by cultivated lowlands.
Bird community: Preliminary inventory only; supports *Ictinaetus malayensis*, *Batrachostomus javensis*, *Berenicornis comatus* (U. Treesucon pers. comm.).
Assessment: Important in view of its size and proximity to Khao Banthad WS (from which separated by a main highway).

KHAO BANTHAD WS 1,267 sq km; maximum elevation 1,350 m. (Code no. 18).
Habitat: Rainforest, with small areas of hill evergreen on steep slopes. Includes approximately 5 sq km of forest below 200 m, along the Namtok Kachong stream at the northern extremity. The largest areas of level lowlands in the south of the reserve are now deforested.
Bird community: Detailed inventory based on recent observations and older records (CWR; Riley 1938). Key lowland species include *Spizaetus nanus*, *Harpactes diardii*, *H. orrhophaeus*, *H. duvaucelii*. May still support *Lophura ignita* and *Napothera macrodactyla*. At least five species of hornbills are present. The montane areas support an endemic race of *Megalaima franklinii* which is unrecorded elsewhere. *Pitta gurneyi* was formerly recorded from lowlands in or near the present day sanctuary (Collar, Round and Wells 1986).
Assessment: KEY SITE for both lowland and montane species.

TON NGA CHANG WS 182 sq km; maximum elevation 932 m. (Code no. 19).
Habitat: Rainforest on hill slopes, with extensive 'semi-plateau' areas. Relatively little forest remains below 200 m. Contiguous with Thaleban NP to the south.
Bird community: Partial list only; 146 species of resident and migrant birds recorded. Closer to the evergreen rainforest zone than other nature reserves and may possibly support some of the species with a restricted range in the far south, such as *Buceros rhinoceros*. The density of *Argusianus argus* may be higher than in most other reserves. *Harpactes diardii*, *Anorrhinus galeritus* and *Buceros bicornis* are all present.
Assessment: KEY SITE

THALEBAN NP 102 sq km; maximum elevation 720 m. (Code no. 13).
Habitat: Rainforest on steep hill slopes, with only small areas of forest below 150 m elevation.

Bird community: Partial inventory; 201 species of resident and migrant birds known. Supports *Argusianus argus* and at least six species of hornbill including *Anthracoceros malayanus* and *Rhinoplax vigil*. *Heliopais personata* (one pair) are regularly present on a small, forest edge pond, though it is not known whether the species is resident here.
Assessment: KEY SITE.

Offshore islands and coastal sites

LAEM SON NP   Area of land and water 315 sq km, including marine area of 267 sq km; maximum elevation 298 m. (Code no. 01).
Habitat: Sandy beach, open water and small, offshore islets. Adjacent inlets supporting degraded mangrove lie outside the park boundary.
Bird community: Not surveyed; probably of limited conservation value for landbirds.

MU KO SURIN NP   Area 135 sq km, including marine area of 102 sq km; maximum elevation 350 m. (Code no. 02). Not shown on map.
Habitat: Forested offshore islets (land area 30 sq km), situated 53 km off the west coast.
Bird community: Partial inventory. Supports *Ducula bicolor, D. aenea* and *Caloenas nicobarica*. *Rhyticeros undulatus* is present. *Halcyon coromanda* is reported common (Brockelman and Nadee 1977).
Assessment: KEY SITE.

MU KO ANG THONG NP   Area 102 sq km, including marine area of 84 sq km; maximum elevation 342 m. (Code no. 03).
Habitat: Islands, situated 30 km off east coast. Disturbed, semi-evergreen rainforest and secondary growth.
Bird community: Preliminary inventory. Supports both *Ducula bicolor* and *D. aenea*.

MU KO SIMILAN NP   Area of land and water 128 sq km, including marine area of 114 sq km; maximum elevation 244 m. (Code no. 07). Not shown on map.
Habitat: Islets, situated 65 km off west coast. Undisturbed semi-evergreen rainforest.
Bird community: Not surveyed; supports *Caloenas nicobarica*.

AO PHANG-NGA NP   Area of land and water 400 sq km, including marine area of 347 sq km; maximum elevation 439 m. (Code no. 06).
Habitat: A large bay, encompassing over 40 wooded, limestone islets. Large areas of low stature, secondary or fringing mangrove. Much of the area has been cut over.
Bird community: Not surveyed; supports *Haliaeetus leucogaster*. Probably supports *Ducula bicolor*, as well as *Pelargopsis amauroptera* and *Pitta megarhyncha* in mangroves.

Assessment: POSSIBLE KEY SITE. The most extensive areas of mangrove in Phang-nga Bay are outside the park boundary, which should be extended.

HAT NAI YANG NP   Area 90 sq km, including marine area of 68 sq km; maximum elevation 335 m. (Code no. 08).
Habitat: Narrow coastal strip, with sandy beach and rocky headlands.
Bird community: Preliminary survey. Of no conservation significance for forest birds.

MU KO PHI PHI NP   Area 390 sq km, including marine area of 326 sq km; maximum elevation 374 m. (Code no. 09).
Habitat: Rocky mainland coast around the town of Krabi and two islands, situated 26 km offshore. Vegetation much disturbed, but small areas of primary forest remain on the steeper, less accessible slopes. Human habitation within park.
Bird community: Well surveyed; supports *Haliaeetus leucogaster*, *Falco peregrinus* and *Ducula bicolor*. *Caloenas nicobarica* is still present on Ko Maa, a small islet outside the park boundary, while areas of mangrove around Krabi Town, adjacent to the park, support *Pelargopsis amauroptera*, *Halcyon coromanda*, *Pitta megarhyncha*, *Trichastoma rostratum* and *Nectarinia calcostetha* (C. Robson pers. comm.).
Assessment: Boundary should be extended to incorporate Ko Maa, together with areas of mangrove on the mainland at Krabi Town

HAT CHAO MAI NP   Area of land and water 231 sq km, including marine area of 137 sq km; maximum elevation 432 m. (Code no. 12).
Habitat: Coastal beach and offshore islets. Encompasses steep, forested hills and degraded mangrove.
Bird community: Not surveyed. Recent unconfirmed reports of the continued presence of *Ephippiorhynchus asiaticus* which formerly bred at this site (Robinson and Chasen 1936).

TARUTAO NP   Area of land and water 1,490 sq km, including marine area of 1,230 sq km; maximum elevation 721 m. (Code no. 14).
Habitat: An island group, extending 26 to 71 km off the west coast. The largest single island has a land area of 151 sq km. Supports semi-evergreen rainforest, secondary growth and small areas of mangrove (Congdon 1982).
Bird community: Partial inventory. Supports *Ardea sumatrana*, *Heliopais personata*, *Ducula bicolor*, *D. aenea*, *Caloenas nicobarica*, *Pelargopsis amauroptera*, *Halcyon coromanda*, *Rhyticeros undulatus*, *Buceros bicornis*, *Pitta megarhyncha* (Congdon 1981, Medway and Wells 1976). *Columba punicea* also recorded, though status uncertain.
Assessment: KEY SITE.

Additional sites

KHLONG MALA – KHLONG SAI ON and surroundings (ca. 10°43'N, 99°00'E).
Map 11.
Habitat: Approximately 910 sq km of rainforest which extends across northern
Chumphon and Ranong provinces to the Burmese border. Until 1984, still
encompassed 150 sq km of forest on mainly level lowlands at 100–200 m
elevation along the Khlong Mala and its major tributary, the Khlong Sai On.
Bird community: Partial survey. Supports a number of key lowland species
including *Harpactes orrhophaeus*, *Platysmurus leucopterus*, *Napothera
macrodactyla*, and *Malacopteron affine*. *Trichastoma bicolor* and *Malacopteron
magnum* are abundant. The area is close to former localities for *Pitta gurneyi*,
which may well occur. *Argusianus argus* and five species of hornbill including
Rhinoplax vigil are also present (CWR).
Assessment: KEY SITE. Of importance because it encompasses an area of
rainforest of unique biological significance, north of the Isthmus of Kra, near the
northern extremity of the Sunda subregion. Surveys carried out by a Cambridge-
based expedition in 1987 revealed that most of the lowlands had been cleared by
illegal settlers, while the most extensive hill slope forests are scheduled for
logging. Part of the area is to receive Wildlife Sanctuary status.

THA CHANA DISTRICT (9°34'N, 98°57'E). Map 12.
Habitat: Rainforest on the gentle, eastern slopes of the peninsular mountain
spine. When first identified in 1984, included approximately 128 sq km of forest
between 100–200 m elevation and a further 116 sq km below 100 m. A survey in
January 1987 revealed that almost all the lowlands had been cleared, though
undisturbed forest remained on the hill slopes.
Bird community: Forest patches still supported a few key lowland species in
January 1987, including *Psittinus cyanurus*, *Dryocopus javensis* and *Napothera
macrodactyla*; *Batrachostomus javensis* fairly abundant. One territory of *Pitta
gurneyi* located.
Assessment: KEY SITE for lowland birds; a park or sanctuary should be
established to encompass primary forest on the hill slopes together with lowland
secondary growth.

MOUNTAINS OF SURAT THANI and NAKHON SI THAMMARAT (ca. 8°50'N,
99°37'E). Maximum elevation 1,530 m. Map 12.
Habitat: Total area approximately 470 sq km, contiguous with Khao Luang NP
(570 sq km) to the south. May still encompass small areas of forest in the
foothills, together with large areas of rainforest on the submontane slopes, and
some areas of hill evergreen forest.
Bird community: Supports most or all of the endemic montane subspecies which
are found on Khao Luang (Medway and Wells 1976) and is certain to still support
large populations of submontane species.
Assessment: One of the largest remaining forest blocks in Peninsular Thailand.
The establishment of an additional park or sanctuary here should be considered.

KHAO PHRA THAEW NON-HUNTING AREA (8°03'N, 98°23'E). Maximum elevation 450 m. Map 12.
Habitat: A semi-evergreen rainforest area of 22 sq km. Supports the endemic palm *Kerriodoxa elegans* J. Dransf. (Dransfield 1983).
Bird community: Partial inventory. Supports a relatively impoverished avifauna, typical of islands. May still support a few hornbills. *Spizaetus alboniger* present.
Assessment: The last remaining patch of primary forest on Phuket Island. Should be upgraded to the status of Wildlife Sanctuary. Illegal hunting continues to pose a threat.

KHAO SI SUK (8°42'N, 98°55'E). Maximum elevation 550 m. Map 12.
Habitat: A small, isolated, forested mountain in an otherwise mainly lowland area with less than 5 sq km of lowland forest and secondary growth around its margins.
Bird community: Partial survey; 156 resident birds recorded, including some important lowland species: *Batrachostomus stellatus*, *Harpactes diardii*, *H. orrhophaeus* and many babblers. *Oriolus xanthonotus* is abundant. Five species of hornbills still present, including *Rhinoplax vigil* (C. Robson and U. Treesucon pers. comm.).
Assessment: POSSIBLE KEY SITE; at present, extremely rich although there may be too little habitat left for the area to be viable. There has been an extremely high level of illegal encroachment into the area by settlers and what little forest remains is under a timber concession.

KHAO WET-KHAO KHAI (8°23'N, 99°12'E). Maximum elevation 415 m. Map 12.
Habitat: A small, isolated mountain in an otherwise mainly lowland area. When originally identified in 1984, forest cover maps showed small areas of lowland forest remaining around the foot of the mountain. This has apparently since been destroyed.
Bird community: Not surveyed, but could still support a few key lowland species.

BAN NAI CHONG (8°11'N, 98°50'E). Maximum elevation 438 m. Map 12.
Habitat: Approximately 5 sq km of logged forest and secondary growth around the base of steep limestone crags. Relatively dry, lacking any permanent watercourses.
Bird community: Partial survey; supports a number of lowland species which are scarce or absent in existing nature reserves, including *Megalaima rafflesii*, *Oriolus xanthonotus*, *Platysmurus leucopterus*, *Napothera macrodactyla* and *Stachyris nigricollis*. *Pitta guajana* is still present, while *Eupetes macrocerus* appears to be fairly common. The site may be too dry to support *Pitta gurneyi*.
Assessment: KEY SITE. The most easily accessible lowland forest fragment remaining anywhere in Peninsular Thailand, though parts of the area have been

encroached upon. The site should be established as a Non-Hunting Area or other category of reserve.

KHAO NOI CHUCHI NON-HUNTING AREA (7°54'N, 99°18'E). Maximum elevation 650 m. Map 12.

Habitat: An isolated, small mountain in an otherwise lowland area. Total area roughly 150 sq km including roughly 30 sq km of logged forest and secondary growth below 200 m elevation.

Bird community: Well surveyed, supporting the most diverse remaining lowland bird fauna of any site so far known in Peninsular Thailand, with over 230 species of resident and migrant birds. The total includes a great many lowland specialists and other species which are scarce elsewhere: *Spizaetus nanus, Rollulus rouloul, Lophura ignita, Treron olax, Ptilinopus jambu, Harpactes diardii, Anthracoceros malayanus, Megalaima rafflesii, Trichastoma bicolor, Malacopteron magnum, Kenopia striata, Napothera macrodactyla, Stachyris maculata* and *S. nigricollis*. This is the only site known to support a potentially viable population of *Pitta gurneyi*, with 12–15 probable territories so far located. *P. caerulea* is also present.

Assessment: KEY SITE for the future of lowland species conservation, in spite of the fact that large areas have been cleared by settlers. At present, it is still threatened by logging, both legal and illegal, and by encroachment for farming. The site has been declared as a Non-Hunting Area, but this alone will be insufficient to protect it unless accompanied by extraordinary protective measures.

KO LIBONG NON-HUNTING AREA (7°15'N, 99°18'E). Maximum elevation 311 m. Map 12.

Habitat: An inhabited island with a small area of terrestrial forest, some plantations and extensive mangrove which, though cut-over, still contains many larger trees.

Bird community: Supports a good variety of mangrove birds, including *Pelargopsis amauroptera* and *Pitta megarhyncha* (Eve and Guigue 1982; CWR).

Assessment: Should be considered for national park status.

PA PHRU NON-HUNTING AREA (6°10'N, 101°58'E). Map 13.

Habitat: A lowland freshwater swamp forest which covers a total area of roughly 340 sq km, of which 98 sq km is still undisturbed primary peat swamp forest, with many tall trees; 146 sq km of *Melaleuca* forest. A detailed description of the vegetation is given by Santisuk and Niyomdham (1985).

Bird community: Preliminary survey; 105 species known. Supports some key level lowland forest species, including *Icthyophaga ichthyaetus, Treron capellei, Anthracoceros malayanus* and *Megalaima rafflesii*. Both *Stachyris nigricollis* and *Macronous ptilosus* are abundant. Local people report the continued presence of *Treron fulvicollis* and the site could also conceivably support *Rhyticeros corrugatus* (U. Treesucon pers. comm.).

Assessment: KEY SITE. The only remaining example of primary peatswamp forest in Thailand, which has been proposed for Biosphere Reserve Status. Part of the area has already been damaged by inappropriate agricultural development; the site should be fully protected.

BUDO MOUNTAIN RANGE (ca. 5°58'N, 101°27'E). Maximum elevation 1,456 m. Map 13.

Habitat: A single forest block of roughly 1,460 sq km on the mountains of Yala and Narathiwat provinces. No forest remains below 200 m elevation, the last such areas along the Khlong Ha La having been flooded by the Bang Lang hydro dam.

Bird community: Preliminary survey only. *Icthyophaga humilis* is still present around the reservoir margins, while the hill slopes are probably still important for the conservation of *Harpactes kasumba*, *Buceros rhinoceros* and other species which are mainly confined to the far south. Significant areas of montane habitat, above 1,000 m.

Assessment: KEY SITE for the establishment of a nature reserve in the Malayan-type rainforest zone; forest contiguous with that on the Malaysian side of the border.

Additional sites established as nature reserves during 1984–1986 for which no data is available:

Mu Ko Phetra NP 494 sq km of land and sea
Khao Lam Pi-Hat Thai Muang NP 72 sq km

Regional assessment

The nature reserve network of Peninsular Thailand occupies over 40 percent of all remaining forest in the region and includes two sites which exceed 1,000 sq km in area. Its most serious shortcoming, however, is the under-representation of extreme lowland forests, along river valleys and in the plains. In the only instance where a major lowland river system has been protected, in the adjacent Khao Sok NP and Khlong Saeng WS, it has subsequently been allowed to be inundated by a hydro-electric dam scheme. Even though 29 of the 43 lowland forest birds listed in Table 12 already occur in existing parks and sanctuaries, because these areas contain so very little lowland forest, the populations of many of these species may be too small to be viable. There is no single forest area remaining which supports a fully representative lowland avifauna.

Deforestation of the Peninsula has now progressed so far that the opportunity to incorporate any extensive areas of plains rainforest has now been already lost. The best strategy for lowland species conservation would therefore be to establish protection at the few additional sites identified in this report and to extend the boundaries of existing parks and sanctuaries, wherever possible, in order to incorporate any small areas of logged lowland forest and secondary growth which may remain around their margins.

A further requirement is for the establishment of a major protected area in the Malayan-type rainforest zone of the extreme southern provinces, which might ensure that the few species which are confined to this biome are represented.

While both island and montane habitats appear to be adequately represented, virtually the entire remaining area of mangrove is either being cut under concession or is in danger of being cleared for aquaculture. The incorporation of additional areas of mangrove along the west coast into the park and sanctuary network should be accorded high priority.

As in other regions of the country, illegal subsistence hunting and the live capture of birds are widely practised and pose major threats. Protection of all existing nature reserves needs to be greatly improved.

Recommendations

Nature reserve establishment. The following areas should be accorded high priority for park or sanctuary status: Khlong Mala-Khlong Sai-On, Tha Chana, Khao Si Suk, Ban Nai Chong and the Budo Mountain range.

The status of the following non-hunting areas should be upgraded to national park or wildlife sanctuary: Khao Phra Thaew, Khao Noi Chuchi, Ko Libong and Pa Phru.

Surveys in existing nature reserves. Of the 21 national parks and wildlife sanctuaries in Peninsular Thailand, none have received full, recent coverage. Priority should be given to surveying the margins of all sites in order to determine the status of lowland habitats, both inside and outside their boundaries.

Boundary changes to existing nature reserves. The boundaries of both Khlong Phraya WS and Khao Phanom Bencha NP should be extended in order to encompass lowland secondary growth and logged forest around their margins. The boundary of Mu Ko Phi Phi NP should be extended in order to incorporate areas of mangrove on the mainland, around Krabi Town. The boundary of Ao Phang-nga NP should be extended to encompass more extensive areas of mangrove.

Species surveys. Priority should be given to determining the present status of all those species which are thought to be lowland specialists, in order to identify those areas which continue to support the greatest lowland species diversity. Particular attention should be paid to *Ciconia stormi, Arborophila charltonii, Rollulus rouloul, Lophura ignita, Polyplectron malacense, Rhyticeros corrugatus, Pitta caerulea* and *P. gurneyi*. Searches should also be made for *Rhizothera longirostris* and *Caloperdix oculea*. Although both species may occur on submontane slopes, they are probably much hunted.

Plate 2: A tall emergent tree at the edge of semi-evergreen forest, 750 m elevation, Khao Yai National Park, North-east Thailand. (U. Treesucon)

Plate 1: A trail through tall, valley bottom rainforest, Khao Banthad Wildlife Sanctuary, Peninsular Thailand. (U. Treesucon)

75

Plate 3: Hill evergreen forest, at 2,000 m elevation, Doi Pha Hom Pok, Northern Thailand. Note the preponderance of mosses and other epiphytes. (P. D. Round)

Plate 4: Dry dipterocarp forest, 600 m elevation, Doi Inthanon National Park, Northern Thailand. Photograph taken in mid April, after the annual dry season burn. Note the flush of new leaves, including the large leaves of *Dipterocarpus tuberculatus*, Roxb. trees and seedlings and the open, grassy ground vegetation. (P. D. Round)

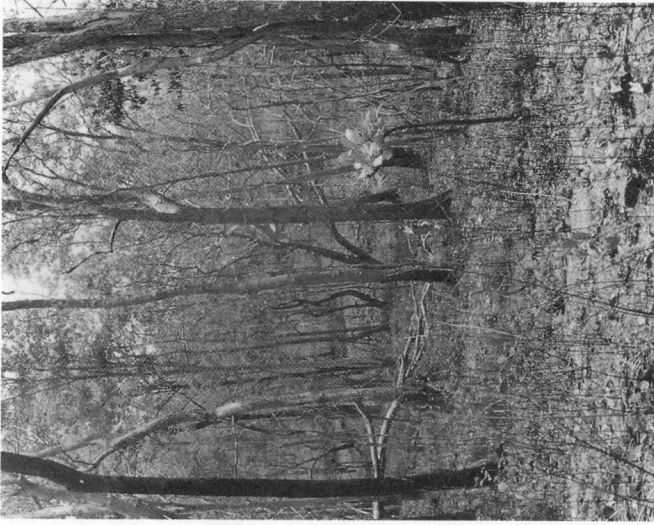

Plate 5: Streamside mixed deciduous forest, 400 m elevation, Huai Kha Khaeng Wildlife Sanctuary, South-west Thailand. Note the preponderance of towering bamboos, *Bambusa arundinacea* Willd. Forest guard in foreground. Photograph taken in January (mid dry season), before onset of annual forest fire. (P. D. Round)

Plate 6: Mixed deciduous forest, 400 m elevation, Huai Kha Khaeng WS. Photograph taken in May, after annual forest fire. Note the very open forest floor. (P. D. Round)

Plate 7: Selectively-logged rainforest near the boundary of Khlong Saeng Wildlife Sanctuary, Peninsular Thailand. (P. D. Round)

Plate 8: Doi Pha Hom Pok, Northern Thailand, November 1983. Hill evergreen forest is now mainly confined to areas above 1,800 m. (P. D. Round)

Plate 9: Kao Sok National Park, Peninsular Thailand. Slash-and-burn encroachment has ascended the foothills to 150 m elevation, within the park boundary. The lowlands in the background now support only secondary growth and cultivation. (P. D. Round)

Plate 10: Illegal bird trapping, Kanchanaburi Province, South-west Thailand. The captive Golden-fronted Leafbird (*Chloropsis aurifrons*) on the right has decoyed a wild individual into the cage trap on the left. (S. Duangkhae)

79

Plate 11: Hill evergreen forest and burnt areas, Om Koi Wildlife Sanctuary, Northern Thailand, March 1982. Note the contrast between Plate 10, photographed in the early dry season and Plate 11, taken in the late dry season when deliberate forest burning is at its height. (P. D. Round)

Plate 12: Khao Yai National Park, North-east Thailand. Much of the park consists of an undulating plateau, above 700 m elevation. Large tracts of little-disturbed semi-evergreen forest are interspersed with grassy fields, relics of former cultivation before the park's establishment in 1962. (P. D. Round)

Plate 14: The interior of semi-evergreen forest, along a streamside. Khao Yai NP, 800 m elevation. (P. D. Round)

Plate 13: Mixed deciduous forest and riverine sandbanks, Huai Kha Khaeng Wildlife Sanctuary. (P. D. Round)

Plate 15: New slash-and-burn in lowland (100 m elevation) rain forest along the Khlong Mala River System, Peninsular Thailand, June 1985. Illegal encroachment by landless settlers has been the principal cause of forest loss in Thailand. (P. D. Round)

Plate 16: Thaleban National Park, Peninsular Thailand. As in most nature reserves in the Peninsula, remaining forest cover is now mostly confined to the submontane slopes, above 100 m elevation. (P. D. Round)

SPECIES STATUS REVIEW

A complete list of resident landbirds, together with information on their distribution, occurrence in protected areas, habitat requirements and status is presented in Appendix I. Those waterbirds which do not show any particular association with forests are listed separately in Appendix III.

The conservation status of resident landbirds and most larger waterbirds is reviewed in the following pages. Six categories are used to assess degrees of threat or potential threat and are defined below. These correspond approximately with those used in IUCN/ICBP Red Data Books (King 1978–1979) save that the 'vulnerable' category has been subdivided into 'threatened' and 'vulnerable' so as to more closely define the degree of threat. Unless otherwise stated, these categories are used only to define a species' status within Thailand and should not be used to make any inference concerning its international conservation status. Many species will, however, face similar types or degree of threat throughout their world ranges.

Extinct. Species believed to have been extirpated in Thailand.

Endangered. A species in which the numbers are believed to have been reduced to such a critical level that it is considered to be in imminent danger of extinction.

Threatened. A species in which the populations have been greatly reduced or have been regionally extirpated so that it may soon become endangered.

Vulnerable. A species which, though still present and even numerous in existing protected areas or elsewhere, is declining due to its susceptibility to current threats. If present levels of direct or indirect disturbances are maintained, the species could enter the 'threatened' category.

Indeterminate. A species which is probably eligible for any of the above categories, but for which insufficient information on status or habitat requirements exists.

Rare. A species with localised populations in restricted habitats, usually on higher mountain summits. Most such species are locally abundant and do not appear to be at risk at present. Grassland species which are similarly restricted (e.g. White-browed Laughing Thrush *Garrulax sannio* which is known from only two mountains) are excluded since the areas of suitable habitat for such species are presumed to be expanding with increased deforestation.

The term 'at risk' is used only to describe those species which are listed in the categories 'endangered', 'threatened', 'vulnerable' or 'indeterminate'.

In assessing the status of any species, the following factors have been considered:

- Number of discrete localities from which known. A species with a small range or one which has disappeared from parts of its former range may be more at risk than a species which is widespread.
- Occurrence in protected areas. A species which is not present in any national park or wildlife sanctuary would be more at risk than one which is.
- Ecological tolerance. A species which inhabits forest and secondary growth across a wide altitudinal range would be less vulnerable than would a species which is only known from, say, lowland forests in the immediate vicinity of streams or rivers.
- Degree of disturbance to preferred habitat. A species which is confined to a forest type which has been largely cleared would be at greater risk than a species which still has abundant habitat remaining.
- Size and relative abundance. Larger birds would, on average, occur at a lower density than would smaller birds and should therefore be less numerous in any forest block. Larger birds would also be at greater risk of being shot for food.
- Number and types of threat. The most vulnerable species would be those which are subject to a combination of threats; namely habitat destruction, hunting for food and live capture for the avicultural trade.

Larger waterbirds

Extinct: *Pseudibis davisoni, P. gigantea, Grus antigone.*

Endangered: *Pelecanus philippensis, Mycteria leucocephala, Ciconia episcopus, C. stormi, Ephippiorhynchus asiaticus, Leptoptilos dubius, L. javanicus, Threskiornis melanocephala, Sarkidiornis melanotos, Cairina scutulata.*

Threatened: *Anhinga melanogaster, Ardea sumatrana.*

Although most of these species are not strictly forest birds, in view of the extreme threats which they face, their status deserves review. Many species (*Pseudibis davisoni, P. gigantea, Ciconia episcopus, Ephippiorhynchus asiaticus, Leptoptilos dubius, Sarkidiornis melanotos, Cairina scutulata* and *Grus antigone*) inhabit, or formerly inhabited, open lowland forests with scattered clearings and small ponds as well as open marshes. Others (*Pelecanus philippensis, Anhinga melanogaster, Mycteria leucocephala* and *Leptoptilos javanicus*) formerly nested in freshwater swamp forests or mangroves. In most cases, direct human persecution, combined with the drainage of wetlands and the loss of secure feeding, roosting and nesting areas rather than deforestation itself, has brought about their decline.

Most of the species listed as endangered now only occur as wandering non-breeders, though a few pairs of *Mycteria* still breed at the Thale Noi Non-Hunting Area in Peninsular Thailand. *Ciconia episcopus* still occurs in lowland forest in the Khao Ang Ru Nai Wildlife Sanctuary, South-east Thailand. It is possible that further pairs of this, and other large waterbirds, may also be found in the extensive lowlands of the upper River Khwae, in the little-explored Thung Yai Wildlife Sanctuary.

The Storm's Stork *Ciconia stormi* has only recently been discovered breeding in valley bottom rainforest in the Khlong Saeng Wildlife Sanctuary (Nakhasathien 1987). Though villagers reportedly knew of two pairs, the area was already being inundated by the Chiew Larn Hydro Dam at the time of discovery. Unless the birds are able to adapt to the modified environment, the species may be facing extinction as no other suitable forested basins exist elsewhere in Peninsular Thailand.

The Comb Duck *Sarkidiornis melanotos* is still reported to breed in one area in Buriram Province, North-east Thailand, and a few pairs may occur elsewhere. The White-winged Duck *Cairina scutulata*, which favours denser forests, close to still water bodies in areas of gentle topography, has been reliably reported from four protected areas (S. Singhapant pers. comm.). Of these, the huge Thung Yai and Huai Kha Khaeng block offer the best hope for the species' survival, though significant numbers may also be present in Yot Dom Wildlife Sanctuary, near the Thai-Kampuchean border. Three individuals were captured near the latter site in winter 1985/86 but the sanctuary has not been properly surveyed, since it is a stronghold of Khmer Rouge insurgents.

The only recent confirmed records of *Ardea sumatrana* are from Tarutao National Park (Congdon 1981). This species appears to be exclusively associated with mangrove coastlines and offshore islets and has almost certainly declined due to mangrove clearance and persecution.

Falconiformes

Extinct: *Gyps indicus.*

Endangered: *Icthyophaga ichthyaetus, Gyps bengalensis, Aegypius calvus.*

Threatened: *Macheirhamphus alcinus, Milvus migrans, Icthyophaga humilis, Spizaetus nanus.*

The great majority of the resident raptors in Thailand are associated with wooded country, including mangroves. Because of the relatively large size of most species and their low breeding densities, they should be among the more vulnerable birds, being affected both by habitat destruction and by hunting. Those species which feed mostly or entirely in forest, however, should be less susceptible to pesticide poisoning than those species which occur in proximity to agricultural land.

Populations of Black Kites *Milvus migrans* and vultures, formerly commensals of man, have collapsed in Thailand and the Long-billed Vulture *G. indicus* may be already extinct. While human persecution and the use of poisoned baits may have contributed to their decline (McNeely 1975), a shortage of available carrion is also probably implicated. The only resident population of the White-rumped Vulture *G. bengalensis* known is up to 21 birds from the vicinity of a slaughter house in Pattani Province, Southern Thailand, where offal is disposed of by throwing it into a field (J. Howes *in litt.*). The Red-headed Vulture *Aegypius calvus* is still found in Huai Kha Khaeng and Thung Yai Wildlife Sanctuaries, where up to 22 individuals have been seen together (T. Prayurasiddhi pers. comm.). The species inhabits the open deciduous forests of remote river valleys and lower hills, feeding primarily on the carcases of large mammals, including the 'kills' of tigers *Panthera tigris* Linnaeus.

The majority of forest raptors appear to be still fairly frequent. The Black Eagle *Ictinaetus malayensis*, for example, is not listed as being at risk because it was still present in Doi Suthep-Pui National Park during 1978–1984 even though the five species of hornbill which formerly occurred there had been extirpated (Round 1984). Although, like many other large birds in Thailand, raptors are widely shot for food, they may be less affected by limited deforestation, since forest clearings might provide additional feeding opportunities. Also, the majority of species inhabit hilly country and should be less vulnerable to lowland forest destruction. Exceptions include the Wallace's Hawk-Eagle *Spizaetus nanus* which, throughout the Malay Peninsula, may be mainly restricted to the level lowlands (Wells 1985) and possibly also the Bat Hawk *Macheirhamphus alcinus*, which may not have been reliably recorded above low altitudes. Both of these species are still present in protected areas, however. Both the Lesser Fish-Eagle *Icthyophaga humilis* and the Grey-headed Fish-Eagle *I. ichthyaetus* are also at risk. The former is still known from forested stream valleys in both South-west and Peninsular Thailand. *I. ichthyaetus* is apparently restricted to the plains and may be close to extinction as there have been only two recent sightings (Eve and Guigue 1982, U. Treesucon pers. comm.). It is not known whether the species utilises any man-made irrigation reservoirs, some of which still possess areas of woodland around their margins.

In this report, a generally cautious approach to the listing of raptors as endangered has been taken, though like most other large birds, their status deserves close monitoring.

Phasianidae

Endangered: *Rhizothera longirostris, Arborophila charltonii, Rollulus rouloul, Lophura ignita, Syrmaticus humiae, Polyplectron malacense.*

Threatened: *Arborophila rufogularis, A. cambodiana, Lophura diardi, Pavo muticus.*

Vulnerable: *Arborophila brunneopectus, Lophura leucomelana, L. nycthemera, Polyplectron bicalcaratum, Argusianus argus.*

This family includes many species which are at risk, both due to forest destruction and to hunting pressure. Not only are most species shot for food, but they are also trapped alive for the illegal cagebird trade. The secretive behaviour of many species can, however, complicate assessment of their status. There are few recent records of the Ferruginous Wood-Partridge *Caloperdix oculea*, for example, yet because this species primarily inhabits submontane slopes, much apparently suitable forest habitat remains within its range. Both Long-billed Partridge *Rhizothera longirostris* and Crested Wood Partridge, *Rollulus rouloul* are probably at risk. Though neither is listed as a lowland specialist by Wells (1985), and *Rhizothera* has been recorded up to 1,500 m in Malaysia (Wells 1983), the only recent records from Peninsular Thailand have come from the lowlands and foothills outside protected areas. According to rural people, both species have disappeared from areas where they were formerly common. Three further endangered species, Chestnut-necklaced Partridge *Arborophila charltonii*, Crested Fireback *Lophura ignita* and Malaysian Peacock Pheasant *Polyplectron malacense* are also restricted to the lowlands. *P. malacense* is almost extinct in Thailand, judging by the reports of rural people and the high prices paid for the few birds which still enter the trade. Davison (1981) considered that *Lophura ignita* was limited to lowland forests close to riverbanks, but villagers' reports would suggest that it is still present in the forested foothills in a few parks and sanctuaries in Thailand.

Although Hume's Pheasant *Syrmaticus humiae*, which inhabits uplands in the north-west has not been reliably recorded for many years and had apparently disappeared from Doi Suthep by 1935 (Deignan 1945), unconfirmed reports of its continued occurrence have been received elsewhere: from Doi Chiang Dao (a former locality) and from Doi Langka (Young 1967). A skin from the Thai-Burmese border area was obtained from a trapper in 1983 (S. Norapuckprutikorn pers. comm.). Both this species and the Rufous-throated Partridge *Arborophila rufogularis* are at risk because their ranges overlap almost completely with the distribution of the various tribes of upland shifting cultivators. Though *A. rufogularis* is still locally numerous, it has disappeared from at least one former locality (Round 1984).

The Chestnut-headed Partridge *Arborophila cambodiana* is restricted to the mountains of South-east Thailand. Though most of its available habitat is already enclosed in protected areas, it is certainly at risk from the high level of hunting pressure. A distinctive race of the Silver Pheasant *Lophura nycthemera lewisi* is also restricted to the same region and is much more vulnerable than the widespread *L. n. jonesi* as it is especially sought after by aviculturists in Bangkok. While both *L. n. jonesi* and the Kalij Pheasant *L. leucomelana* are still locally common, the Siamese Fireback *L. diardi* is at greater risk. It inhabits lowland semi-evergreen forests in the eastern part of the country and is therefore now limited to a relatively narrow zone, above the upper limit of cultivation but below those areas occupied by *L. nycthemera*, with which it scarcely overlaps altitudinally. In addition, even where forest remains, its habitat is extremely patchy since large parts of the lowlands are dominated by unsuitable, deciduous formations.

The Green Peafowl *Pavo muticus* has disappeared from most of the country due to human persecution. However, a population of at least 200 individuals occurs in the Huai Kha Khaeng Wildlife Sanctuary, in the open deciduous woodlands and clearings of a lowland river system. A few birds also occur elsewhere, in Thung Yai Wildlife Sanctuary (Phumpakapun and Kutintara 1983), Salawin Wildlife

Sanctuary (B. Stewart-Cox pers. comm.) and perhaps also in Yot Dom Wildlife Sanctuary. Riparian habitats elsewhere, on the lower Khwae Yai and Khwae Noi Rivers, and on the Ping and Nan Rivers, have either been cleared or settled or inundated by hydro-electric reservoirs. Reports of its continued occurrence elsewhere (Bain and Humphrey 1982, King 1978–79) are probably erroneous. The species is still illegally shot for food and in the past, males were hunted solely for their ornamental upper tail coverts (N. Phumpakapun pers. comm.). More often, however, these are collected where they have fallen, after the post nuptial moult. Young birds which may be wild-taken still appear from time to time in the Bangkok Weekend Market (Mrs S. Dobias pers. comm.).

Turnicidae

Three species of buttonquail (*Turnix* spp.) are found in Thailand and all are fairly common in grassland or in open cultivated areas and are not subject to any known threat.

Rallidae

Of ten species of crake and rail species, only the Slaty-legged Crake *Rallina eurizonoides* and the Red-legged Crake *R. fasciata* are primarily forest-living and both have recently been found in moist areas on the low-lying deciduous forests of Huai Kha Khaeng. *R. fasciata* may also be fairly widespread in forests and secondary growth in the Peninsula. Most other recent records probably concern passage or wintering individuals. In addition, the Black-tailed Crake *Porzana bicolor* has recently been discovered in Thailand (Seriot *et al.* 1986). An apparently resident population exists along a streamside in a deforested area of Doi Inthanon National Park and the species could well be widespread in Northern Thailand (Inskipp and Round in prep.).

Heliornithidae

Threatened: *Heliopais personata*

The Masked Finfoot *Heliopais personata* is thought to be at risk due to the destruction of its forest pond or streamside and mangrove habitat. While the species has been recently recorded at various sites in Peninsular Thailand, and also in Thung Yai Wildlife Sanctuary in the South-west (Phumpakapun and Kutintara 1983), it is not known whether it is resident there. Medway and Wells (1976) consider that *Heliopais* is a non-breeding visitor to the Malay Peninsula and both the Thai and Malaysian records span a similar period, from November to July. It is unrecorded whether *Heliopais* utilises larger water-bodies, such as hydro dams which have inundated areas of formerly suitable, lowland riverine habitats.

Columbidae

Threatened: *Treron fulvicollis, T. olax, T. capellei, Caloenas nicobarica.*

Vulnerable: *Treron pompadora, T. phoenicoptera, Ducula aenea, Columba pulchricollis.*

Many pigeons occur in secondary, disturbed habitats as well as in primary forest. The only species which utilise dry dipterocarp forests to any extent are the Spotted Dove *Streptopelia chinensis* and the Oriental Turtle Dove *S. orientalis* and this may be correlated with the scarcity of smaller fruits and seeds in this habitat. Most species are subject to considerable hunting pressure and this, combined with forest destruction, has reduced their numbers. Nonetheless, because pigeons are apparently able to disperse among isolated forest patches (Terborgh and Winter 1980, Wells 1976), they may be less vulnerable to local extinctions than many other similar-sized forest birds. Thus, although illegal hunting has greatly reduced the numbers of the Mountain Imperial Pigeon *Ducula badia* in Doi Suthep-Pui National Park, other species which are equally heavily hunted such as the Pin-tailed Pigeon *Treron apicauda* and Wedge-tailed Pigeon *T. sphenura* are still frequently seen.

Of the species listed above, lowland forest destruction is the principal threat faced by six species. The Cinnamon-headed Pigeon *Treron fulvicollis*, Little Green Pigeon *T. olax* and Large Green Pigeon *T. capellei* are all restricted to the level lowlands of the Peninsula. *T. capellei* is still present in primary peat swamp forest of the Pa Phru Non-Hunting Area and it is conceivable that the same area might also support *T. fulvicollis*. *T. olax* is at present only known from two sites, of which one is protected. The Pompadour Pigeon *T. pompadora*, which is found in Continental Thailand, is also very scarce and though occasionally found as high as 800 m, is primarily a bird of the plains. Both the Yellow-footed Pigeon *T. phoenicoptera* and the Green Imperial Pigeon *Ducula aenea*, which were formerly widespread and common in the lowland deciduous forests of Continental Thailand, have disappeared from most areas and may be prevented from recolonising secondary habitats by hunting pressure. Both species are still fairly numerous, however, in the remoter regions of South-west Thailand. *D. aenea* also occurs on forested offshore islands, together with the Pied Imperial Pigeon *D. bicolor*, which is not listed above. The status of the Pale-capped Pigeon *Columba punicea*, also unlisted, needs clarifying and while it has been recorded from mainland sites, it too may be resident in island forests.

The Nicobar Pigeon *Caloenas nicobarica* is entirely restricted to island forests and, while it has undoubtedly declined due to human disturbance, it may be fairly secure on the few uninhabited islands which have been granted national park status, such as Ko Surin and Ko Similan.

The Ashy Wood-Pigeon *Columba pulchricollis*, a montane species from the north, is extremely vulnerable to hunting and deforestation. Most records have come from the few mountains which possess significant areas of forest above 1,800 m, the usual upper limit of the zone of hilltribe cultivation, though it has been recorded as low as 1,500 m and may perhaps disperse more widely.

The status of three further pigeon species, Yellow-vented Pigeon *Treron seimundi*, White-bellied Pigeon *T. sieboldii* and Jambu Fruit-Dove *Ptilinopus jambu*, is unclear though none are known to be especially at risk. Although there are only two records of *T. seimundi* from the north and from near Bangkok (Deignan 1963), this montane species occurs in Malaysia and might therefore be expected to occur also in the mountains of Peninsular Thailand.

Psittacidae

Threatened: *Psittacula eupatria, Psittinus cyanurus.*

All the parakeets *Psittacula* spp. occur primarily in association with lowland deciduous forests. Although these habitats have been much reduced in area, most species can nevertheless utilise secondary habitats including open country and croplands provided that scattered clumps of taller trees remain as secure nesting and roosting sites. However, all species have declined very markedly in numbers and are now very scarce and local in all the more densely populated parts of the country as a result of human persecution. Large numbers of young birds are taken from the nest for the cagebird trade while the adults are frequently shot as pests. Flocks of over 1,000 Red-breasted Parakeets *Psittacula alexandri* were formerly recorded from the plains in Chiang Mai Province (Deignan 1945), in areas from which the species has since vanished. The largest numbers of this species, together with the Blossom-headed Parakeet *P. roseata* and the Grey-headed Parakeet *P. finschii*, are now found in the least disturbed lowlands and lower hills along the western margin of the country.

The Alexandrine Parakeet *P. eupatria* is believed to be at risk because there are few recent sightings. Each year, however, many hundreds of young birds are illegally sold in the Bangkok Weekend Market and probably come from the remoter areas of South-west Thailand and perhaps Burma.

There are very few recent records of the Blue-rumped Parrot *Psittinus cyanurus* which is restricted to the level lowlands (Wells 1985). Although the species has reportedly become a pest of oil palm in Malaysia (Ward and Wood 1967), it may be prevented from exploiting the increasing areas of this habitat in Peninsular Thailand by the lack of adjacent forests to provide nesting or roosting sites.

Cuculidae

Although the majority of cuckoos inhabit forests and other wooded habitats, no species are considered to be immediately at risk and almost all are known from existing nature reserves. Those species which could be vulnerable to further deforestation, however, are those which are mainly confined to the lower hills slopes and lowlands, including the Moustached Hawk-Cuckoo *Cuculus vagans*, Violet Cuckoo *Chrysococcyx xanthorhynchus*, Black-bellied Malkoha *Phaenicophaeus diardi* and Chestnut-bellied Malkoha *P. sumatranus*.

The Coral-billed Ground-Cuckoo *Carpococcyx renauldi* is not listed because it is still quite numerous in the semi-evergreen forests of the North-east and South-east, up to at least 800 m and at two sites has also been found in selectively logged forest. However, because of its terrestrial habits, it is frequently caught in noose traps and is taken both for food and for the illegal cagebird trade. Its status should be closely monitored.

Strigiformes

Threatened: *Otus sagittatus, O. rufescens.*

Indeterminate: *Bubo coromandus.*

The majority of owl species are known from existing nature reserves. However, assessment of the status of some species is compounded by difficulties in their detection.

Both the White-fronted Scops-Owl *Otus sagittatus* and the Reddish Scops-Owl *O. rufescens* are probably restricted to the rainforests of the level lowlands and the foothills (D. R. Wells *in litt.*). The only known population of *O. rufescens* is in primary peat swamp forest at Pa Phru Non-Hunting Area. The Dusky Eagle-Owl *Bubo coromandus* is also listed as a lowland specialist by Wells (1985) although because this species frequents the more open wooded country, it may not be at risk. The only recent record is from Khao Sam Roi Yot National Park (G. Clark *in litt.*).

Podargidae

Threatened: *Batrachostomus auritus, B. stellatus.*

The frogmouths are among the most difficult forest birds to detect, owing to their nocturnal habits and relatively unobtrusive or infrequently uttered calls. With the exception of the Hodgson's Frogmouth *Batrachostomus hodgsoni*, which inhabits hill evergreen forests of the north, the Thai species are primarily birds of lowland forests and both species listed above are confined to the extreme lowlands of the Peninsula (Wells 1985), where very little forest remains.

The Javan Frogmouth *B. javensis* occurs up to 800 m in Khao Yai National Park and has been found in mixed deciduous as well as in evergreen forests and rainforest (Marshall 1978). Even so, it is extremely scarce on the hill slopes and common only in the extreme lowlands.

Caprimulgidae

Most of the nightjars occur in a variety of open or open wooded situations and are not considered to be at risk. Although both the Malaysian Eared Nightjar *Eurostopodus temminckii* and the Great Eared Nightjar *E. macrotis* are primarily forest birds, both apparently occur across a fairly wide altitudinal range and neither should be at risk from deforestation. *E. temminckii* is only known from the extreme southern provinces of Yala and Narathiwat (Holmes 1973, Holmes and Wells 1975) and is therefore not represented in any of the parks or sanctuaries in Thailand. An assessment of its status would probably, therefore, be timely.

Apodidae

The swifts, though aerial feeders, are dealt with because many species, such as the swiftlets *Aerodramus* spp., White-bellied Swiftlet *Collocalia esculenta* and Silver-rumped Swiftlet *Rhaphidura leucopygialis* feed wholly or largely over forest (Waugh and Hails 1983). The Brown Needletail *Hirundapus giganteus*, which feeds both over forest and open country, together with *Rhaphidura*, is probably also dependent upon lofty forest trees to provide hollows in which to nest.

None of these species is thought to be at risk in Thailand though any assessment of the status of *Aerodramus* spp. is complicated by their great similarity in the field. Since the nests of the Edible-nest Swiftlet *A. fuciphagus* and, to a lesser extent, the Black-nest Swiftlet *A. maximus* are harvested for food, threats might be more likely to stem from disturbance of their breeding colonies rather than from deforestation. No assessment of the effects of nest-harvesting is possible within the scope of this report, however.

Hemiprocnidae

None of three species of treeswift in Thailand is at risk. Both the Crested Treeswift *Hemiprocne coronata* of Continental Thailand and the Grey-rumped Treeswift *H. longipennis* of the Peninsula feed and nest in a variety of wooded habitats including secondary growth and plantations. The Whiskered Treeswift *H. comata*, though mostly restricted to forest, occurs in hills as well as lowlands and is not considered immediately vulnerable to deforestation.

Trogonidae

Threatened: *Harpactes kasumba, H. diardii, H. orrhophaeus.*

Vulnerable: *H. duvaucelii.*

All of the trogons are mainly restricted to primary forests. The Orange-breasted Trogon *Harpactes orekios*, which occurs in evergreen and in the moister mixed deciduous forests from the plains to 1,100 m elevation throughout the country, is probably the most ecologically tolerant species and has also been found occasionally in secondary growth. The Red-headed Trogon *H. erythrocephalus*, though primarily a montane species, follows the evergreen forests down to the foothills in Continental Thailand. Both species are common and are found in a great number of protected areas.

All four remaining species, which are restricted to the Peninsula, are considered to be at risk from lowland deforestation and are much less common in logged, regenerating forests than in primary forest (Johns 1986, Wong 1985). Though Wells (1985) only lists the Cinnamon-rumped Trogon *H. orrhophaeus* as a lowland specialist, in Thailand both Diard's Trogon *H. diardii* and the Scarlet-rumped Trogon *H. duvaucelii* are extremely scarce on hill slopes. There are only two recent records of the Red-naped Trogon *H. kasumba*, from the extreme lowlands of Khlong Phraya Wildlife Sanctuary (Craig Robson, Uthai Treesucon pers. comm.) and in Pa Phru Non-Hunting Area. This species was previously thought to be confined to the Malayan rainforest zone of the extreme southern provinces, where clearance of both lowland and hill-slope forests has been exceptionally severe. Even though it is more widely distributed than hitherto known, it must be considered threatened.

Alcedinidae

Threatened: *Megaceryle lugubris.*

Indeterminate: *Pelargopsis amauroptera, Halcyon coromanda.*

The great majority of kingfishers are represented in existing nature reserves. The Crested Kingfisher *Megaceryle lugubris* is considered to be at immediate risk since it inhabits the banks of wooded or little-disturbed rivers and streams in the lowlands and lower hills and has disappeared from those areas of Northern Thailand where it was formerly recorded. The only site known to support the species at present is the River Khwae in Thung Yai Wildlife Sanctuary, South-west Thailand (Phumpakapun and Kutintara 1983). This area is threatened by the proposed Nam Choan hydro-electric project.

Two further species, the Brown-winged Kingfisher *Pelargopsis amauroptera* and the Ruddy Kingfisher *Halcyon coromanda* occur in mangroves in Peninsular Thailand and may be at risk from their continued destruction. The former species is still locally common, even in logged mangrove while the latter occurs in secondary mangrove and in other coastal vegetation (Medway and Wells 1976) and is also known from some terrestrial forests on offshore islands. There is also one breeding season record of a bird in rainforest of the level lowlands at Khao Noi Chuchi.

The Chestnut-collared Kingfisher *Halcyon concreta* inhabits rainforest in the Peninsula but, though scarce and local, may not be at risk since it occurs on the hill slopes as well as in the lowlands, having been found up to 750 m in Malaysia (Medway 1972).

Meropidae

Of the six species of bee-eater which occur in Thailand only two, the Red-bearded Bee-eater *Nyctyornis amictus* and the Blue-bearded Bee-eater *N. athertoni* are strictly forest birds. However, because both species occur across a wide altitudinal range and are present in a great many nature reserves, neither is at immediate risk.

Coraciidae

The Dollarbird *Eurystomus orientalis* inhabits the more open forests, small clearings and forest edge. It is also frequent in more open cultivated areas in the Peninsula and is not thought to be at risk.

Upupidae

The Hoopoe *Upupa epops* inhabits open country and cultivation as well as open woodlands. A common and widespread bird in Thailand, it is not at risk.

Bucerotidae

Endangered: *Rhyticeros corrugatus.*

Threatened: *Aceros nipalensis, Rhyticeros subruficollis, Anthracoceros malayanus, Buceros rhinoceros.*

Vulnerable: *Berenicornis comatus, Ptilolaemus tickelli, Anorrhinus galeritus, Rhyticeros undulatus, Buceros bicornis, Rhinoplax vigil.*

Hornbills are among the forest birds which are most at risk, owing to their large size, vulnerability to hunting and dependence upon large tracts of primary forest. All species are still widely shot for food by rural people and all five species of hornbills which formerly occurred in Northern Thailand have already been extirpated from the more accessible parts of that region (Round 1984). Accordingly, all species other than the Pied Hornbill *Anthracoceros albirostris*, the smallest and ecologically most tolerant hornbill, are considered to be vulnerable, threatened or endangered. Only one species, the Rhinoceros Hornbill *Buceros rhinoceros* is not known from any protected area, since it appears to be almost entirely restricted to the Malayan rainforest zone of the extreme south, where no nature reserves have yet been established. While the species may still occur widely on forested hill slopes, much of its habitat has been lost. Of the other hornbills which are most at risk, two species, the Wrinkled Hornbill *Rhyticeros corrugatus* and the Black Hornbill *Anthracoceros malayanus* are extreme lowland specialists, restricted to the Peninsula. Although both are still found around the margins of a small number of protected areas, *Rhyticeros corrugatus*, in particular, may be close to extinction.

The status of the Plain-pouched Hornbill *Rhyticeros subruficollis* remains somewhat unclear because of potential confusion with the Wreathed Hornbill *R. undulatus*. It is listed as threatened, however, because on present evidence it is restricted to lowland river valleys of South-west Thailand, in the Huai Kha Khaeng and Thung Yai Wildlife Sanctuaries.

Of the remaining species, the Rufous-necked Hornbill *Aceros nipalensis* may be the most acutely threatened, since its range in the north and west overlaps almost totally with that of the hill-tribe upland shifting cultivators. It is probably close to extinction in Northern Thailand, though populations remain in at least two nature reserves of the South-west, where the hill-tribes have so far had less impact upon forest cover.

All of the remaining species are widely distributed in nature reserves and in some cases are locally common. Even the Helmeted Hornbill *Rhinoplax vigil*, listed in the IUCN/ICBP Red Data Book, and assigned endangered status by Bain and Humphrey (1982), is still found fairly widely. The largest contiguous forest block within the Thai range of this species exceeds 4,000 sq km, so the species may not be at immediate risk from deforestation provided that the Thai Government maintains a strong commitment to protect watersheds. This species is certainly much scarcer than the other members of the 'vulnerable' group and its status deserves close monitoring, especially as it may be hunted for its casque, the source of hornbill 'ivory'.

A major consideration in the long-term conservation of hornbills and other forest birds which occur at low density is the maintenance of forest patches which are sufficiently large to support viable populations. Three species, *Rhyticeros undulatus*, *Anthracoceros albirostris* and the Great Hornbill *Buceros bicornis*, are found on forested offshore islands, but most other hornbills may have a very limited capacity to disperse for any distance between isolated forest blocks. Increased fragmentation of remaining habitats could therefore lead to the insularisation and possible extinction of local populations. Unfortunately, there are few published estimates of hornbill densities for South-East Asian forests. Tentative estimates of one individual per 200 ha for larger species and 4–5 per 200 ha for smaller species (Medway and Wells 1971) were based on very small plots in level lowland forest and may not be representative. Poonswad *et al.* (1987) give densities of 0.38 and 0.7 nests per sq km for two larger species, *Rhyticeros undulatus* and *Buceros bicornis* respectively, in 26 sq km of primary evergreen forest at Khao Yai National Park. Many of Thailand's parks and sanctuaries have been selectively logged, however, and may support much lower hornbill densities. Johns (1986) mentions that Bushy-crested Hornbill *Anorrhinus galeritus*, one of the smaller species, survives well in logged forest but the larger species, which usually require trees of more than 1 m diameter in which to nest (Poonswad *et al.* 1987), may be much less tolerant.

Capitonidae
Threatened: *Megalaima rafflesii.*

While two species of barbet, the Lineated Barbet *Megalaima lineata* and the Coppersmith Barbet *M. haemacephala* are common and ecologically tolerant, inhabiting open country with scattered trees and even gardens and cultivated areas, most other species are associated only with forests. Most barbets can, however, tolerate a moderate degree of habitat disturbance. The Great Barbet *M. virens*, for example, is still present in many smaller forest patches of the mountains and most other species are common in nature reserves.

The only species at immediate risk in Thailand is the Red-crowned Barbet *M. rafflesii* which is restricted to forest on flat lowlands of the Peninsula (Wells 1985). The species has disappeared from most of its former range and the only recent records are from terrestrial forest and secondary growth at Ban Nai Chong, Khao Noi Chuchi and from Pa Phru, an area of primary peat swamp forest in Narathiwat.

Indicatoridae
Of three recent records of the Malaysian Honeyguide *Indicator archipelagicus* in Peninsular Thailand, two were found in the level lowlands, at Tha Chang district, Surat Thani (J. Nabhitabhtata pers. comm.) and at Khlong Phraya Wildlife Sanctuary (C. Robson and U. Treesucon pers. comm.). The species has not been listed as a lowland specialist, however, as a further sighting, at Khao Noi Chuchi was at 300 m, while in Malaysia, the honeyguide has been recorded up to 900 m elevation (Medway and Wells 1976). The species has also been recorded from South-west Thailand (Deignan 1963).

Picidae

Threatened: *Gecinulus grantia.*

Vulnerable: *Dryocopus javensis, Picoides cathpharius.*

Indeterminate: *Picus xanthopygaeus, Picoides mahrattensis.*

The Pale-headed Woodpecker *Gecinulus grantia* is considered to be threatened because it has only been recorded once from lowland evergreen woodland on the banks of the Mekong River (King 1966). Although this area is now almost completely deforested, there is a possibility of its continued occurrence as the species primarily inhabits bamboo. The Bamboo Woodpecker *G. viridis*, with which this species is sometimes considered conspecific (Short 1982), is much more common and widespread. Thailand is, however, somewhat peripheral to the main range of both *G. grantia* and the Yellow-crowned Woodpecker *Picoides mahrattensis* and this may explain their scarcity.

The lack of recent records of the Streak-throated Woodpecker *Picus xanthopygaeus* is puzzling. Like *Picoides mahrattensis*, however, it is an inhabitant of lowland deciduous woodlands and may have suffered from the great reduction in the areas of these habitats.

The remaining lowland species listed, the White-bellied Woodpecker *Dryocopus javensis*, may be a useful indicator of the least-disturbed lowland forests since it requires large trees for both foraging and nesting (Short 1982). The race *D. j. feddeni* of Continental Thailand inhabits deciduous woodlands of the plains and foothills,ascending the slopes to no more than 500–600 m. The Peninsular subspecies *D. j. javensis* has an even narrower altitudinal range and does not usually occur above the hill-foot boundary (Wells 1985). It is today very scarce. The continental subspecies is still fairly plentiful, however, and is widely represented in nature reserves. The Great Slaty Woodpecker *Muelleripicus pulverulentus* is not listed above. Although it too is restricted to the level lowlands in the Peninsula, it is less constrained by altitude in Continental Thailand and inhabits both deciduous and evergreen forests up to at least 900 m.

The Crimson-breasted Woodpecker *Picoides cathpharius* is known only from two largely deforested mountains of the far north, Doi Pha Hom Pok and Doi Ang Khang, neither of which has nature reserve status. Although the species is still present, it is very scarce.

Eurylaimidae

Vulnerable: *Cymbirhynchus macrorhynchos.*

Although the broadbills are almost entirely forest birds, six of the seven Thai species are not thought to be at risk. Most are fairly common and widespread and are represented in many nature reserves. The Black-and-Red Broadbill *Cymbirhynchus macrorhynchos* is highly vulnerable because it only inhabits lowlands below 300 m in the immediate vicinity of streams or rivers. Unlike the Banded Broadbill *Eurylaimus javanicus* which, in the vicinity of water, can utilise mixed deciduous as well as evergreen forests, *Cymbirhynchus* is restricted to the evergreen zone. Throughout Continental Thailand, therefore, where deciduous forests dominated most of the lowlands, it must necessarily have been very patchy and local in distribution and was probably most common in the least seasonal areas of the South-east, where it may still be present.

In the Peninsula, *Cymbirhynchus* is still widely present, largely because it shows some ability to survive in deforested country where relict taller trees and moist secondary growth remain along riverbanks. Its status will need careful monitoring, however, as in many areas such cover is being gradually lost due to the repeated burning of natural vegetation, the unchecked spread of human settlements and the gradual intensification of agriculture.

Pittidae

Endangered: *Pitta granatina, P. elliotti, P. gurneyi.*

Threatened: *P. caerulea.*

Indeterminate: *P. megarhyncha.*

Rare: *P. soror.*

Most pitta species in Thailand are principally lowland forest birds. The exceptions are the Rusty-naped Pitta *Pitta oatesi* of the northern highlands and the Blue-rumped Pitta *P. soror* which is restricted to the small upland areas of the South-east. Some species, such as the Blue Pitta *P. cyanea* and Eared Pitta *P. phayrei*, which occur up to 1,500 m (Deignan 1945) display a fairly wide altitudinal tolerance.

Although the Mangrove Pitta *P. megarhyncha*, which is restricted to the west coast of the Peninsula, occurs in secondary or logged mangroves as well as in primary formations, its habitat is rapidly being reduced as huge areas are being cleared to establish shrimp ponds.

The other species listed are believed to be wholly or mainly restricted to the evergreen forests of the extreme lowlands. The Bar-bellied Pitta *P. elliotti* is known only from a few market-purchased specimens reputed to have come from South-east Thailand (J. Nabhitabhata pers. comm.). The Garnet Pitta *P. granatina* may be mainly confined to the Malayan rainforest zone of the extreme southern provinces where it has been recorded by Holmes (1973). No parks or sanctuaries have yet been established in its Thai range. The plight of Gurney's Pitta *P. gurneyi* may be the most severe, however, owing to its small world range in Peninsular Thailand and Burma. Until its rediscovery in 1986, the species had not been recorded in the wild for 34 years and its near extirpation is correlated with the virtually complete deforestation of the lowlands in its Thai range (Collar, Round and Wells 1986; Round and Treesucon 1986). The survival of the small population of Gurney's Pittas subsequently found will almost certainly depend upon the maintenance of patches of well-watered forest and secondary growth in the level lowlands, in proximity to remaining submontane slope forests. The Giant Pitta *P. caerulea* may also be mainly restricted to similar situations but is listed as threatened, rather than endangered, as there is one reliable record at over 800 m elevation (Medway and Wells 1976). Both the Blue-winged Pitta *P. moluccensis* and the Hooded Pitta *P. sordida* are fairly common in moist secondary growth and scrub, even including overgrown rubber plantations, while *P. phayrei* is also fairly widespread in secondary and scrub habitats. Banded Pitta *P. guajana*, the only other pitta recorded for Thailand, seems to be rather more confined to the forest interior. It is already known from most protected areas in the Peninsula, and since it occurs up to at least 600 m elevation (Robinson 1915), is not considered to be at immediate risk from habitat destruction. However, this species, together with *P. moluccensis*, occurs frequently in the illegal cagebird trade.

Alaudidae

Three species of lark are resident in Thailand, inhabiting dry, open country. No species are at risk.

Hirundinidae

Endangered: *Pseudochelidon sirintarae.*

An assessment of the status of the White-eyed River Martin *Pseudochelidon sirintarae* is outside the scope of this report. The species is only known in winter from Beung Boraphet, a lake in Central Thailand and its breeding grounds remain unknown (Thonglongya 1968, King and Kanwanich 1978). There have been no reliable reports since 1980 and, in addition, the concentrations of roosting Barn Swallows *Hirundo rustica* with which *Pseudochelidon* was formerly associated have been reduced, both due to cutting of *Phragmites* and direct disturbance by illegal trappers (Sophasan and Dobias 1984). This species is not treated further in this report.

Campephagidae

Threatened: *Coracina striata.*

Indeterminate: *Hemipus hirundinaceus.*

Most species of campephagid are common and widespread in existing nature reserves. The Bar-bellied Cuckoo-Shrike *Coracina striata* is restricted to the forests of the level lowlands of the Peninsula (Wells 1985) and is therefore at risk.

The status of the Black-winged Flycatcher-Shrike *Hemipus hirundinaceus* deserves examination since it has a restricted range in the extreme southern provinces. Though not usually regarded as a lowland specialist, the only recent Thai records are from primary peat swamp forest at Pa Phru, Narathiwat.

Irenidae

Three species of iora, five species of leafbird together with the Asian Fairy Bluebird *Irena puella*, are the representatives of this family in Thailand. (Note that in Appendix I, which follows King *et al.* 1975, *Irena* is placed immediately after the Orioles *Oriolus* spp.) All species are represented widely in nature reserves and none are at immediate risk.

Pycnonotidae

Threatened: *Pycnonotus zeylanicus.*

Vulnerable: *P. eutilotus.*

Most bulbuls are common and ecologically tolerant species. Many of the *Pycnonotus* bulbuls in Continental Thailand inhabit scrub or grassland and some, such as the Red-whiskered Bulbul *P. jocosus*, have probably expanded their ranges with increased deforestation. While a higher proportion of Sundaic *Pycnonotus* species are associated with forest, most are frequent on hill slopes. The two species listed above, the Straw-headed Bulbul *P. zeylanicus* and the Puff-backed Bulbul *P. eutilotus* are mainly or entirely confined to the lowlands in Thailand and are extremely scarce, though neither is listed as a lowland specialist by Wells (1985). In addition, *P. zeylanicus*, which chiefly inhabits secondary growth along riverbanks, is much sought after as a cagebird and this has undoubtedly contributed to its decline.

Bulbuls of the genera *Criniger* and *Hypsipetes* are all mainly forest birds, though of these only the Finsch's Bulbul *Criniger finschii*, which is limited to the Malayan rainforest zone, is not found in any existing nature reserve. The White-headed Bulbul *Hypsipetes thompsoni*, endemic to Northern Thailand and the Shan States in Burma, is still fairly numerous and inhabits hill evergreen forests and secondary growth.

Dicruridae

Most of the drongos are common and widely distributed birds, inhabiting both forests and secondary growth. The Black Drongo *Dicrurus macrocercus* breeds in open areas and scrubland while the Greater Racket-tailed Drongo *D. paradiseus*, though more arboreal, nevertheless enters gardens and orchards. Most other species are more closely associated with forest or forest edge and clearings.

No species are at risk. The Crow-billed Drongo *D. annectans* is the most scarce and local species and is so far only known to breed in the lowland mixed deciduous woodlands of the Huai Kha Khaeng Wildlife Sanctuary.

Oriolidae

Vulnerable: *Oriolus xanthonotus.*

Of the three species of oriole which breed in Thailand, only the Dark-throated Oriole *Oriolus xanthonotus*, which is restricted to the rainforests of the Peninsula, is listed. It is seldom found away from the lowlands and lower foothills. The Black-hooded Oriole *O. xanthornus* of lowland deciduous woodlands and secondary growth and the Maroon Oriole *O. traillii* of the moister hill evergreen forests of the North and North-east are both fairly common, though both species would undoubtedly be affected by further deforestation.

Breeding is suspected in a further species, the Slender-billed Oriole *O. tenuirostris*, hitherto known only as a winter visitor to the North and therefore not listed in Appendix I. Since this species occurs in the more open hill evergreen forests and secondary growth, it would probably be little affected by continued habitat disturbance.

Corvidae

Extinct: *Corvus splendens.*

Vulnerable: *Platysmurus leucopterus.*

Rare: *Cissa thalassina.*

The Black Magpie *Platysmurus leucopterus* is mainly restricted to the forests of the lowland and foothills of the Peninsula and although it is not completely confined to areas below the hill-foot boundary, its scarcity on hill slopes suggests that populations there may not be self-supporting (D. R. Wells *in litt.*). The Short-tailed Magpie *Cissa thalassina* is restricted to the remaining patches of evergreen forest in the South-east but is not thought to be at immediate risk since it occurs in most protected areas of the region and is found across a wide altitudinal range.

The House Crow *Corvus splendens*, a common commensal of man elsewhere in its range, may be extinct in Thailand. It was formerly known only from Prachuap and Phetchaburi Provinces of the South-west (Deignan 1963) where it has not been seen for many years. This species, which is generally regarded as an undesirable pest since it preys upon the nests and eggs of other birds, could conceivably become re-established as there is a large and expanding population in Malaysia (Medway and Wells 1976).

Both the Green Magpie *Cissa chinensis* and the Blue Magpie *Urocissa erythrorhyncha* are taken in considerable numbers for the illicit cagebird trade.

Aegithalidae, Paridae

Rare: *Aegithalos concinnus, Sylviparus modestus.*

Two species of tits are very local in distribution, in hill evergreen forests of the north. The Black-throated Tit *Aegithalos concinnus* is known only from Doi Pha Hom Pok, which lacks nature reserve status, while the Yellow-browed Tit *Sylviparus modestus* is known both from there and from Doi Inthanon and may be expected to occur elsewhere on the few other high peaks which possess significant areas of hill evergreen forest above 1,800 m elevation. Neither species is thought to be at risk, though both would be vulnerable with further deforestation.

Sittidae

Vulnerable: *Sitta formosa, S. magna.*

The Beautiful Nuthatch *Sitta formosa* is known in Thailand only from dense hill evergreen forests near the summit of Doi Pha Hom Pok, where it was discovered in early 1986 (P. Hopkin, A. J. Merritt pers. comm.). The Giant Nuthatch *S. magna* is very scarce and local in the north and appears to be restricted to the more open hill evergreen forests where pines *Pinus kesiya* are frequent, between 1,200–1,800 m. This zone has been very largely deforested by shifting cultivators. In addition, pines may be selectively cut as fuelwood owing to their combustibility. *Sitta magna* could not be relocated in Doi Suthep-Pui National Park, a former locality, during 1978–1984 (Round 1984). Nevertheless, it is still present at a number of other sites, including at least three nature reserves (Eve and Guigue 1984 and *in litt.*).

Certhiidae
Vulnerable: *Certhia discolor.*

The Brown-throated Treecreeper *Certhia discolor* inhabits taller hill evergreen forest in North Thailand in areas with a high proportion of large-girth trees. Selective cutting of larger trees by hill-tribes, together with repeated annual burning of undergrowth in standing forest is degrading or destroying such forests. Although the species is still fairly common in Doi Inthanon National Park, it may have disappeared from Doi Suthep-Pui (Round 1984).

Cinclidae
Indeterminate: *Cinclus pallasii.*

The present status of the Brown Dipper *Cinclus pallasii* is unclear as there are very few recent sightings. Past records are from the months August, September, December, April and May (Deignan 1945, King 1966). The species is presumed to be resident (Deignan 1963, Legakul and Cronin 1974), though the nest has never been found in Thailand.

Timaliidae
Threatened: *Malacopteron affine, M. magnum, Kenopia striata, Napothera macrodactyla, Stachyris maculata, S. nigricollis.*

Vulnerable: *Trichastoma rostratum, T. bicolor, Macronous ptilosus.*

Indeterminate: *Stachyris leucotis, Alcippe rufogularis.*

Rare: *Stachyris rodolphei, Garrulax merulinus, G. milnei, Minla strigula, Alcippe peracensis, Yuhina humilis, Y. flavicollis.*

All of the babblers listed in the 'threatened', 'vulnerable' or 'indeterminate' categories are believed to be at risk from lowland deforestation. Of these, only the Rufous-throated Babbler *Alcippe rufogularis* occurs in Continental Thailand and the remainder are restricted to the Peninsula. The White-chested Babbler *Trichastoma rostratum*, Ferruginous Babbler *T. bicolor*, Sooty-capped Babbler *Malacopteron affine*, Striped Wren Babbler *Kenopia striata*, Large Wren-Babbler

Napothera macrodactyla and Fluffy-backed Tit-Babbler *Macronous ptilosus* are considered to be wholly or mainly restricted to the level lowlands (Wells 1985, D. R. Wells *in litt.*). In addition the Rufous-crowned Babbler *Malacopteron magnum*, Chestnut-rumped Babbler *Stachyris maculata*, White-necked Babbler *S. leucotis* and Black-throated Babbler *S. nigricollis*, none of which is listed as a lowland specialist by Wells (1985), are all extremely scarce in Thailand and are thought to be restricted to the well-watered lowlands. The future of such species may well depend upon their ability to survive in small patches of secondary growth. *T. bicolor* has been found in an overgrown rubber plantation (author's observation) and both *Malacopteron affine* and *Macronous ptilosus* are regarded as 'forest edge' species in Malaysia. However, the extent of forest clearance and the intensification of agriculture in Peninsular Thailand is such that even regenerating secondary woodland is a very scarce habitat.

Most babblers in Continental Thailand are relatively ecologically tolerant, inhabiting both forests and secondary growth. Some montane forms, such as minlas *Minla* spp. and fulvettas *Alcippe* spp., take a proportion of small fruits in their diet and consequently are frequent along the forest edge where there is an abundance of pioneer shrubs and smaller trees. Even the more strictly arboreal species such as shrike-babblers *Pteruthius* spp. and sibias *Heterophasia* spp. are still fairly common where relict forest patches alternate with scrub and grassland.

Neither the Spot-breasted Laughingthrush *Garrulax merulinus* nor the Red-tailed Laughingthrush *G. milnei* occur in any nature reserve, although both apparently inhabit secondary growth and scrub and should therefore not be at risk (King *et al.* 1975). Deignan's Babbler *Stachyris rodolphei* is apparently endemic to Doi Chiang Dao, today a wildlife sanctuary, where it inhabits bamboo (Deignan 1939, 1945). Any assessment of its status is complicated by the likelihood that the species is inseparable in the field from the common and widespread Rufous-fronted Babbler *S. rufifrons*.

The Limestone Wren-Babbler *Napothera crispifrons*, though extremely local in distribution, is not listed. It does not appear to be at risk since it inhabits moist forested crevices and ravines in areas of steep limestone crags. There seems little likelihood of its habitat becoming deforested.

Panuridae

Rare: *Paradoxornis atrosuperciliaris.*

The parrotbills inhabit the mountains of the North and a small part of North-east Thailand. No species is entirely restricted to forest and all frequent bamboo and grassland to some degree. The Grey-headed Parrotbill *Paradoxornis gularis* is the most arboreal species but is still fairly common and widespread. The Lesser Rufous-headed Parrotbill *P. atrosuperciliaris* has only been recorded from Doi Pha Hom Pok, in association with bamboo and forest edge of high elevation (King 1966, Lekagul and Cronin 1974).

Turdidae

Threatened: *Saxicola jerdoni.*

Vulnerable: *Cochoa purpurea.*

Indeterminate: *Zoothera interpres.*

Rare: *Brachypteryx montana, Cinclidium frontale.*

The Jerdon's Bushchat *Saxicola jerdoni*, though not a forest bird, is listed because its status has hitherto received little attention. It inhabits tall grass of riverine floodplains in the North and appears to be very scarce. It has disappeared from some former haunts as these have been drained or cleared for agriculture. The usual practice is to burn reedbeds in marshy lowlands and along riverbanks as the water levels drop in the early part of the year, in order to plant vegetables.

The habitat requirements of the Chestnut-capped Thrush *Zoothera interpres*, which occurs in rainforests of the Peninsula, are not well known. Although the species has been recorded up to 750 m in Malaysia, all of the Thai records are from the lowlands and foothills.

The remaining species listed are all montane forms. The Purple Cochoa *Cochoa purpurea* inhabits evergreen forest and has so far been found from three northern peaks of which two, Doi Suthep and Doi Mon Chong, lie within nature reserves (Deignan 1945, Round 1983a). The few records come from elevations between 1,000 m to 1,800 m, with one record at roughly 400 m. *C. purpurea* thus shows considerable altitudinal overlap with Green Cochoa *C. viridis*, though why it should be so much rarer is unknown. Though both species inhabit the moister hill evergreen forests, *C. viridis* should be less at risk because it is the more widely distributed.

Neither of the remaining species is known to be at immediate risk. The White-browed Shortwing *Brachypteryx montana* is found only on those few mountains which exceed 2,000 m, although it apparently descends, and may possibly breed, as low as 1,500 m (King 1966, author's observations). There is only one record of the Blue-fronted Robin *Cinclidium frontale* from forest at approximately 2,000 m on Doi Pha Hom Pok (King 1966). The species is presumed to be resident there.

Sylviidae

Extinct: *Graminicola bengalensis.*

Indeterminate: *Abroscopus albogularis, Tesia cyaniventer.*

Rare: *Phylloscopus maculipennis.*

The Large Grass Warbler *Graminicola bengalensis*, though not a forest bird, is listed above in order to draw attention to its status. The species formerly occurred in an area of tall, marshy, riverine grassland north of Bangkok (Herbert 1923) which has long since been drained for agriculture and has become progressively urbanised. Nonetheless, although *Graminicola* is also limited to lowland grassland in India (Ali and Ripley 1968–1974), it has recently been discovered breeding in dry grassland at 750 m elevation in Hong Kong (Melville and Chalmers 1984) and there is thus a slight possibility that it may persist elsewhere in Thailand.

The other species listed are all forest birds. The Rufous-faced Warbler *Abroscopus albogularis* is only known from four specimens and one sight record on four different mountains of the North, including both Doi Inthanon and Doi Suthep (Deignan 1945). The species was found in evergreen forest between 850–1,350 m, a zone which has been subject to much deforestation. The Grey-bellied Tesia *Tesia cyaniventer* is only known by one specimen from Doi Phu Kha in the collection of Dr Boonsong Lekagul, Bangkok. This mountain has no nature reserve status and has been badly deforested. The species is probably still present, however, as the Slaty-bellied Tesia *T. olivea*, which has similar habitat requirements, still occurs along moist stream gullies with secondary growth on other deforested mountains, such as Doi Ang Khang.

The Ashy-throated Leaf-Warbler *Phylloscopus maculipennis* is only found in hill evergreen forest on Doi Inthanon where it breeds above 2,000 m. Its habitat is still mostly intact and the species is not thought to be at immediate risk.

Muscicapidae

Rare: *Rhipidura hypoxantha.*

None of the 27 resident species of flycatcher is known to be at risk. The Yellow-bellied Fantail *Rhipidura hypoxantha*, which inhabits hill evergreen forests, is found on only a few of the highest mountains in the North. Some other montane flycatchers, including the White-gorgetted Flycatcher *Ficedula monileger* and Small Niltava *Niltava macgrigoriae*, are restricted to the moister areas of lush, shady forest undergrowth, especially along streamsides and are probably affected by habitat disturbance, such as the use of fire. The Large Niltava *N. grandis*, which inhabits dense middle storey vegetation, may have disappeared from Doi Suthep-Pui National Park during 1978–1984 as a result of such habitat disturbance (Round 1984).

Among lowland Sundaic flycatchers, the Grey-chested Flycatcher *Rhinomyias umbratilis* appears to be unrepresented in any nature reserve and may be confined to the Malayan rainforest zone of the far south. There is an unconfirmed report from Thaleban National Park, however. The Spotted Fantail *Rhipidura perlata* may also have a similarly restricted distribution in Thailand and although it extends further northwards into Khao Banthad Wildlife Sanctuary, it is rather scarce. Neither species appears to be confined to the extreme lowlands, however.

Pachycephalidae

The Mangrove Whistler *Pachycephala cinerea*, though listed as threatened by Bain and Humphrey (1982), is not believed to be at risk. It is still fairly common in both logged and secondary mangrove and it occurs also in dry coastal woodland, secondary growth and in island forests.

Motacillidae

The Richard's Pipit *Anthus novaeseelandiae* is a common and widespread resident of open areas in Thailand. There are no threats to this species.

Artamidae

The Ashy Wood Swallow *Artamus fuscus* is a common resident in drier open country and is not at risk.

Laniidae

Both the Burmese Shrike *Lanius collurioides* and the Long-tailed Shrike *L. schach* breed in Thailand. Although the latter is much more common and widespread while the former breeds only on the hills of the North, both species inhabit open country, and neither is at risk.

Sturnidae

This family includes many species which are abundant in open country. Some, such as the Common Myna *Acridotheres tristis*, Black-collared Starling *Sturnus nigricollis* and Vinous-breasted Starling *S. burmannicus* have been able to expand their ranges with increased deforestation. Two species, the Golden-crested Myna *Ampeliceps coronatus* and the Hill Myna *Gracula religiosa* are primarily lowland forest birds, the former species being much the scarcer. Both species have been found nesting in relict stands of taller trees in open secondary growth and are also present in a number of protected areas and so neither is listed. Although in Continental Thailand, the Hill Myna occurs across a wide altitudinal range, the subspecies *G. r. religiosa* of the Peninsula appears to be restricted to the level lowlands (Wells 1985) and is now extremely scarce. The Hill Myna is one of the mainstays of the cagebird trade in Thailand, the overwhelming majority of birds being taken illegally.

Nectariniidae

Rare: *Aethopyga nipalensis.*

Most sunbirds and spiderhunters inhabit the canopy of forest where they feed to a great extent upon nectar from flowering trees. However, many species have also adapted to forest edge, clearings and secondary growth where smaller flowering trees and shrubs are similarly abundant and they may be less immediately vulnerable to deforestation than many other small, mainly insectivorous birds. The species which have been most successful in colonising open country, however, are primarily inhabitants of mangrove, deciduous woodlands or scrub such as the Brown-throated Sunbird *Anthreptes malacensis*, Purple-throated Sunbird *Nectarinia sperata* and Olive-backed Sunbird *N. jugularis* (Wells 1976).

   Although no species are thought to be at risk, the Green-tailed Sunbird *Aethopyga nipalensis* is listed above because it is extremely local. One race, *A. n. angkanensis*, is endemic to the summit of Doi Inthanon, inhabiting forests above 2,000 m while another, *A. n. australis*, is endemic to the mountains of Surat Thani and Nakhon Si Thammarat in the Peninsula. Both races are represented in existing nature reserves.

The apparent scarcity of the Copper-throated Sunbird *Nectarinia calcostetha* (Appendix I) may merely reflect the poor coverage of its mangrove habitat in the Peninsula and South-east.

All of the spiderhunters *Arachnothera* spp. are known from existing nature reserves. The Long-billed Spiderhunter *A. robusta* is the scarcest member of the genus and is apparently much less common in Thailand than in Malaysia.

Dicaeidae

Rare: *Dicaeum melanoxanthum.*

No species of flowerpecker is thought to be at risk. Most species in Continental Thailand either inhabit both deciduous and evergreen forests, or are found across a wide altitudinal range while those species limited to the Peninsula also ascend the hill slopes. The Scarlet-breasted Flowerpecker *Prionochilus thoracicus* is the scarcest of the Sundaic flowerpeckers, but has been recorded up to 1,260 m in Malaysia (Medway and Wells 1976).

The Yellow-breasted Flowerpecker *Dicaeum melanoxanthum*, previously thought to be a winter visitor (Deignan 1963), may possibly breed on the summit of Doi Inthanon (Round 1983a).

Zosteropidae

The Oriental White-Eye *Zosterops palpebrosa* is a common and ecologically tolerant species which occurs in a variety of wooded habitats while the Everett's White-Eye *Z. everetti* inhabits forests, up to high elevation. Neither species is at risk.

Ploceidae

The sparrows *Passer* spp. and weavers *Ploceus* spp. all inhabit open country and no species are believed to be at risk from habitat disturbance. However, weaver populations have undoubtedly declined as there is considerable illegal netting of large communal roosts of weavers and the wintering Yellow-breasted Bunting *Emberiza aureola*. The birds are sold both for food and also for the cagebird trade. Baya Weavers *Ploceus philippinus* are also disturbed at their breeding colonies and their nests sold as souvenirs.

Estrildidae

Although most estrildines are open country birds, the Pin-tailed Parrotfinch *Erythrura prasina* is found in forest, usually in areas where bamboos are in seed. It also exploits crops to a limited extent, where these occur in proximity to forest. Though scarce, the species is not thought to be at risk even though large numbers are taken for the cagebird trade.

Fringillidae

The Spot-winged Grosbeak *Coccothraustes melanozanthos* frequents forest edge, secondary growth and cultivation in the mountains of the north and though rather scarce, it is not known to be at risk. The status of the Scarlet Finch *Haematospiza sipahi*, which frequents similar areas, is unknown. It may only occur as a non-breeding visitor since summer records from Nepal are at over 2,400 m (Inskipp and Inskipp 1984).

Crested Fireback *Lophura ignita* (male and female). An increasing rare lowland forest species of Peninsular Thailand, classed as Endangered in this publication. *Illustration by* Kamol Komolphalin

DISCUSSION AND RECOMMENDATIONS

NATURE RESERVE COVERAGE

The present coverage of national parks and wildlife sanctuaries, both in terms of their geographical distribution and the habitats which they enclose, is fairly good and 521 of the 595 species of resident birds listed in Appendix I are already known from one or more protected areas. Of the 74 species which appear to be unrepresented (Table 14), 17 are mainly open country birds, most of which are locally common and which should remain unaffected by any further deforestation while a further 11 species, all of which are at risk, are primarily associated with wetlands or open lowlands. Of the 40 species of forest birds which are, as yet, unrecorded from any protected area, at least seven may be expected to be present, on the basis of their known ranges and habitat requirements. There are two subregions where an expansion of the present nature reserve network is needed. Ten species of montane forest bird are confined to the extreme north of the country (Table 14; 3.i) and the establishment of a park or sanctuary on Doi Pha Hom Pok would provide protection for all of these species apart from *Tesia cyaniventer*, together with at least five of the seven open country montane birds listed (Table 14; 1.ii). Similarly the establishment of one or more protected area in the lowland rainforest of the extreme south could provide protection for a further seven species of forest bird (Table 14; 3.v).

The wide coverage of parks and sanctuaries also offers an opportunity, with minimal expansion of the present network, to ensure that not only most extant species but also subspecies of birds are represented. No full analysis of subspecies distribution is presented here, but of the 63 subspecies of birds which are apparently endemic to Thailand (Table 15), all but five are thought to occur in existing nature reserves. Only two of those which are unrepresented (*Garrulax erythrocephalus subconnectens*, recorded from Doi Phu Kha in Nan Province and *Napothera crispifrons calcicola* from the limestone hills outside the north-west boundary of Khao Yai National Park) are forest birds.

While lowland hill slope habitats, from 200–900 m elevation, are extremely well represented, there are very few parks or sanctuaries which possess extensive areas of forest on level ground or in valley bottoms, close to major streams and rivers. Most such areas had already been cleared and settled before nature reserve establishment. In many cases, planners have chosen not to enclose lowland waterways within nature reserves but instead to use them to delimit their boundaries.

Table 14: List of resident birds which are not known from existing national parks or wildlife sanctuaries.

1. Relatively common, open country species, not known to be at risk:

    (i)   Lowlands:
            Coturnix coromandelica, Turnix sylvatica, Chrysococcyx minutillus, Ceryle rudis, Riparia paludicola, Megalurus palustris, Passer domesticus, Ploceus hypoxanthus, Amandava amandava, Padda oryzivora.

    (ii)   Mountains, extreme north:
            Bambusicola fytchii, Hirundo rustica, Pycnonotus xanthorrhous, Garrulax sannio, Paradoxornis guttaticollis, Saxicola torquata, Bradypterus luteoventris.

2. Open country or wetland species which are considered to be at risk:
    Pelecanus philippensis, Anhinga melanogaster, Mycteria leucocephala, Ephippiorhynchus asiaticus, Leptoptilos javanicus, Threskiornis melanocephala, Sarkidiornis melanotos, Milvus migrans, Icthyophaga ichthyaetus, Gyps bengalensis, Saxicola jerdoni.

3. Forest birds:

    (i)   Extreme north, mountains:
            Picoides cathpharius, Aegithalos concinnus, Sitta formosa, Garrulax merulinus, G. milnei, Liocichla phoenicea, Yuhina flavicollis, Paradoxornis atrosuperciliaris, Cinclidium frontale, Tesia cyaniventer.

    (ii)   Extreme north, plains:
            Gecinulus grantia.

    (iii)   South-east, lowlands:
            Pitta elliotti

    (iv)   Peninsula, level lowlands:
            Rhizothera longirostris, Arborophila charltonii, Rollulus rouloul, Polyplectron malacense, Treron fulvicollis, T. capellei, Otus rufescens, Batrachostomus auritus, B. stellatus, Megalaima rafflesii, Pitta gurneyi, Pycnonotus zeylanicus, Malacopteron affine, Stachyris maculata.

    (v)   Peninsula, extreme south.'Malayan-type' rainforest zone:
            Eurostopodus temminckii, Buceros rhinoceros, Pitta granatina, Hemipus hirundinaceus, Criniger finschii, Trichastoma sepiarium, Rhinomyias umbratilis.

Table 14   contd

(vi)   Species which, on the basis of their known range and habitat, may
be expected to occur in existing reserves:
*Treron seimundi, T. sieboldii, Strix seloputo, Collocalia
esculenta, Picus xanthopygaeus, Picoides mahrattensis,
Pycnonotus melanoleucos.*
4.   Species which are probably extinct:
*Pseudibis davisoni, P. gigantea, Gyps indicus, Grus antigone, Corvus
splendens, Graminicola bengalensis.*

Table 15: List of subspecies of birds which are apparently endemic to Thailand.
(Sources: Deignan 1963, Howard and Moore 1984)

Subspecies	Range	Present in Nature Reserve
Arborophila cambodiana diversa	SE, mountains	X
Lophura lineata crawfurdi	SW	X
Turnix suscitator thais	N, NE, SE, C	X
Ducula badia obscurata	SE, mountains	X
Harpactes erythrocephalus klossi	SE, islands	X
Lacedo pulchella deignani	Pen.	X
Actenoides concreta peristephes	Pen.	X
Megalaima franklinii trangensis	Pen., mountains	X
M. asiatica chersonesus	Pen., mountains	X
Megalaima incognita elbeli	NE	X
Calorhamphus fuliginosus detersus	Pen.	X
Picus flavinucha lylei	SW	X
Muelleripicus pulverulentus celadinus	Pen.	X
Psarisomus dalhousiae cyanicauda	SE	X
Pitta guajana ripleyi	Pen.	X
Mirafra assamica subsessor	N, open country	
Hirundo daurica vernayi	SW	X
Tephrodornis virgatus vernayi	SW	X
Chloropsis cochinchinensis serithai	Pen.	X
Pycnonotus melanicterus elbeli	SE, islands	X
P. m. negatus	SW	X
P. aurigaster thais	SE	X
Criniger pallidus isani	NE	X
Pellorneum ruficeps indistinctum	N	X
P. r. chthomium	N	X
P. r. elbeli	NE	X
P. r. smithii	SE, islands	X
Trichastoma abbotti obscurius	SE	X
Napothera crispifrons calcicola	NE	
Stachyris rufifrons obscura	Pen.	X
S. striolata nigrescentior	Pen.	X

Table 15   contd

Subspecies	Range	Present in Nature Reserve
Macronous gularis connectens	SW, SE, C	X
M. g. inveteratus	SE, islands	X
Timalia pileata patriciae	C, open country	
Garrulax erythrocephalus subconnectens	N	
Alcippe peracensis eremita	SE	X
Myophonus caeruleus crassirostris	SE, Pen.	X
Zoothera dauma affinis	Pen., mountains	X
Seicercus castaniceps collinsi	N, mountains	X
S. c. youngi	Pen., mountains	X
Abroscopus superciliaris bambusarum	Pen.	X
A. albogularis hugonis	N, mountains	X
Orthotomus cuculatus thais	Pen., mountains	X
Prinia hodgsonii erro	N, SW, NE, SE, C, open country	X
P. rufescens peninsularis	Pen., open country	X
P. flaviventris delacouri	N, NE, C, open country	X
Cisticola exilis equicaudata	N, NE, C, open country	X
Muscicapa latirostris siamensis	N	X
Cyornis banyumas deignani	SE	X
C. b. lekakhuni	NE	X
Culicicapa ceylonensis antioxantha	SW, SE, Pen.	X
Rhipidura albicollis celsa	N, SW, NE	X
Lanius schach longicaudatus	SE, C, open country	X
Anthreptes singalensis interposita	Pen.,	X
Aethopyga nipalensis angkanensis	N, mountains	X
A. n. australis	Pen., mountains	X
A. saturata galenae	N, mountains	X
A. s. anomala	Pen., mountains	X
A. siparaja trangensis	Pen.	X
Dicaeum cruentatus siamense	N, SW, NE, SE, C	X
Zosterops palpebrosa williamsoni	SW, Pen.	X
Z. everetti wetmorei	Pen.	X
Ploceus philippinus angelorum	C, open country	

The only extensive, little-disturbed areas of lowland riverine forest which are completely enclosed within nature reserves are in the Thung Yai and Huai Kha Khaeng Wildlife Sanctuaries of South-west Thailand, yet even these may be at risk from proposed hydro-electric development. The lack of level lowland, evergreen forests in the nature reserves of South-east and Peninsular Thailand is a particularly unfortunate short-coming of the present site network since at least 15 species which are wholly or mainly restricted to such habitats are currently unknown from nature reserves (Table 14; 3.iii, iv). Since most nature reserves have been established in hilly terrain, such valley bottom and foothill habitats as exist are located around their margins and are therefore subject to continuing 'slash-and-burn' encroachment. The establishment of additional nature reserves, or the extension of existing reserves, to encompass what few fragments of extreme lowland forest remain is an urgent and critical requirement.

NATURE RESERVE AREA

A key realisation of modern conservation theory is that most nature reserves are destined to resemble islands of natural or semi-natural vegetation in a 'sea' of grossly man-modified habitats. The tenets of island biogeography (MacArthur and Wilson 1967) would suggest that nature reserves, like other habitat isolates, will eventually support an equilibrium number of species, the value of which will be determined by the size of the reserve area and its distance from sources of further colonists. Larger forest nature reserves which are close to other forest blocks might be expected to maintain a greater species diversity than smaller, more distant sites. Larger areas can be expected to support more individuals per species; larger populations would be more likely to be self-sustaining and less likely to crash due to normal population fluctuation or mishap (Wilcox 1980). There is little known concerning the minimum area which might be necessary to support a viable population of any given species, but it has been observed that, for birds, doubling of the area is associated with an approximately 10 percent increase in the number of species, right on up to areas of continental size. Thus, there is no 'minimal' reserve size for the conservation of diversity.

Studies of both habitat isolates and land bridge islands suggest that bird species from a variety of trophic levels, body sizes and taxonomic groups have suffered extinctions, but that the initial rarity of a species is the best indication of its vulnerability (Terborgh and Winter 1980). Species such as pheasants, hornbills, woodpeckers and babblers are apparently susceptible to extinctions on land bridge islands, while pigeons, cuckoos, kingfishers, thrushes and warblers are among those which show unusual resistance. In part, this may be related to the dispersal capabilities of these birds; pigeons are unusually strong fliers while pheasants and babblers are weak fliers. Many of the bird families which appear to be extinction prone are large frugivores which may not be able to cope with a seasonal dearth of food when the habitat becomes fragmented.

This would suggest that the hornbills would be especially sensitive to the insularisation of habitats, because they are not only frugivorous but are also relatively large and presumably occur at low density. Although they appear to be strong fliers, with the possible exception of the Wreathed Hornbill *Rhyticeros undulatus*, no species has been observed to regularly fly for any significant distance over open deforested country. A population of 50 to 500 individuals has been suggested as the minimum effective size which may be necessary to maintain the short-term fitness and long-term genetic adaptability of any given species (Franklin 1980, Soulé 1980). While recognising that, in the absence of precise data on the breeding structure or genetic variability of different species or populations, such a projection may be oversimplified (Shaffer 1981), it can still provide a useful guideline. In order to conserve a population of 500 hornbills, for example, extrapolating from the known densities of 0.38 and 0.7 nests per sq km for *R. undulatus* and *Buceros bicornis* respectively (Poonswad *et al.* 1987) and assuming two adult individuals per nest, an area of forest of between 658 and 357 sq km might be sufficient. It is important to recognise, however, that the above densities were found in primary forest in the centre of Khao Yai National Park. Large areas of many other parks and sanctuaries have already been logged and, with fewer large nesting trees, probably support considerably lower densities. In addition, Khao Yai exceeds 2,000 sq km in area; smaller nature reserves might also be expected to support lower densities since, having a greater perimeter to area ratio, they would suffer more from human disturbance and other factors. Over half of the existing parks and sanctuaries are less than 400 sq km in area (Figure 5) and the present richness of many of these sites can probably be attributed to the fact that they constitute portions of much larger blocks of National Reserve Forest. Since present government policy dictates that no more than 15 percent of the land area of the country should be maintained as forest for watershed protection and nature conservation, with remaining forest being utilised for productive forestry (which, in practice, implies eventual clear-felling), nature reserves will become increasingly isolated from each other and this may lead to a long-term reduction in the diversity of species which they support. Nonetheless, the proportion of protected areas in Thailand which exceed 1,000 sq km is actually higher than the average for parks and sanctuaries elsewhere in the Indo-Malayan realm (IUCN 1980b). In addition, the strategy of siting parks and sanctuaries adjacent to each other so that they share boundaries and, in effect, constitute larger nature reserve units should help to maximise their conservation potential. Only South-east Thailand lacks any nature reserve larger than 1,000 sq km (Table 16).

Table 16: Areas (sq km) of the largest nature reserves and contiguous nature reserve blocks in the five regions of Thailand.

	N	SW	NE	SE	PEN
Largest individual park/ sanctuary	Om Koi WS 1,224	Thung Yai WS 3,200	Tab Lan NP 2,240	Khao Soi Dao WS 745	Khao Banthad WS 1,267
Largest contiguous nature reserve block	Om Koi-Mae Tuen-Mae Ping 3,400	Thung Yai-Huai Kha Khaeng 5,775	Tab Lan-Pang Sida 3,084	Khao Soi Dao-Khao Kitchakut 803	Khao Sok-Khlong Nakha-Khlong Saeng 2,280

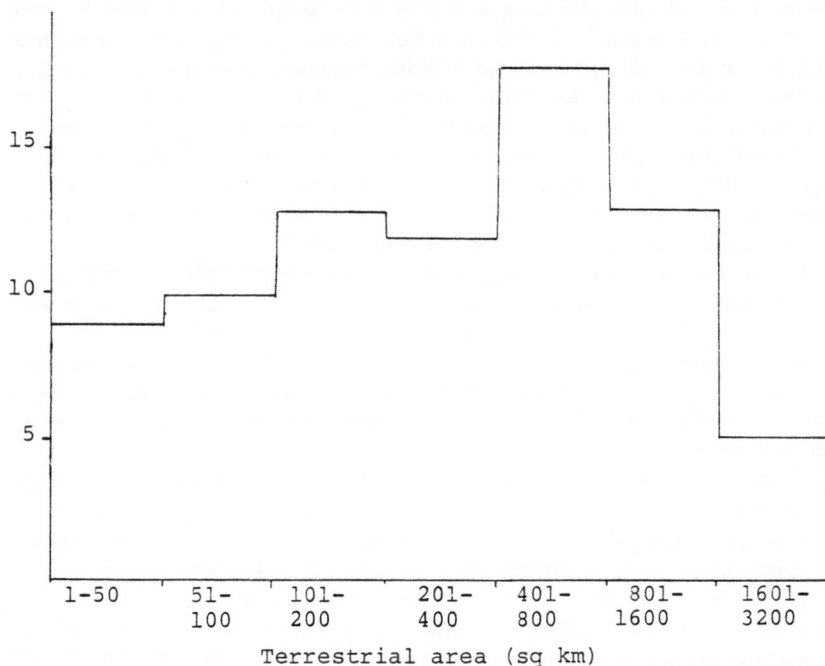

Figure 5: Size classes of national parks and wildlife sanctuaries in Thailand. (Land areas only, marine areas excluded)

CONSERVATION PRIORITIES

Although large scale habitat destruction usually poses the primary threat to wild bird populations, the imminence of this threat may be postponed through the establishment of nature reserves. However, as habitats and populations become increasingly fragmented, so the threats posed by hunting or live capture will increase in relative importance. If direct persecution is not halted by the establishment of nature reserves, many populations may be greatly reduced or even extirpated even where suitable habitat remains. This has already happened in the case of some gamebirds and most hornbills in Northern Thailand.

Table 17 summarises the threats to 93 species of birds considered endangered, threatened or vulnerable. A further 31 species of rare or indeterminate status, together with six species already deemed extinct, are omitted from consideration.

Eleven species (those marked *) are considered to be primarily birds of wetlands or open swamp woodlands. Many of these species have been affected by a combination of drainage and direct persecution rather than by deforestation *per* se, as their lowland haunts have been cleared for agriculture and settled by man. Some of these species might benefit from improved protection of terrestrial forests (e.g. *Ciconia episcopus* and *Cairina scutulata*) or mangrove forests (e.g. *Ardea sumatrana* and *Leptoptilos javanicus*). For most, however, a separate assessment of wetland conservation priorities, outside the scope of this report, is needed. Both extant vultures, neither of which is strictly a forest bird, have been subject to similar pressures: lack of undisturbed areas in which to roost or nest, combined with direct persecution and (very probably) an inadequate food supply has brought them to the brink of extinction.

Of the remaining 79 species, destruction of lowland forest is implicated in threats to 55, of which the majority (38 species) are restricted (or mainly restricted) to the Peninsula. The position of many of these Sundaic species is extremely precarious, because they are almost wholly confined to the level lowlands, where very little forest remains. The populations, even of those species which are known from existing nature reserves, must be extremely small and potentially unviable.

Of the 17 lowland species which occur in Continental Thailand, or which are found throughout the entire country, those inhabiting evergreen forests are usually less altitudinally restricted than Sundaic species, occurring widely on the submontane slopes up to around 700 m elevation (e.g. *Lophura diardi*). Others (e.g. *Ducula aenea*) inhabit both evergreen and deciduous habitats and appear to be more ecologically tolerant. While continuing encroachment around the margins of parks and sanctuaries will continue to pose some threat to all the birds in this group, the species which are most at risk are those which occur in association with forested lowland water bodies, such as *Cairina scutulata*, *Icthyophaga ichthyaetus* and *Pavo muticus*.

Of the remaining 23 species, for all but five small montane birds (*Picoides cathpharius*, *Sitta magna*, *S. formosa*, *Certhia discolor* and *Cochoa purpurea*), hunting or live capture is thought to be the main immediate threat or is assigned the same importance as forest destruction. All are medium to large birds, many of which are reasonably abundant on forested submontane slopes, and most are found widely in existing nature reserves (e.g. *Lophura nycthemera*, *Argusianus argus* and *Buceros bicornis*). Among this group, the most acutely threatened species are those montane birds with ranges which overlap entirely with the distribution of hill tribe shifting cultivators in the north and west (*Arborophila rufogularis*, *Syrmaticus humiae* and *Aceros nipalensis*); those species with an extremely restricted geographical distribution (*Arborophila cambodiana*) or which are restricted to islands (*Caloenas nicobarica*).

The widespread and almost universal occurrence of illegal hunting in Thailand's protected areas has already been commented on (see Section 'Threats'). Khao Yai National Park is one of the better protected nature reserves, and has 12 guard stations, supporting over 100 forest guards, to patrol its 2,168 sq km area (RFD 1985). Yet there are more than 100 villages around the park's perimeter and villagers from most of these sites regularly enter the park in order to hunt larger birds and mammals. Forest trails in some areas of the park were littered with the feathers of Silver Pheasants *Lophura nycthemera* and other birds which had been shot in March and April 1985 (R. J. Dobias pers. comm.) while within less than one kilometre of the park headquarters, gun shots are frequently heard and noose traps found (Brockelman 1987 and pers. comm.). The majority of nature reserves are even less well protected so that hunting pressure may be even higher and encroachment by loggers and settlers more frequent.

It is clear, therefore, that while some additional nature reserves need to be established in key habitats, such as forested lowlands, especially in the vicinity of rivers, this should be combined with much better protection of existing sites. In addition, improved monitoring on the conservation status of both habitats and species, inside and outside of protected areas, is required. Only in this way can the limited resources, which are available to conservation agencies, in the face of escalating pressures upon the environment, be allocated with maximum benefit.

Table 17: Conservation status summary for endangered, threatened and vulnerable birds.

K = Known; S = Known + Suspected; H = Hunting; T = Trade; HL = Habitat Loss. (Threats: 1 = primary threat, 2 = secondary threat. Numbers indicate relative importance of diffent threats for each species and are not necessary comparable among species. L = species restricted to level lowlands or lower submontane slopes, S = species which frequent on upper submontane slopes, M = exclusively montane species, * = primarily associated with wetlands, C = restricted to Continental Thailand, P = restricted to Peninsular Thailand)

Species	Number of nature reserves in which present		Threats				
	K	S	H	T	HL		
Pelecanus philippensis	0	0	1=		1=	L	*
Anhinga melanogaster	0	0	1=		1=	L	*
Ardea sumatrana	1	4	1=		1=	islands	*
Mycteria leucocephala	0	0	1=		1=	L	*
Ciconia episcopus	1	3	1=		1=	L	*
C. stormi	1	2	2		1	LP	
Ephippiorhynchus asiaticus	0	0	1=		1=	L	*
Leptoptilos dubius	1	2	1=		1=	LC	*
L. javanicus	0	0	1=	2	1=	L	*
Threskiornis melanocephalus	0	0	1=		1=	L	*
Sarkidiornis melanotos	0	0	1=		1=	LC	*
Cairina scutulata	4	6	1=		1=	L	
Macheirhamphus alcinus	2	10			1	LP	
Milvus migrans	0	0	1	2			
Icthyophaga humilis	3	5	1=		1=	L	

Table 17   contd

Species	Number of nature reserves in which present		Threats			
	K	S	H	T	HL	
I. ichthyaetus	0	0	1=		1=	L
Gyps bengalensis	0	0	1			
Aegypius calvus	3	3	1=		1=	
Spizaetus nanus	2	6–10	2		1	LP
Rhizothera longirostris	0	2	1=		1=	L
Arborophila rufogularis	5	6–12	1=		1=	MC
A. brunneopectus	7	21–30	1			SC
A. cambodiana	2	3	1	2		MC
A. charltonii	0	2	1=		1=	LP
Rollulus rouloul	0	2	1=	1=	1=	LP
Lophura leucomelana	4	11–20	1		1	SC
L. nycthemera	12	21–30	1=	1=		SC
L. ignita	1	4	2=	2=	1	LP
L. diardi	5	11–20	2=	2=	1	LC
Syrmaticus humiae	0	1	1		2	MC
Polyplectron bicalcaratum	6	11–20	1=	1=	2	SC
P. malacense	0	0	2=	2=	1	LP
Argusianus argus	9	10	1=	1=		SP
Pavo muticus	3	5	1=	1=		L
Heliopais personata	4	6			1	L
Treron pompadora	4	21–30	2		1	LC
T. fulvicollis	0	1	2		1	LP
T. olax	1	4	2		1	LP
T. capellei	0	2	2		1	LP
T. phoenicoptera	2	21–30	2		1	LC
Ducula aenea	5	21–30	2		1	L
Columba pulchricollis	1	2	1		2	MC
Caloenas nicobarica	3	4	1=	1=	2	P islands
Psittacula eupatria	3	11–20	1=	1=	2	LC
Psittinus cyanurus	2	5			1	LP
Otus sagittatus	1	4			1	LP
O. rufescens	0	2			1	LP
Batrachostomus auritus	0	2			1	LP
B. stellatus	0	2			1	LP
Harpactes kasumba	1	5			1	LP
H. diardii	4	6–10			1	LP
H. orrhophaeus	3	5			1	LP
H. duvaucelii	6	10			1	LP
Megaceryle lugubris	1	4			1	LC
Berenicornis comatus	8	10	1=	1=	2	SP

Table 17 contd

Species	Number of nature reserves in which present		Threats			
	K	S	H	T	HL	
Ptilolaemus tickelli	6	21–30	1=	1=	2	SC
Anorrhinus galeritus	8	10	1=	1=	2	SP
Aceros nipalensis	3	5	1=		1=	SC
Rhyticeros corrugatus	1	1	2		1	LP
R. undulatus	22	>40	1=	1=	2	S
R. subruficollis	2	5	1=		1=	L
Anthracoceros malayanus	2	5	1=		1=	LP
Buceros rhinoceros	0	0	1=		1=	SP
B. bicornis	25	>40	1=	1=	2	S
Rhinoplax vigil	6	10	1=	1=	2	SP
Megalaima rafflesii	0	4			1	LP
Gecinulus grantia	0	0			1	LC
Dryocopus javensis	7	21–30			1	L
Picoides cathpharius	0	0			1	MC
Cymbirhynchus macrorhynchos	3	6–10			1	L
Pitta caerulea	4	6–10			1	LP
P. granatina	0	0			1	LP
P. elliotti	0	2			1	LC
P. gurneyi	0	2			1	LP
Coracina striata	1	2			1	LP
Pycnonotus zeylanicus	0	2		1	2	LP
P. eutilotus	1	6–10			1	LP
Oriolus xanthonotus	4	6–10		2	1	LP
Platysmurus leucopterus	3	6–10			1	LP
Sitta magna	4	6			1	MC
S. formosa	0	0			1	MC
Certhia discolor	1	4			1	MC
Trichastoma rostratum	2	5–6			1	LP
T. bicolor	4	5–6			1	LP
Malacopteron affine	0	4			1	LP
M. magnum	1	5–6			1	LP
Kenopia striata	1	5–6			1	LP
Napothera macrodactyla	3	5–6			1	LP
Stachyris maculata	0	4			1	LP
S. nigricollis	1	4			1	LP
Macronous ptilosus	1	2–4			1	LP
Cochoa purpurea	2	4–5			1	MC
Saxicola jerdoni	0	0			1	LC *

RECOMMENDATIONS

1. Establishment of additional nature reserves

Detailed recommendations for the establishment of additional nature reserves are made at the regional level (see Section 'Regional Analysis'). The major habitats and geographical areas where the network should be extended in order to further bird species conservation are summarised below.

(i) *Montane habitats in Continental Thailand*: Doi Pha Hom Pok (North) should be established as a park or sanctuary. The eastern boundary of Hui Kha Khaeng (South-west) should be extended in order to encompass the entire Khao Manorom massif. Surveys should be carried out at a further three sites in Northern Thailand (Khao Kha Khaeng; Doi Langka-Doi Mae Tho and Doi Phu Kha) in order to determine their suitability for nature reserve status.

(ii) *Lowland riverine areas in Continental Thailand*: The southern boundary of Huai Kha Khaeng WS (South-west) should be extended downstream. The boundary of Yot Dom WS (North-east) should be extended in order to encompass forest on both banks of the Lam Dom Yai. A further three areas in Northern Thailand are recommended for survey.

(iii) *Lowland semi-evergreen forest in Continental Thailand*: The Chachoengsao-Chanthaburi watershed area (South-east) is the last remnant of extreme lowland semi-evergreen forest remaining in Continental Thailand. The southern and eastern boundaries of Khao Ang Ru Nai WS should be extended in order to encompass all areas of forest which remain. Two further areas to the east (Khao Sam Ngam and Khlong Pun Piak) are recommended for survey.

(iv) *Rainforests in Peninsular Thailand*: Additional protected areas should be established at six sites (Khlong Mala-Khlong Sai-On; Tha Chana and elsewhere in the mountains of Surat Thani; Khao Si Suk, Ban Nai Chong and in the Budo Mountain range). The status of two further sites, Khao Phra Thaew and Khao Noi Chuchi, should be upgraded from Non-Hunting Area to National Park or Wildlife Sanctuary.

Owing to the almost complete clearance of the level lowland forests, the opportunity to incorporate any single extensive area of extreme lowland rainforest has now been lost. A useful strategy would be to extend the boundaries of existing parks and sanctuaries in order to encompass any remaining areas of forest (including logged forest) and secondary growth around their margins. Boundary extensions to Khlong Phraya WS and the adjacent Khao Phanom Bencha NP are recommended; the lowland margins of all other parks and sanctuaries in the Peninsula should also be surveyed.

(v) *Peat Swamp Forest*: The status of the Pa Phru Non-Hunting Area should be upgraded to wildlife sanctuary.

(vi) *Mangrove*: The boundaries of Ao-Phangnga NP and Mu Ko Phi Phi NP (Peninsula) should be extended in order to encompass more extensive areas of mangrove. Ko Libong should be upgraded from Non-Hunting Area to either National Park or Wildlife Sanctuary. The mangrove inlets along the coast of Chanthaburi and Trat provinces should be surveyed in order to determine their present conservation value.

Because of the under-representation of mangroves in the park and sanctuary network, the establishment of further parks or sanctuaries specifically aimed at protecting significant areas of this habitat, preferably on the west coast of the Peninsula, should be considered.

2. Surveys and monitoring

This report constitutes the only detailed evaluation of the likely effectiveness of Thailand's national park and wildlife sanctuary network in conserving the biotic diversity of any class of animals. Yet, with no fewer than 80 protected areas having been establishment up to April 1986, this can only be regarded as a preliminary assessment which has been impeded by inadequate information on both species distributions and the present status of forested habitats.

While neither the National Parks Division nor the Wildlife Conservation Division has made any systematic effort to maintain species inventories for protected areas, bird lists for many sites have nevertheless been compiled by both Thai and expatriate researchers, tourists and by members of non-governmental bodies such as the Bangkok Bird Club and the Siam Society, and these form the main source of data on which this report is based. All species and habitat data is being collated on computer at the Center for Wildlife Research, Mahidol University as part of a programme to establish a national conservation monitoring centre.

Forest cover data obtained from satellite imagery is of limited value unless ground-checked by biologists. This is both due to the heterogeneity of lowland forest habitats, in which deciduous forests of relatively low species diversity alternate with richer, semi-evergreen and evergreen formations, and to the difficulties in distinguishing between primary forests and selectively logged or degraded areas or even, in some cases, tree plantations. In part, obscuring the distinction between these categories may be a deliberate, unwritten policy of commercial foresters, in order to provide justification for continued logging. At the very least, foresters are concerned chiefly with the identification of potential timber resources rather than with the identification and protection of areas of high biotic diversity. There is a need for much closer liaison between conservation planners in the National Parks and Wildlife Conservation Divisions and officials of the Forest Mapping and Remote Sensing Sections of the Forest Management Division.

There is a clear need for a much expanded programme of field surveys in order to establish the current status of both habitats and species.

3. Species protection legislation

Under the Wild Animals Reservations and Protection Act (1960), although the great majority of bird and mammal species are protected (see Section 'Conservation Measures, Species Protection Legislation'), any Thai National may hold in captivity up to two individuals of any native species. This constitutes a major loophole of the present law, since the burden of proving illegal capture, sale or purchase of any bird is then placed upon the Wildlife Conservation Division. Traders can therefore avoid prosecution by claiming that the species in their possession, which are otherwise fully protected by the law, are not for sale.

Most illegal hunting or capture takes place in relatively remote areas where wildlife protection legislation is extremely difficult to enforce. The one significant area where law enforcement could have a real impact in lessening persecution is in the wildlife trade, since most retailers or animal wholesalers are active in and around major population centres. The law should be amended to prohibit private ownership of all those bird species which are considered to be at risk. Some allowance would have to be made for those species which are easily bred in captivity, such as pheasants. This might be done through issuing licences to the few reputable aviculturists, for example.

4. Nature reserve protection

Greatly improved protection of existing nature reserves is required if populations of pheasants, hornbills and some other large birds are to be maintained. Conventional park protection measures, however, have had limited success in Thailand as most villagers choose to ignore wildlife protection legislation. Few villagers receive any immediate benefits from the establishment of parks and sanctuaries and because many communities around the margins of remaining forests live close to subsistence level, they may not be able to forgo the opportunities for hunting or collecting forest products which these areas offer. Most villagers are well-armed and efforts by park guards to arrest poachers have occasionally ended in gunfights and loss of life. As a result, few routine patrols by forest guards are now carried out in nature reserves (Brockelman 1987).

Although increased emphasis has been placed upon the need to ensure that rural people receive some benefit from National Parks and other areas set aside for wildlife conservation (IUCN 1982), there are, as yet, very few examples where this has occurred in Thailand. Part of the revenue from tourism and other rural developments associated with parks should be channelled to rural communities in order to provide some financial incentives for conservation (Brockelman 1987). With such an objective in mind, a forest trekking programme which employs villagers as skilled guides has been promoted at one village on the boundary of Khao Yai National Park and there are undoubtedly many other sites where such projects would be feasible.

Such financial incentives, however, need to be combined with more rigorous patrolling of protected areas and by improved enforcement of existing wildlife legislation, if they are to be successful.

5. Birdwatching and tourism

According to Royal Forest Department statistics, Thailand's national parks alone received almost four million visitors during October 1983 to September 1984, of whom the vast majority were Thai Nationals. While most park visitors are content to relax in beautiful scenery, close to flowing water and with tall, shady trees, an increasing proportion also appreciate opportunities to observe wildlife. As most mammals are scarce or difficult to observe, birds are the only vertebrates which most visitors will encounter and because of their relative conspicuousness and often bright plumage, they have great potential to further environmental awareness. Yet the majority of parks and sanctuaries lack any interpretive or display material on the birds or other wildlife that occurs within their boundaries. A program for species conservation monitoring should also lead to the production of popular and informative leaflets for all protected areas, listing the bird species which occur there.

Increasing numbers of overseas tourists are visiting Thailand specifically in order to see forest birds. In winter 1984/85 alone, five different bird tour companies from Britain and the USA brought groups to Thailand, all of which stayed in National Parks for part of their visit. Approximately 50 independent birdwatchers also visited the country. Although some nature tour companies have a policy of donating a small proportion of their profits to national conservation bodies in the countries they visit, in practice, very little of the income generated by tours actually reaches rural people. Villagers might, however, benefit from combined trekking/birdwatching tours which might appeal to the more specialised forest birdwatcher. For example, any person who wishes to see species such as the Chestnut-headed Partridge *Arborophila cambodiana* or Blue-rumped Pitta *Pitta soror* in the field could only do so by hiking into the mountains of Khao Soi Dao Wildlife Sanctuary, a trip of at least one or two weeks. Since there are no employees of the Wildlife Conservation Division at the sanctuary who are skilled enough to undertake such an expedition without getting lost, the only practicable means of entering such a remote area is through hiring villagers who might otherwise hunt these birds and who are familiar with the forest trails.

Such tourism within parks and sanctuaries should be actively encouraged, particularly if it leads to the employment of villagers. If legitimised, it could in addition enable officials to more effectively monitor or limit the activities of rural people within the areas under their jurisdiction.

REFERENCES

Agricultural Regulatory Division (1982) Poisonous articles brought in or imported (1981). Department of Agriculture, Bangkok.

Ali, S. and Ripley, S. D. (1968–1974) *Handbook of the Birds of India and Pakistan.* Oxford University Press, Bombay. 10 Vols.

Anon. (1987) *Assessment of National Parks, Wildlife Sanctuaries and other preserves development in Thailand. Final Report.* Faculty of Forestry, Kasetsart University, Bangkok. xii + 138 pp.

Bain, J. R. and Humphrey, S. R. (1982) *A Profile of the Endangered Species of Thailand.* Vol. 1. University of Florida, Gainesville. 344pp.

Brockelman, W. Y. (1977a) A survey of pileated gibbons in Khao Soi Dao Wildlife Sanctuary, Chanthaburi, Thailand. Special report to the Wildlife Conservation Division, Royal Forest Department. Unpublished typescript.

Brockelman, W. Y. (1977b) Second survey of pileated gibbons in Khao Soi Dao Wildlife Sanctuary, Chanthaburi, Thailand. Special report to the Wildlife Conservation Division, Royal Forest Department. Unpublished typescript.

Brockelman, W. Y. (1987) Nature conservation. Pp. 91–119 in A. Arbhabirama, D. Phanthumvanit and J. Elkington (eds.), *Thailand Natural Resources Profile.* Thailand Development Research Institute, Bangkok. xxv + 310 pp.

Brockelman, W. Y. and Nadee, N. (1977) Preliminary survey and bio-geographic analysis of the birds of the Surin Islands. *Nat. Hist. Bull. Siam Soc.* 26: 211–226.

Brockelman, W. Y. and Sophasan, S. (1979) Bird list of Khao Chamao, East Thailand. Unpublished typescript.

Bunjavejchewin, S. (1983) Analysis of tropical dry deciduous forest of Thailand, I. Characteristics of the dominance types. *Nat. Hist. Bull. Siam Soc.* 31: 109–122.

Chumnankid, C. (1985) Application of aerial photographs in land use and forest production studies in Huai Kha Khaeng Wildlife Sanctuary, Uthai Thani and Tak Province. Unpublished MSc. Dissertation, Faculty of Forestry, Kasetsart Univserity, Bangkok. (In Thai.)

Chunkao, K. (1987) Forest Resources. Pp. 73–88 in A. Arbhabirama, D. Phanthumvanit and J. Elkington (eds.), *Thailand Natural Resources Profile.* Thailand Development Research Institute, Bangkok. xxv + 310 pp.

Collar, N. J., Round, P. D. and Wells, D. R. (1986) The past and future of Gurney's Pitta. *Forktail* 1: 29–51.

Congdon, G. (1981) Tarutao National Marine Park: Birds. Unpublished typescript.

Congdon, G. (1982) The vegetation of Tarutao National Park. *Nat. Hist. Bull. Siam Soc.* 30: 135–198.

Davison, G. W. H. (1981) Habitat requirements and the food supply of the Crested Fireback. *W.P.A. Journal* 6: 40–52.

Davison, G. W. H. (1982) Systematics within the Genus *Arborophila* Hodgson. *Fed. Mus. J.* 27: 125–134.

Deignan, H. G. (1939) Three new birds of the genus *Stachyris*. *Field. Mus. Nat. Hist. Zool. Ser.* 24(90): 109–114.

Deignan, H. G. (1945) The birds of Northern Thailand. *US Nat. Mus. Bull.* 186.

Deignan, H. G. (1963) Checklist of the birds of Thailand. *US Nat. Mus. Bull.* 226.

Delacour, J. (1929) On the birds collected during the fourth expedition to French Indo-China. *Ibis* 12: 193–220; 403–429.

Dickinson, E. C. and Chaiyaphun, S. (1968) Notes on Thai Birds 1. *Nat. Hist. Bull. Siam Soc.* 22: 307–315.

Dickinson, E. C. and Chaiyaphun, S. (1970) Notes on Thai Birds 2. A first contribution to our knowledge of the birds of Thung Salaeng Luang National Park, Phitsanulok Province. *Nat. Hist. Bull. Siam Soc.* 23: 515–525.

Dickinson, E. C. and Chaiyaphun, S. (1973) Notes on Thai Birds 4. Birds collected in Phu Kradeung National Park, Loei Province. *Nat. Hist. Bull. Siam Soc.* 25: 33–38.

Dobias, R. J. (1982) *The Shell Guide to the National Parks of Thailand.* Shell, Bangkok. 137 pp.

Dransfield, J. (1983) *Kerriodoxa*, a new Coryphoid Palm genus from Thailand. *Principes* 27(1): 3–11.

Enderlein, P. (1976) Report from the second expedition to the Dongrak Mountain Range in Eastern Thailand in search for Kouprey *Bos sauveli*. FAO Bangkok. Unpublished typescript.

Eve, R. and Guigue, A. M. (1982) Birds on Ko Libong, Southern Thailand. *Nat. Hist. Bull. Siam Soc.* 30: 91–104.

Eve, R. and Guigue, A. M. (1984) Birds observed in Lum Nam Pai Wildlife Sanctuary, 23–29 July 1984. Unpublished typescript.

FAO (1981) *Forest Resources of Tropical Asia.* FAO and UNEP Rome. ix + 475 pp.

Franklin, I. R. (1980) Evolutionary change in small populations. Pp. 135–149 in M. E. Soulé and B. A. Wilcox (eds.). *Conservation Biology: An Evolutionary-Ecological Perspective.* Sinuaer, Sunderland, USA. xv + 395 pp.

Herbert, E. G. (1923) Nests and eggs of birds in Central Siam. *J. Nat. Hist. Siam Soc.* 6: 39–66.

Holmes, D. A. (1973) Bird notes from southernmost Thailand, 1972. *Nat. Hist. Bull. Siam Soc.* 25: 39–66.

Holmes, D. A. and Wells, D. R. (1975) Further observation on the birds of South Thailand. *Nat. Hist. Bull. Siam Soc.* 26: 61–78.

Inskipp, C. and Inskipp, T. P. (1984) *A Guide to the Birds of Nepal.* Croom Helm, London and Sydney. 392 pp.

Inskipp, T. P. and Round, P. D. (in prep.) [A review of the Black-tailed Crake *Porzana bicolor*.]

IUCN (1979) *Conservation for Thailand. Policy Guidelines.* IUCN Morges. 2 Vols.

IUCN (1980a) *World Conservation Strategy.* IUCN, Gland.

IUCN (1980b) *1980 United Nations List of National Parks and Equivalent Reserves.* IUCN and UNEP, Gland. iii + 121 pp.

IUCN (1982) Recommendations. World National Parks Congress, Bali, Indonesia, 11–22 October 1982. IUCN, Gland.

Johns, A. D. (1986) Effects of selective logging on the ecological organisation of a peninsular Malaysian rainforest avifauna. *Forktail* 1: 65–79.

King, B. (1966) List of bird skins and specimens collected in Thailand from 1 March 1964 to 30 June 1966 under MAPS programme. Centre for Thai National Reference Collections, Bangkok.

King, B. (1984) The birds of South-East Asia. Revised Checklist, October 1984. Unpublished typescript.

King, B., Dickinson, E. C. and Woodcock, M. W. (1975) *A Field Guide to the Birds of South-East Asia.* Collins, London. 480 pp.

King, B. and Kanwanich, S. (1978) First wild sighting of the White-eyed River Martin *Pseudochelidon sirintarae. Biol. Conserv.* 13: 183–186.

King, W. B. (1978–1979) *Red Data Book, 2. Aves.* Second edition. IUCN, Morges, Switzerland.

Klankamsorn, B. and Charuppat, T. (1984) Application of remote sensing in forest inventory and change detection. Paper presented at the Third Agricultural Remote Sensing Symposium, Chiang Mai, Thailand. Unpublished typescript.

Kloss, C. B. (1915) Zoogeographical divisions for Siam. *J. Nat. Hist. Soc. Siam* 1: 250–251.

Kunstadter, P., Chapman, E. C. and Sabhasri (eds.) (1978) *Farmers in the Forest. Economic Development and Marginal Agriculture in Northern Thailand.* East-West Center, Hawaii. 402 pp.

Lekagul, B. and Cronin, E. W. Jr. (1974) *Bird Guide of Thailand.* 2nd edition. Association for the Conservation of Wildlife, Bangkok. xiv + 324 pp.

Lekagul, B. and McNeely, J. A. (1977) *Mammals of Thailand.* Association for the Conservation of Wildlife, Bangkok. li + 758 pp.

MacArthur, R. H. and Wilson E. O. (1967) *The Theory of Island Bio-geography.* Princeton University, Princeton. xi + 203 pp.

Marshall, J. T. (1978) Systematics of the smaller Asian nightbirds based on voice. *Ornith. Monogr.* 25: 1–58.

Maxwell, J. F. (1980) Vegetation of Khao Khieo Game Sanctuary, Chonburi Province, Thailand. *Nat. Hist. Bull. Siam Soc.* 28: 9–24.

McClure, H. E. (1974) Some bionomics of the birds of Khao Yai National Park, Thailand. *Nat. Hist. Bull. Siam Soc.* 24: 41–78.

McClure, H. E. and Chaiyaphun, S. (1971) The sale of birds at the Bangkok 'Sunday Market', Thailand. *Nat. Hist. Bull. Siam Soc.* 24: 41–78.

McNeely, J. A. (1975) Draft report on wildlife and national parks in the Lower Mekong Basin. Committee for the Coordination of Investigations of the Lower Mekong Basin, Bangkok. Unpublished typescript.

Medway, Lord (1972) The Gunong Benom Expedition 1967: 6. The distribution and altitudinal zonation of birds and mammals on Gunong Benom. *Bull. Brit. Mus. Nat. Hist. Zool.* 23: 103–154.

Medway, Lord and Wells, D. R. (1971) Diversity and density of birds and mammals at Kuala Lompat, Pahang. *Malay Nat. J.* 24: 238–247.

Medway, Lord and Wells, D. R. (1976) *The Birds of the Malay Peninsula.* Vol. 5. Witherby in association with Penerbit Universiti Malaya. London and Kuala Lumpur. xxxi + 448 pp.

Melville, D. S. and Chalmers, M. (1984) Large Grass Warblers in Hong Kong. The discovery of *Graminicola bengalensis* with a review of the records of *Prinia criniger* and *Prinia atrogularis. Hong Kong Bird Report* 1981/82: 87–97.

Meyer de Schauensee, R. (1946) On Siamese birds. *Proc. Acad. Nat. Sci. Philadelphia* 98: 1–82.

Nakhasathien, S. (1987) The discovery of Storm's Stork *Ciconia stormi* in Thailand. *Forktail* 3: 43–49.

National Economic and Social Development Board (1981) Fifth National Economic and Social Development Plan 1982–1986. Office of the Prime Minister, Bangkok.

Neal, D. G. (1967) *Statistical description of the forests of Thailand.* Joint Thai-US Military Research and Development Center, Bangkok. xvi + 346 pp.

Phumpakapun, N. and Kutintara, U. (1983) *Wild Fauna of Thung Yai Naresuan.* Faculty of Forestry, Kasetsart University, Bangkok. Unpublished typescript.

Phumpakapun, N., Kutintara, U. and Naksatit, N. (1986) Wild Fauna of Huai Kha Khaeng. Pp. 1–63 in Wildlife Conservation Division Technical Section, *Khao Nang Rum Research Station Report* No. 1. Royal Forest Department, Bangkok.

Poonswad, P., Tsuji, A. and Ngampongsai, C. (1987) A comparative study on breeding biology of sympatric hornbill species (Bucerotidae) in Thailand with implications for breeding in captivity. *Proc. Jean Delacour/IFCB Symposium on breeding birds in captivity*, pp. 250–315. IFCB, Los Angeles.

Riley, J. H. (1938) Birds from Siam and the Malay Peninsula in the United States National Museum collected by Drs. Hugh M. Smith and William L. Abbott. *US Nat. Mus. Bull.* 172.

Robbins, R. G. and Smitinand, T. (1966) A botanical ascent of Doi Inthanon. *Nat. Hist. Bull. Siam Soc.* 21: 205–227.

Robinson, H. C. (1915) On a collection of birds from the Siamese province of Bandon. NE Malay Peninsula. *J. Fed. Malay States Mus.* 5(3): 83–110.

Round, P. D. (1982) Notes on breeding birds in North-west Thailand. *Nat. Hist. Bull. Siam Soc.* 30: 1–14.

Round, P. D. (1983a) Some recent bird records from Northern Thailand. *Nat. Hist. Bull. Siam Soc.* 31: 123–138.

Round, P. D. (1983b) A pilot survey of the Green Peafowl (*Pavo muticus*) in Huai Kha Khaeng Wildlife Sanctuary, Uthai Thani Province, Western Thailand. Preliminary report to the Wildlife Conservation Division and World Pheasant Association, Thailand. Unpublished typescript.

Round, P. D. (1984) The status and conservation of the bird community in Doi Suthep-Pui National Park, North-west Thailand. *Nat. Hist. Bull. Siam Soc.* 32: 21–46.

Round, P. D. and Treesucon, U. (1986a) Gurney's Pitta: an object lesson in forest preservation. *World Birdwatch* 8(1): 1–2.

Round, P. D. and Treesucon, U. (1986b) The rediscovery of Gurney's Pitta. *Forktail* 2: 53–66.

Royal Forest Department (1983a) Forest Types Map. RFD, Bangkok.

Royal Forest Department (1983b) *List of Protected Animal Species.* RFD, Bangkok. iii + 71 pp. (In Thai.)

Royal Forest Department (1985) *Khao Yai National Park Management Plan 1985-1989.* RFD, Bangkok.

Royal Forest Department (1986) *Forestry Statistics of Thailand 1985.* RFD, Bangkok. 74 pp.

Santisuk, T. and Niyomdham, C. (1985) Some conservation problems of peat swamp forest in Thailand. Pp. 205–220 in W. Y. Brockelman (ed.) *Nature conservation in Thailand in relation to social and economic development.* Siam Society, Bangkok. vi + 324 pp. (In Thai.)

Sayer, J. A. (1981) *A review of the nature conservation policies and programmes of the Royal Forest Department.* FAO, Bangkok. 104 pp.

Seriot, J., Pineau, O. de Schatzen, R. and Dubois, P. J. (1986) Black-tailed Crake *Porzana bicolor*: a new species for Thailand. *Forktail* 2: 101–103.

Shaffer, M. L. (1981) Minimum population sizes for species conservation. *Bioscience* 31: 131–134.

Short, L. L. (1982) *Woodpeckers of the World.* Delaware Museum of Natural History, Greenville, USA. xviii + 676 pp.

Smitinand, T. (1968) Vegetation of Khao Yai National Park. *Nat. Hist. Bull. Siam Soc.* 22: 289–305.

Smitinand, T. and Scheible, W. R. (1966) *Survival manual for Thailand and adjacent areas.* Joint Thai-US Military Research and Development Center, Bangkok. vii + 134 pp.

Smitinand, T., Na Lamphun, A. and Vanek, D. (1967) Map of Thailand showing types of forest. Map supplement to D. G. Neal, *Statistical description of the forests of Thailand.* Joint Thai-US Military Research and Development Center, Bangkok. xvi +346 pp.

Smythies, B. E. (1953) *The Birds of Burma*, second (revised) edition, Oliver and Boyd, Edinburgh. xiii + 668 pp.

Sophasan, S. and Dobias, R. (1984) The fate of the "Princess Bird" or White-eyed River Martin (*Pseudochelidon sirintarae*). *Nat. Hist. Bull. Siam Soc.* 32: 1–10.

Soulé, M. E. (1980) Thresholds for survival: monitoring fitness and evolutionary potential. Pp. 151–169 in M. E. Soulé and B. A. Wilcox (eds.), *Conservation Biology: An Evolutionary-Ecological Perspective.* Sinauer, Sunderland, USA. xv + 395 pp.

Srikosamatara, S. and Doungkhae, S. (1982) Dry dipterocarp forest as a barrier to gibbon dispersal: A survey in Phu Phan National Park, North-east Thailand. *Nat. Hist. Bull. Siam Soc.* 30: 25–32.

Starks, J. (1985) Interwader surveys in Thailand. Pp. 27–42 in D. Parish and D. Wells (eds.), *Interwader Annual Report 1984.* Interwader, Kuala Lumpur. 164 pp.

Storer, P. J. (1980) A preliminary biological survey of Khao Khieo Wildlife Sanctuary. *Nat. Hist. Bull. Siam Soc.* 28: 25–46.

Terborgh, J. and Winter, B. (1980) Some causes of extinction. Pp. 119–133 in M. E. Soulé and B. A. Wilcox (eds.), *Conservation Biology: An Evolutionary-Ecological Perspective.* Sinauer, Sunderland, USA. xv + 395 pp.

Thonglongya, K. (1968) A new martin of the genus *Pseudochelidon* from Thailand. *Thai Nat. Sci. Papers, Fauna Series* No. 1. Applied Scientific Research Corporation of Thailand, Bangkok.

Tuntawiroon, N. and Samootsakorn, P. (1986) Thailand's dam building programme: past, present and future. Pp. 291–303 in E. Goldsmith and N. Hildyard (eds.), *The Social and Environmental Effects of Large Dams. Vol. 2: Case Studies,* Wadebridge Ecological Centre, Camelford. 331 pp.

Ward, P. and Wood, B. (1967) Parrot damage to oil palm fruit in Johore. *The Planter* 43: 1–3.

Waugh, D. R. and Hails, C. J. (1983) Foraging ecology of a tropical aerial feeding bird guild. *Ibis* 125: 200–217.

Wells, D. R. (1976) Resident Birds. Pp. 1–33 in Lord Medway and D. R. Wells, *The Birds of the Malay Peninsula.* Vol. 5. Witherby in association with Penerbit University Malaya. London and Kuala Lumpur. xxxi + 448 pp.

Wells, D. R. (1983) Bird Report: 1976 and 1977. *Malay Nat. J.* 36: 197–218.

Wells, D. R. (1985) The forest avifauna of Western Malaysia and its conservation. Pp. 213–232 in A. W. Diamond and T. E. Lovejoy (eds.), *Conservation of Tropical Forest Birds.* ICBP Techn. Publ. No. 4, Cambridge.

Wells, D. R., Hails, C. J. and Hails, A. J. (in prep.) A mist netting study of avifaunal variation in lowland tropical forest in Malaysia.

Wharton, C. H. (1969) Man, fire and cattle in South-east Asia. *Proc. Ann. Tall Timbers Fire Ecology Conference* 8: 107–167.

Whitmore, T. C. (1975) *Tropical Rain Forests of the Far East.* Clarendon, Oxford. xiii + 282 pp.

Wilcox, B. A. (1980) Insular ecology and conservation. Pp. 95–117 in M. E. Soulé and B. A. Wilcox (eds.), *Conservation Biology: An Evolutionary-Ecological Perspective.* Sinauer, Sunderland, USA. xv + 395 pp.

Wiles, G. J. (1980) The birds of Salak Phra Wildlife Sanctuary, South-western Thailand. *Nat. Hist. Bull. Siam Soc.* 28: 101–120.

Wong, M. (1985) Understorey birds as indicators of regeneration in a patch of selectively logged west Malaysian rainforest. Pp. 249–263 in A. W. Diamond and T. E. Lovejoy (eds.), *Conservation of Tropical Forest Birds*. ICBP Techn. Publ. No. 4, Cambridge.

Young, G. (1967) *Tracks of an Intruder*. Souvenir, London. 191 pp.

APPENDIX I

DISTRIBUTIONAL LIST OF RESIDENT LANDBIRDS

Order and nomenclature follows King, Dickinson and Woodcock (1975) or King (1984).

Habitat

DD	dry dipterocarp	PE	pinewoods
MD	mixed deciduous	BO	bamboo
SE	semi-evergreen	MA	mangroves
TR	rainforest	SG	secondary forest or forest patches with scattered clearings
HE	hill evergreen	F	forest (all categories)

O   Open, deforested country or other man-made or natural/semi-natural habitats which are remote from forest. (Includes plantations, scrub, gardens, orchards, grassland, marshland, cultivated fields.)

*   Upper altitudinal limit not established for Thailand. Data obtained from Medway and Wells (1976) for Malaysia.

Distribution

Numbers refer to National Parks or Wildlife Sanctuaries which are listed in Appendix II. Numbers in parenthesis ( ) indicate that records pre-date 1978. Detailed distribution data is presented only for those populations which are resident or which are presumed to breed in the region.

◩   Out of range; species not likely to occur in region.

Threats

1	forest destruction	3	live capture for trade
2	hunting	4	pesticides

Threats listed in declining order of importance.

Status

X	extinct	V	vulnerable
E	endangered	Ind.	indeterminate
T	threatened	Rare	

(See Section "Species Status Review" for definition of the terms used).

SPECIES	HABITAT	DISTRIBUTION						THREATS	STATUS
		N	SW	NE	SE	PEN.	C		
SPOT-BILLED PELICAN *Pelecanus philippensis*	swamp forests	formerly present	present	present		formerly present	present	1,2	E U
ORIENTAL DARTER *Anhinga melanogaster*	swamp forests	formerly present		formerly present		formerly present	present	1,2	T U
GREAT-BILLED HERON *Ardea sumatrana*	MA (islands, seacoasts).				present	14		1,2	T
MALAYAN NIGHT HERON *Gorsachius melanolophus*	SE, up to 1200 m	present	present	(04) 08	04 07 08	migrant only	migrant only	2,1	
PAINTED STORK *Mycteria leucocephala*	swamp forests		migrant only	migrant only		present	migrant only	2,1	E U
WOOLLY-NECKED STORK *Ciconia episcopus*	DD MD SE SG, plains	formerly present	formerly present	formerly present	07	formerly present	formerly present	1,2	E
STORM'S STORK *Ciconia stormi*	TR, plains					16		1,2	E
BLACK-NECKED STORK *Ephippiorhynchus asiaticus*	swamp forests	formerly present				present/ formerly present	formerly present	2,1	E U
GREATER ADJUTANT *Leptoptilos dubius*	DD SG, swamp forests	formerly present	08	present	formerly present	migrant only	migrant only	1,2	E
LESSER ADJUTANT *Leptoptilos javanicus*	MA, swamp forests			migrant only		present	migrant only	2,1	E U

SPECIES	HABITAT	DISTRIBUTION						THREATS	STATUS
		N	SW	NE	SE	PEN.	C		
BLACK-HEADED IBIS Threskiornis melanocephala	swamp forests		migrant only			migrant only	present	2,1	E U
WHITE-SHOULDERED IBIS Pseudibis davisoni	swamp forests	formerly present				formerly present	formerly present	1,2	X
GIANT IBIS Pseudibis gigantea	swamp forests					formerly present	formerly present	1,2	X
COMB DUCK Sarkidiornis melanotos	DD MD close to water	formerly present		present			formerly present	2,1	E U
WHITE-WINGED DUCK Cairina scutulata	F, close to water	formerly present	07 08	13	formerly present	formerly present		1,2	E
JERDON'S BAZA Aviceda jerdoni	MD SE plains-1200 m	migrant only	present	08	(08)	04		3	
BLACK BAZA Aviceda leuphotes	DD MD SE HE, plains-1500 m	02 03 13,16	07 09	08	07	migrant only	present		
CRESTED HONEY BUZZARD Pernis ptilorhyncus	DD MD SG, plains - 1200 m	02 03	05 07	08 15	07 08	04 13 (10) 15 17 18 19	migrant		
BAT HAWK Macheirhamphus alcinus	TR plains, foothills					13 17		1	T

SPECIES	HABITAT	DISTRIBUTION						THREATS	STATUS
		N	SW	NE	SE	PEN.	C		
BLACK-SHOULDERED KITE Elanus caeruleus	O, plains - 1500 m	03 08	05 06 07	08	06 08	03	present	3	
BLACK KITE Milvus migrans	O, plains.	migrant only	formerly present	migrant only	migrant only	migrant only	present	2, 4, 3	T U
BRAHMINY KITE Haliastur indus	MA O, rivers, seacoasts	formerly present	06	formerly present	present	14 (18)	present	3	
WHITE-BELLIED SEA-EAGLE Haliaeetus leucogaster	MA, wooded cliffs of seacoasts.	/	06		01	02 03 06 09 13 14	/	3	
LESSER FISH-EAGLE Icthyophaga humilis	F, close to rivers of plains and foothills	formerly present	07	/	/	04 13	/	1, 2	T
GREY-HEADED FISH-EAGLE Icthyophaga ichthyaetus	F, close to rivers, coasts. Extreme lowlands	formerly present	formerly present	/	/	present	formerly present	1, 2, 4	E U
WHITE-RUMPED VULTURE Gyps bengalensis	O, plains - 1350 m.	formerly present	present	present	/	present	formerly present	2, 4	E U
LONG-BILLED VULTURE Gyps indicus	O, chiefly plains	formerly present	/	formerly present	formerly present	formerly present	formerly present	2, 4	X/E
RED-HEADED VULTURE Aegypius calvus	MD DD O chiefly plains foothills.	present	07 08 09		formerly present	formerly present	formerly present	1, 2	E

SPECIES	HABITAT	N	SW	NE	SE	PEN.	C	THREATS	STATUS
CRESTED SERPENT-EAGLE Spilornis cheela	DD MD SE TR HE, up to 1500 m.	02 03 04 06 14 18	03 04 05 06 07 09	03 08 13	02 (04) 06 08	03 04 11 13 15 18 19	present	3	
BESRA Accipiter virgatus	MD SE, plains - 2000 m.	02 (03)	present	08	(08)				
CRESTED GOSHAWK Accipiter trivirgatus	MD SE TR HE, plains - 1800 m.	02 03 04 13 14	05 07	present	01 06 08	04 15 16 17	present		
SHIKRA Accipiter badius	DD MD SE HE, O,plains-1500 m.	02 03 04 06 13 14 16	03 04 05 06 07 09	03 08 11 13	06 07 08	migrant only	present	None	
RUFOUS-WINGED BUZZARD Butastur liventer	DD MD SG, plains, foothills	(02) 03		13			present	3	
BLACK EAGLE Ictinaetus malayensis	SE TR HE, plains - 2600 m	02 03 14 18	07	08 13	(08)	04 11 17			
BONELLI'S EAGLE Hieraaetus fasciatus	HE (near cliffs) above 1000 m	03 13							
RUFOUS-BELLIED EAGLE Hieraaetus kienerii	MD SE TR HE, foothills-2000 m	02 03 14	07	08	08	13 16			
CHANGEABLE HAWK-EAGLE Spizaetus cirrhatus	MD SE TR HE SG, plains - 2000 m	02 04 13 18	04 05 07	08	06 08	19	formerly present	3	
MOUNTAIN HAWK-EAGLE Spizaetus nipalensis	HE SG, 1000 - 2590 m	03	07	probably migrant only	migrant only	migrant only	migrant only	3	

SPECIES	HABITAT	N	SW	NE	SE	PEN.	C	THREATS	STATUS
BLYTH'S HAWK-EAGLE Spizaetus alboniger	TR, foothills - 1800 m					13 15 17 19		3	
WALLACE'S HAWK-EAGLE Spizaetus nanus	TR, level lowlands & foothills					04 18		1	T
WHITE-RUMPED FALCON Polihierax insignis	DD MD SG, plains - 700 m	(02) 03 14	07	present					
COLLARED FALCONET Microhierax caerulescens	DD MD HE SG, plains - 1800 m	02 03 13 16	04 05 07 08 09	03 (08)	07			3	
BLACK-THIGHED FALCONET Microhierax fringillarius	TR, (clearings) SG up to 1500 m		02 (03) 07	08		13 16 17 18		3	
ORIENTAL HOBBY Falco severus	MD SE TR, foothills-1500m	present		08	present	04	present		
PEREGRINE FALCON Falco peregrinus	MD SE TR, cliffs	present 06		08		04 09 13	migrant only		
CHINESE FRANCOLIN Francolinus pintadeanus	O, plains - 1500 m	02 03 13 16 18	07 09	(02) 03 (08)	06		present	None	Common
LONG-BILLED PARTRIDGE Rhizothera longirostris	SE TR BO, chiefly lowlands		present	present	present	present		1, 2	E U
RAIN QUAIL Coturnix coromandelica	O, plains	present	present	present					U
BLUE-BREASTED QUAIL Coturnix chinensis	O, plains - 1300 m	03		08 13		present	present		

SPECIES	HABITAT	DISTRIBUTION						THREATS	STATUS
		N	SW	NE	SE	PEN.	C		
RUFOUS-THROATED PARTRIDGE Arborophila rufogularis	HE 1200 - 2590 m	03 14 18	07	13				2, 1	T
BAR-BACKED PARTRIDGE Arborophila brunneopectus	SE HE, 700 - 1300 m	14	07 05	(02) 03 (04) 15				2, 1	V
CHESTNUT-HEADED PARTRIDGE Arborophila cambodiana	SE HE, 700 -				(04)(08)			2, 1	T
SCALY-BREASTED PARTRIDGE Arborophila chloropus	MD SE BO, plains - 1000 m	02 (04) 14	05 07 09	(04) 08	02 (04) 06 07 08			2	E
CHESTNUT-NECKLACED PARTRIDGE Arborophila charltonii	TR, level lowlands					present		1, 2	
FERRUGINOUS WOOD-PARTRIDGE Caloperdix oculea	SE TR, hill slopes up to 900 m					(10) 13 17		2	
CRESTED WOOD PARTRIDGE Rollulus rouloul	TR SE, chiefly lowlands		present			present		2, 3	E U
MOUNTAIN BAMBOO-PARTRIDGE Bambusicola fytchii	O SG BO, above 1200 m	present	03 07 08 09					2	U
KALIJ PHEASANT Lophura leucomelana	SE HE, 600 - 1200 m	present						2,3,1	V
SILVER PHEASANT Lophura nycthemera	SE HE, 750 - 2000 m	02 03 (04) 14		03(04)08 13 15	02 (04) 08			2, 3	V

SPECIES	HABITAT	DISTRIBUTION						THREATS	STATUS
		N	SW	NE	SE	PEN.	C		
CRESTED FIREBACK Lophura ignita	TR, level lowlands, close to stream banks					16 (18)		1, 2, 3	E
SIAMESE FIREBACK Lophura diardi	SE lowlands to 800 m	present		(04) 08 15	07 08			1, 2, 3	T
RED JUNGLEFOWL Gallus gallus	F SG BO, plains - 1800 m	02 03 06 13 14	03 05 06 07 08 09	03 (04) 08 11 13 15	02 06 07 08	04 13 16 18 19		2 / 2	
HUME'S PHEASANT Syrmaticus humiae	HE SG, clearings above 1200 m	(14)						2, 1	E
GREY PEACOCK PHEASANT Polyplectron bicalcaratum	SE HE, 600 - 1800 m	present	present 05 07 08	(04)13 15		present		1, 2, 3	V
MALAYSIAN PEACOCK-PHEASANT Polyplectron malacense	TR, level lowlands, extreme lower hill slopes					present		1, 2, 3	E U
GREAT ARGUS Argusianus argus	TR, foothills - 900 m					04(05)10 13 15 16 17 18 19		2, 3, 1	V
GREEN PEAFOWL Pavo muticus	MD SG close to rivers, below 500 m	12	07 08	present/ formerly present		formerly present		2, 3, 1	T
LITTLE BUTTON QUAIL Turnix sylvatica	O plains						present	None	U
YELLOW-LEGGED BUTTON QUAIL Turnix tanki	SG O, plains - 1800 m	(02) 03	present 08				present	None	

SPECIES	HABITAT	N	SW	NE	SE	PEN.	C	THREATS	STATUS
				DISTRIBUTION					
BARRED BUTTON QUAIL Turnix suscitator	SG O, plains - 1500 m	13 18	present	08		06	04 16 (18)	present	None	
SARUS CRANE Grus antigone	DD O, plains	formerly present		formerly present			formerly present	formerly present		X
RED-LEGGED CRAKE Rallina fasciata	MD SE TR, moist areas below 400 m	present	07				17			
SLATY-LEGGED CRAKE Rallina eurizonoides	MD SE SG, lowlands-1300 m	(03)	07				migrant only	migrant only		
BLACK-TAILED CRAKE Porzana bicolor	SG O, streams, moist areas 1300m	03								
MASKED FINFOOT Heliopais personata	MD SE MA, (rivers) lowlands	formerly present	08		formerly present	04, 13, 14			1, 2	V
PIN-TAILED PIGEON Treron apicauda	SE HE 600 - 1800 m	02 (03) 14		present					2	
YELLOW-VENTED PIGEON Treron seimundi	SE HE, mountains	present						migrant only	2	U
WEDGE-TAILED PIGEON Treron sphenura	SE HE SG, 700 - 2590 m	02 03 04	07	08					2	
WHITE-BELLIED PIGEON Treron sieboldii	mountain forests	present		present					2	U
THICK-BILLED PIGEON Treron curvirostra	MD SE TR HE MA SG,plains-1200 m	06 0	03 05 07 09	(04) 08	02 (04) 06 07 08	(10) 11 14 15 16	present	2	U

SPECIES	HABITAT	DISTRIBUTION						THREATS	STATUS
		N	SW	NE	SE	PEN.	C		
POMPADOUR PIGEON Treron pompadora	SE plains - 800 m	present 07		08	07 (08)	18 19		1, 2	V
CINNAMON-HEADED PIGEON Treron fulvicollis	TR MA, level lowlands					present		1, 2	T U
LITTLE GREEN PIGEON Treron olax	TR, level lowlands					17		1, 2	T
PINK-NECKED PIGEON Treron vernans	MD SE TR MA SG, O, lowlands	present 06			(05)	03 (14)	present	2	
ORANGE-BREASTED PIGEON Treron bicincta	MD SE MA SG, O, lowlands - 800 m		(06) 07	08	08	present		2	
LARGE GREEN PIGEON Treron capellei	TR level lowlands					present		1, 2	T U
YELLOW-FOOTED PIGEON Treron phoenicoptera	MD SE SG, plains, foothills	formerly present	07	08				2, 1	V
JAMBU FRUIT-DOVE Ptilinopus jambu	MA, TR, lowlands - 1200 m*			present/formerly present	formerly present	(18)			
GREEN IMPERIAL PIGEON Ducula aenea	MD SE plains, islands	formerly present	07 08			02 03 14		2, 1	V

SPECIES	HABITAT	DISTRIBUTION N	SW	NE	SB	PEN.	C	THREATS	STATUS
PIED IMPERIAL PIGEON *Ducula bicolor*	wooded islands	/	/	/	present	02 03 09 14	/	2	
MOUNTAIN IMPERIAL PIGEON *Ducula badia*	SE HE, hill up to 2000 m	02 03 (04) 13 14 18	07	(02) 03 08 13	02 06 08	/	/	2	
ASHY WOOD-PIGEON *Columba pulchricollis*	HE 1600-2500 m	03	/	08	/	/	/	1, 2	V
PALE-CAPPED PIGEON *Columba punicea*	SE up to 800 m especially islands	/	08	08	present	14	/	1, 2	
BARRED CUCKOO-DOVE *Macropygia unchall*	SE HE, 500 - 1800 m	02 03 18 (04)	07	(02) 03 (04) 08	08	/	/	2	
LITTLE CUCKOO-DOVE *Macropygia ruficeps*	SE HE, 500 - 1800 m	(02)(04)	07	13	/	/	/		
ORIENTAL TURTLE-DOVE *Streptopelia orientalis*	DD HE SG O, foothills - 1800 m	03 (04) 13		03		/	/	2	
RED TURTLE-DOVE *Streptopelia tranquebarica*	O plains	present	03 06 07	08 13	06 07		present		
SPOTTED DOVE *Streptopelia chinensis*	O plains - 1800 m	02 03 08 13 18	06 07 09	03 08 13	(05) 06 08	14 15	present	None	
PEACEFUL DOVE *Geopelia striata*	O, SG	present	03		01	present	present	None	

SPECIES	HABITAT	DISTRIBUTION						THREATS	STATUS
		N.	SW	NE	SE	PEN.	C		
GREEN-WINGED PIGEON Chalcophaps indica	MD SE TR HE, plains - 1500 m	02 03 06 08 13 14 16	03 04 05 06 07 08 09	03(04) 08 13	06 (04) 07 08	02 04 11 13 14 15 16 18 19 10	/	2	
NICOBAR PIGEON Caloenas nicobarica	island forests	/	/	/	/	02 07 14	/	2,3,1	T
ALEXANDRINE PARAKEET Psittacula eupatria	MD SG, plains and foothills	present	03 07 08	formerly present	/	/	formerly present	3,1	T
RED-BREASTED PARAKEET Psittacula alexandri	DD MD SG O, plains - 1200 m	present	07 08	03 08	07 08	formerly present	present	2,1	
BLOSSOM-HEADED PARAKEET Psittacula roseata	DD MD SG O, plains - 900 m	present	07	03 08	/	/	present		
GREY-HEADED PARAKEET Psittacula finschii	DD MD SG, plains - 1300 m	02 03 16 18	07 08 09	present	/	/	/		
BLUE-RUMPED PARROT Psittinus cyanurus	TR SG, level lowlands	/	/	/	/	17 18	/	1	T
VERNAL HANGING PARROT Loriculus vernalis	MD SE TR SG, plains - 1500 m	02 03 06	03 05 07 08 09	03 08 13 15	04 (05) 06 07 08	04 10 11 13 15 16 18 19	present		
BLUE-CROWNED HANGING PARROT Loriculus galgulus	TR, plains - 1200 m*		/	/	/	13 19	/		
CHESTNUT-WINGED CUCKOO Clamator coromandus	MD SG O, plains, foothills	03	07 08 09	08		migrant only	present		
LARGE HAWK-CUCKOO Cuculus sparverioides	SE HE, 600 - 2500 m	02 03 (04) 14 16 18	03 05 07	(02) 08	probably migrant only	migrant only	migrant only		

SPECIES	HABITAT	DISTRIBUTION						THREATS	STATUS
		N	SW	NE	SE	PEN.	C		
MOUSTACHED HAWK-CUCKOO Cuculus vagans	SE TR, plains - 900 m				(08)	10 13 19		1	
HODGSON'S HAWK-CUCKOO Cuculus fugax	SE TR, plains - 900 m	02	07	08	06	(05) 10 19			
INDIAN CUCKOO Cuculus micropterus	SE TR HE, plains - 1800 m	02 03 16	07 08 09	08	present	13 19	present		
BANDED BAY CUCKOO Cacomantis sonneratii	DD MD SE TR HE, plains - 1650 m	02 03 13 16 18	07 05	03 08	07 08	(05) 10 11 13 15 17 18 19			
PLAINTIVE CUCKOO Cacomantis merulinus	MD SG O, plains - 1800 m	02 03 06 13 16 18	03 06 07	08 13	06 07 08	04 19 13	present	None	
BRUSH CUCKOO Cacomantis variolosus	TR MA SG, plains - 600 m*	02 03				(05) 10 13			
ASIAN EMERALD CUCKOO Chrysococcyx maculatus	HE 1000 - 2100 m		probably migrant only	probably migrant only	migrant only	migrant only	migrant only		
VIOLET CUCKOO Chrysococcyx xanthorhynchus	MD SE TR, plains and foothills	present	03 05 07	present	07 08	04 (05) 10 13	migrant only	1	
MALAYAN BRONZE CUCKOO Chrysococcyx minutillus	MA O, plains - 1300 m					present			U
DRONGO CUCKOO Surniculus lugubris	MD SE TR, plains - 1200 m	02 03 06	06 07	08	07	04 10 13 17 19	migrant only		
COMMON KOEL Eudynamys scolopacea	O SG MA, mostly lowlands	present	06 08	08	present	03	present	None	Common

SPECIES	HABITAT	DISTRIBUTION						THREATS	STATUS
		N	SW	NE	SE	PEN	C		
BLACK-BELLIED MALKOHA Phaenicophaeus diardi	TR, below 200 m					04 10 13 15 16 18		1	
CHESTNUT-BELLIED MALKOHA Phaenicophaeus sumatranus	MA TR SG, lowlands and lower hills					13 17 18 19		1	
GREEN-BILLED MALKOHA Phaenicophaeus tristis	MD SB TR HB SG, O plains - 1685 m	02 03 04 06 13 14 16 18	03 04 05 06 07 08 09	03 08 11 13 15	02 04 (05) 06 07 08	(18)	present	None	Common
RAFFLES'S MALKOHA Phaenicophaeus chlorophaeus	TR, plains - 900 m					04 (05) 10 11 13 15 16 17 18 19			
RED-BILLED MALKOHA Phaenicophaeus javanicus	TR SG, plains - 1000 m					04 (05) 10 13 15 16 18 19			
CHESTNUT-BREASTED MALKOHA Phaenicophaeus curvirostris	TR SG, plains - 1000 m					04(05)10 11 13 15 16 18 19			
CORAL-BILLED GROUND-CUCKOO Carpococcyx renauldi	SB, plains - 900 m	15		03 (04) 08	07 08			2, 3	
GREATER COUCAL Centropus sinensis	O, plains - 1300 m	03 04 06 08 13 14 16 18	03 04 05 06 07 08 09	03 08 11 13 15	06 07 08	02 03 04 14 15 16 19	present	None	
LESSER COUCAL Centropus bengalensis	O, plains - 1800 m	02 03 04 08 18	05 07 09	03 08 13	06	04 11 16 18	present	None	

SPECIES	HABITAT	DISTRIBUTION						THREATS	STATUS
		N	SW	NE	SE	PEN.	C		
BARN OWL Tyto alba	O, plains – lower hills	present	06	present		present	present		
BAY OWL Phodilus badius	SE TR HE, plains – 2000 m	(02)(04)	05 07 08	03 08	02 08	13 18	/		
WHITE-FRONTED SCOPS-OWL Otus sagittatus	TR, level lowlands, foothills	/	/	/	/	(18) 16	/	1	T
REDDISH SCOPS-OWL Otus rufescens	TR, level lowlands	/	/	/	/	present	/	1	T U
MOUNTAIN SCOPS-OWL Otus spilocephalus	SE HE, 500 – 2000 m	02 03 14	05 07 08 09	(02) 03 (04) 08 13	07 08	present	/		
ORIENTAL SCOPS-OWL Otus sunia	MD, plains, lower hills	(02)(03)	03 07	03	probably migrant only	probably migrant only	migrant only		
COLLARED SCOPS-OWL Otus bakkamoena	MD SE TR HE O plains – 2100 m	02 03 (04) 13 16 18	03 05 06 07 08 09	(04) 08 03	(04) 06 08	11 13 17 19	present	None	Common
SPOT-BILLIED EAGLE-OWL Bubo nipalensis	MD SE HE foothills–1888 m	03 (04)	07	03 08	08	/	/		
BARRED EAGLE-OWL Bubo sumatranus	TR SG O, plains – 600 m	/	/	/	/	13 17	/		
DUSKY EAGLE-OWL Bubo coromandus	open forests of extreme lowlands	/	06	/	/	/	/		Ind.

SPECIES	HABITAT	DISTRIBUTION						THREATS	STATUS
		N	SW	NE	SB	PBN.	C		
BROWN FISH-OWL Ketupa zeylonensis	MD SG O, streams, open water, plains - 800 m	present	05 07 08	03 08		present	present		
BUFFY FISH-OWL Ketupa ketupa	SE TR SG, streams plains - 800 m		present	08	08	17 18			
COLLARED OWLET Glaucidium brodiei	SE HE, foot-hills - 2000 m	02 03 04 06 14 18	03 05 07 08 09	03 08 13	02 06 08	(05) 13		None	Common
ASIAN BARRED OWLET Glaucidium cuculoides	DD MD SE HE SG, O, plains-1400 m	02 03 04 06 08 13 14 16 18	03 05 07 08 09	(02) 03 (04) 08 13	01 06 08	present	present	None	Common
BROWN HAWK-OWL Ninox scutulata	MD SE BD SG O, plains - 1200 m	06	03 05 07	08	06 08	present	present		
SPOTTED OWLET Athene brama	O plains - 800 m	present	06	08	01		present	None	Common
SPOTTED WOOD OWL Strix seloputo	SG O MA, below 800 m			present		present	present		U
BROWN WOOD-OWL Strix leptogrammica	MD SE TR HE, plains - 2100 m	02 03	07	08 15		04 10 11 13 18	18		
LARGE FROGMOUTH Batrachostomus auritus	TR, level lowlands					present		1	T U
GOULD'S FROGMOUTH Batrachostomus stellatus	TR, level lowlands, lower hills					present		1	T U

SPECIES	HABITAT	DISTRIBUTION						THREATS	STATUS
		N	SW	NE	SB	PEN.	,C		
HODGSON'S FROGMOUTH Batrachostomus hodgsoni	SE HE, 300 - 1800 m	02 (03)							
JAVAN FROGMOUTH Batrachostomus javensis	SE TR, plains - 800 m.	06	03	08	present	(05) 11 19			
MALAYSIAN EARED NIGHTJAR Eurostopodus temminckii	TR SG, plains - 750 m.					present			U
GREAT EARED NIGHTJAR Eurostopodus macrotis	DD MD SE TR, plains-1200 m.	03	07 09	(04) 08	06 07 08	15 18	formerly present		
GREY NIGHTJAR Caprimulgus indicus	HE, 1200-1800 m.	02 03 18	07	probably migrant		migrant only	migrant only		
LARGE-TAILED NIGHTJAR Caprimulgus macrurus	DD MD SE HE SG O, plains-1200 m.	03	05 06 07 08	(04) 08	06 07 08	15 18	present	None	Common
INDIAN NIGHTJAR Caprimulgus asiaticus	O, plains	present	06 07	present	07		present	None	Common
SAVANNA NIGHTJAR Caprimulgus affinis	DD PE SG O, foothills-1000 m	03	present	present	present		present		
EDIBLE-NEST SWIFTLET Aerodramus fuciphagus	feeds over forest,open areas					09 17			
BLACK-NEST SWIFTLET Aerodramus maximus	feeds over forest,open areas					09			

SPECIES	HABITAT	DISTRIBUTION N	SW	NE	SE	PEN.	C	THREATS	STATUS
HIMALAYAN SWIFTLET *Aerodramus brevirostris*	feeds over forest, open areas	02 06 13 14	03 04 07 09	probably migrant only		probably migrant only			
WHITE-BELLIED SWIFTLET *Collocalia esculenta*	feeds mainly over forest, hills					present			U
BROWN NEEDLETAIL *Hirundapus giganteus*	MD SE TR, plains-1800 m	02 03 (04) 08 14	03 04 07 09	08	01 06 08	04 10 14 18 19	present		
SILVER-RUMPED SWIFT *Rhaphidura leucopygialis*	TR, plains - 1200 m.					04 10 13 15 18			
FORK-TAILED SWIFT *Apus pacificus*	feeds mainly over forest, secondary growth	02 03	07	08	status uncertain	status uncertain	migrant only		
HOUSE SWIFT *Apus affinis*	O plains - 1800 m	02 03 13	present	08	01	13	present	None	Common
ASIAN PALM SWIFT *Cypsiurus balasiensis*	O SG F, plains - 1800 m	03 13 18	03 05 06 07	08 13	04 06	04 10 13	present	None	Common
CRESTED TREESWIFT *Hemiprocne coronata*	DD MD SG O, plains - 1400 m	02 03 04 06 13 14 16 18	05 07 09	03 13					
GREY-RUMPED TREESWIFT *Hemiprocne longipennis*	TR SG MA O, plains - 1200 m					10 13 15 17 18 19			
WHISKERED TREESWIFT *Hemiprocne comata*	TR SG, plains - 750 m					04 (05) 13 15 17 18 19			

SPECIES	HABITAT	DISTRIBUTION						THREATS	STATUS
		N	SW	NE	SE	PEN.	C		
RED-NAPED TROGON Harpactes kasumba	TR, extreme lowlands, lower hill slopes					17		1	T
DIARD'S TROGON Harpactes diardii	TR, level lowlands, foothills					(05) 13 18 19		1	T
CINNAMON-RUMPED TROGON Harpactes orrhophaeus	TR, below 180 m					(05) 16 18		1	T
SCARLET-RUMPED TROGON Harpactes duvaucelii	TR, below 400 m					05 (10) 13 15 17 18		1	V
ORANGE-BREASTED TROGON Harpactes oreskios	MD SE TR, plains - 1100 m	02 (04) 08 13 14	07 05 09	03 (04) 08 15	02 (04) 06 07 08	04 05 10 13 (14) 15 16 18 19			
RED-HEADED TROGON Harpactes erythrocephalus	SE HE, 400 - 1800 m	02 03 (04) 14 18	07	(02) 03 (04) 08 15	02 (04) (05) 06 07 08	(05)			
CRESTED KINGFISHER Megaceryle lugubris	SE, close to streams, rivers below 600 m.	formerly 08 present						1	T
PIED KINGFISHER Ceryle rudis	O rivers, lakes of plains	present	present		present		present	None	
COMMON KINGFISHER Alcedo atthis	O SE MA, close to water	present	07 05	08	present 13	13 15 16 18	present		
BLUE-EARED KINGFISHER Alcedo meninting	MD SE TR, close to streams plains - 900 m	present	07	08 03	08	13 15 16 18	formerly present		

SPECIES	HABITAT	DISTRIBUTION						THREATS	STATUS
		N	SW	NE	SE	PEN.	C		
BLUE-BANDED KINGFISHER Alcedo euryzona	TR, close to streams	/	/	/	/	04 (05) 15 16 18	/		
ORIENTAL DWARF KINGFISHER Ceyx erithacus	SE TR, plains - 300 m	formerly present	present	probably migrant only	07 08 (04)	03 (05) 13 15 16 17 18	migrant only	1	
BANDED KINGFISHER Lacedo pulchella	MD SE TR, plains - 1150 m	02 06 08 14	07 05	03 08	(04) 06 07 08	04 (05) 11 13 17 18 19	/		
BROWN-WINGED KINGFISHER Pelargopsis amauroptera	MA	/	/	/	/	14	/	1	Ind.
STORK-BILLED KINGFISHER Pelargopsis capensis	MD SE O, streams. MA, plains - 800 m	present	03 07 09	08	08	13	present		
RUDDY KINGFISHER Halcyon coromanda	MA, island forests	migrant only	migrant only	migrant only	present	02 14	/	1	Ind.
WHITE-THROATED KINGFISHER Halcyon smyrnensis	O, plains - 1500 m	02 03 06 08 13 18	03 05 06 07 09	03 08 13 15	04 06	02 03 04 13 14 18	present	None	Common
COLLARED KINGFISHER Halcyon chloris	MA O, lowlands	/	06	/	present	present 03 14	present		
RUFOUS-COLLARED KINGFISHER Actenoides concreta	TR, plains - 750 m*	/	/	/	/	05 13 17(18)	/		
CHESTNUT-HEADED BEE-EATER Merops leschenaulti	DD MD SG O, plains - 1500 m	02 03 08 13 18	03 05 07 09	(04) 08 13 15	present	03 04 15	present		

SPECIES	HABITAT	DISTRIBUTION						THREATS	STATUS
		N	SW	NE	SE	PBN.	C		
BLUE-TAILED BEE-EATER Merops philippinus	O mostly plains	present	03 06 09	present	present	present	present	None	Common
GREEN BEE-EATER Merops orientalis	O plains - 1500 m	02 08 13	06 09	08	01 06		present	None	Common
BLUE-THROATED BEE-EATER Merops viridis	MD SE SG O, plains, foothills		migrant only	08	01 06 08	13	present		
RED-BEARDED BEE-EATER Nyctyornis amictus	SE TR, plains - 1200 m		05			03 (05) 10 13 15 16 17 18 19			
BLUE-BEARDED BEE-EATER Nyctyornis athertoni	DD MD SE HE, plains - 2200 m	02 03 13 14 18	03 07 09 05	03 (04) 08 13 15	06 07 08				
INDIAN ROLLER Coracias benghalensis	O plains - 1500 m	03 08 13 18	01 03 04 05 06 07 09	03 08	02 06 07 08	02	present	None	Common
DOLLARBIRD Eurystomus orientalis	F SG MA, plains - 1200 m	02 03 18	03 04 07 09	08	06 07 08	03 15 18 19	formerly present		
HOOPOE Upupa epops	MD SG O, plains - 1500 m	02 (03) 13 16 18	03 05 06 07 09	03	06	present	present		
WHITE-CROWNED HORNBILL Berenicornis comatus	TR, foothills - 900 m					05 10 11 13 16 17 18 19		2,1	V
BROWN HORNBILL Ptilolaemus tickelli	SE HE, 500 - 1500 m	formerly present	07 08	(02) 03 (04) 08				2,1	V

SPECIES	HABITAT	N	SW	NE	SE	PEN.	C	THREATS	STATUS
BUSHY-CRESTED HORNBILL *Anorrhinus galeritus*	TR, plains - 1200 m					04 10 13 15 16 17 18 19		2,1	V
RUFOUS-NECKED HORNBILL *Aceros nipalensis*	SE HE, 700 - 1800 m	03	07 08	08				1,2	T
WRINKLED HORNBILL *Rhyticeros corrugatus*	TR, plains, foothills					17		1,2	E
WREATHED HORNBILL *Rhyticeros undulatus*	SE TR HE MA, plains - 1800 m	formerly present	05 07 08 09	08	02 (05) 06 07 08	04 10 13 14 15 17 18 19		2,1	V
PLAIN-POUCHED HORNBILL *Rhyticeros subruficollis*	MD SE, plains, foothills		07 08			formerly present		1,2	T
BLACK HORNBILL *Anthracoceros malayanus*	TR, plains, foothills					13 10		2,1	T
PIED HORNBILL *Anthracoceros albirostris*	MD SE TR HE SG, plains - 1400 m	present	04 05 06 07 09	03 (04) 08	(05) 07	03 14 15	formerly present	2,1	
RHINOCEROS HORNBILL *Buceros rhinoceros*	TR, plains - 1200 m‡					present		2,1	T U
GREAT HORNBILL *Buceros bicornis*	SE TR HE, plains - 1500 m	13	03 05 07 08 09	03 (04) 08 15	02 (05) 06 07 08	04(05)10 13 14 15 16 17 18 19		2,1	V
HELMETED HORNBILL *Rhinoplax vigil*	TR, plains - 1200 m					04 10 13 15 16 17		2,1	V

SPECIES	HABITAT	DISTRIBUTION						THREATS	STATUS
		N	SW	NE	SE	PEN.	C		
GREAT BARBET Megalaima virens	DD MD SE HB, 800 - 2500 m	02 03 13 04 06 16 18 14 16 18	07 08	03 13 15					
LINEATED BARBET Megalaima lineata	DD MD SG O, plains - 800 m	02 03 06 13 16 18	03 06 07 09	03 08 07 08	02 06	present	present		
GREEN-EARED BARBET Megalaima faiostricta	MD SE, plains - 900 m	(04)	03 05 07 09	03 (04) 08	02 (04) 06 07 09				
GOLD-WHISKERED BARBET Megalaima chrysopogon	TR, plains - 1000 m					04 (05) 13 15 18 19			
RED-CROWNED BARBET Megalaima rafflesii	TR, level lowlands							1	T U
RED-THROATED BARBET Megalaima mystacophanos	TR plains - 750 m			13		04 05 (10) 11 13 15 16 18 19 (18)			
GOLDEN-THROATED BARBET Megalaima franklinii	HE, above 1200 m	02 03 13 18	07	13					
BLUE-THROATED BARBET Megalaima asiatica	SE HB, 600 - 1800 m	02 03 (04) 13	07	(02) 03 13 15		(05)			
MOUSTACHED BARBET Megalaima incognita	SE,HB 600 - 1700 m	present		03 (04) 08 13	02 (04) 06 08				
YELLOW-CROWNED BARBET Megalaima henricii	TR, plains - 800 m*					10 18 19			

SPECIES	HABITAT	N	SW	NE	SE	PEN.	C	THREATS	STATUS
BLUE-EARED BARBET Megalaima australis	MD SE TR SG, plains - 1500 m	(02)(03) 04 06 13 14	03 04 05 07	03 (04) 08 15	04 06 07 08	04(05)10 11 13 15 16 18 19	/		
COPPERSMITH BARBET Megalaima haemacephala	DD MD SG O, plains - 800 m	04 08 13	03 05 06 07 09	03 08	06 08	13 18	present	None	Common
BROWN BARBET Calorhamphus fuliginosus	TR SG, plains - 1000 m*	/				04 (05) 13 17 18 19	/		
MALAYSIAN HONEYGUIDE Indicator archipelagicus	SE TR, plains - 900 m*	/	present			17 (18)	/		
SPECKLED PICULET Picumnus innominatus	MD SE HE BO, foothills-1800 m	02 03 04	07	03 (04) 13		15	/		
WHITE-BROWED PICULET Sasia ochracea	MD SE HE BO, plains - 1800 m	02 03 06 14 16	04 07	03 08			/		
RUFOUS PICULET Sasia abnormis	TR BO SG, plains - 1200 m*	/	07 09			04 (05) (10)13 16 17 18	present		
RUFOUS WOODPECKER Celeus brachyurus	MD SE TR SG, plains - 900 m	02 03 (04) 13	07 09	(04) 08	(04)(08)	04 (05) 13 15 16 17	present		
LACED WOODPECKER Picus vittatus	MD SE BO SG TR, MA O, plains - 1500 m	(02)	05 07 09	(04) 08	04 06 07 08	(05)	present		
STREAK-THROATED WOODPECKER Picus xanthopygaeus	probably DD or MD, lowlands		present	present		/			Ind. U

SPECIES	HABITAT	DISTRIBUTION						THREATS	STATUS
		N	SW	NE	SB	PEN.	C		
GREY-HEADED WOODPECKER Picus canus	DD MD SE HE PE, plains - 1800 m	02 03 04 06 13	03 07 09	03 08 11	06				
BLACK-HEADED WOODPECKER Picus erythropygius	DD MD, plains - 800 m	(02) 03 13 18	03 07 09	03 (04)					
GREATER YELLOWNAPE Picus flavinucha	DD MD SE HE, plains - 1700 m	02 03 04 13 14 18	03 05 07 09	03 08 15	06 08				
CRIMSON-WINGED WOODPECKER Picus puniceus	TR SG, plains - 800 m					04 (05) 10 13 17 18 19			
LESSER YELLOWNAPE Picus chlorolophus	MD SE HE, foothills - 1800 m	02 03 04 18	07 09	03 08 15	(08)				
CHECKER-THROATED WOODPECKER Picus mentalis	TR, plains 1200 m					(05) 11 13 18 19			
BANDED WOODPECKER Picus miniaceus	TR SG MA, plains - 1200 m					04(05)13 15 18 19			
COMMON FLAMBBACK Dinopium javanense	DD MD MA O, plains - 1500 m	02 13 14	05 06 07 09	03 08 15	08	present	present	None	
OLIVE-BACKED WOODPECKER Dinopium rafflesii	TR, plains - 1000 m					04 16 18			
PALE-HEADED WOODPECKER Gecinulus grantia	BO, lowlands	formerly present							T U

SPECIES	HABITAT	DISTRIBUTION						THREATS	STATUS
		N	SW	NE	SE	PEN.	C		
BAMBOO WOODPECKER Gecinulus viridis	BO, plains – 1400 m	(04) 14	03 07 09	03 (04)	(08)	04 (05) 15 17			
BUFF-RUMPED WOODPECKER Meiglyptes tristis	TR, plains – 750 m					04 (05) (10) 13 16 18 19			
BLACK-AND-BUFF WOODPECKER Meiglyptes jugularis	MD SE, plains – 900 m	(04)	07	(04) 08 03	(04) 06 08				
BUFF-NECKED WOODPECKER Meiglyptes tukki	TR, plains – 1000 m					(05)(10) 13 15 18			
GREAT SLATY WOODPECKER Mulleripicus pulverulentus	DD MD SE TR, plains – 900 m	03 08 13	03 07 05	03 08	07 (08)	(05)(10) 17			
WHITE-BELLIED WOODPECKER Dryocopus javensis	DD MD SE TR SG, MA, plains – 600 m	03 13	07 08 09	03		17		1	V
CRIMSON-BREASTED WOODPECKER Picoides cathpharius	HE, above 1200 m	present							
RUFOUS-BELLIED WOODPECKER Picoides hyperythrus	DD, 600-1000 m	13		present				1	V U
STRIPE-BREASTED WOODPECKER Picoides atratus	HE, 1000-2000 m	02 03 (04) 13 14 18	07	13					
FULVOUS-BREASTED WOODPECKER Picoides macei	MD O, plains	present 07					present		

SPECIES	HABITAT	DISTRIBUTION						THREATS	STATUS
		N	SW	NE	SB	PEN.	C		
YELLOW-CROWNED WOODPECKER Picoides mahrattensis	MD, plains	present		present					Ind. U
GREY-CAPPED WOODPECKER Picoides canicapillus	DD MD SE HE SG SG O, plains - 1800 m	02 03 (04) 13 14 18	03 06 07 09	03 (04) 15	08 (04)	15 18			
GREY-AND-BUFF WOODPECKER Hemicircus concretus	TR, plains - 1100 m*					(10) 13 16 17 18 19			
HEART-SPOTTED WOODPECKER Hemicircus canente	MD,SE, plains - 900 m	08	03 05 07	03 08	07 08 (04)	status uncertain present	formerly present		
BAY WOODPECKER Blythipicus pyrrhotis	SE,HE, 500 - 2000 m	02 03 (04) 14 18	05 07	03 13					
MAROON WOODPECKER Blythipicus rubiginosus	TR, plains - 1500 m					04 (05) 13 15 16 17 18 19			
ORANGE-BACKED WOODPECKER Reinwardtipicus validus	TR, plains - 700 m*					(05) 11 13 18 19			
GREATER FLAMEBACK Chrysocolaptes lucidus	DD MD SE HE MA SG, plains - 1600 m	02 03	04 06 07 09	03 08	(04)(05) 06 07 08	02 04 10 13 14 15 16 18			
DUSKY BROADBILL Corydon sumatranus	MD SE TR, plains - 1000 m	(04)	05 07	08	02 04 06 08	04(05) (10) 13 16 18 19			
BLACK-AND-RED BROADBILL Cymbirhynchus macrorhynchos	SE TR SG, close to streams,rivers, below 300 m		05	formerly present	formerly present	04 18		1	V

SPECIES	HABITAT	DISTRIBUTION						THREATS	STATUS
		N	SW	NE	SE	PEN.	C		
BANDED BROADBILL Eurylaimus javanicus	MD SE TR, plains - 1000 m	(04) 08 14	05 07	03 08	04 06 07 08	(05) 10 13 18 19			
BLACK-AND-YELLOW BROADBILL Eurylaimus ochromalus	TR, plains - 700 m					04 10 13 15 16 17 18 19			
SILVER-BREASTED BROADBILL Serilophus lunatus	MD SE TR HB BO, foothills - 1800 m	02 03 04 13 14	03 05 07 09	(02) 03 (04) 08 15	08	(05)			
LONG-TAILED BROADBILL Psarisomus dalhousiae	SE HB, foothills - 1800 m	02 03 04 13 14	07	03 (04) 08	02 04 08				
GREEN BROADBILL Calyptomena viridis	TR, plains - 750 m	02 03 (04)				04 10 11 13 15 16 18 19			
RUSTY-NAPED PITTA Pitta oatesi	HB, 900-2590 m		07	03					
BLUE-RUMPED PITTA Pitta soror	SE HB, 900 - 1670 m				(08)				Rare
GIANT PITTA Pitta caerulea	TR SG, plains, foothills (once 870 m)					(05)(18) (10) 15		1	T
BLUE-WINGED PITTA Pitta moluccensis	MD SE TR SG BO, plains - 700 m	08	03 07 09	(02) 08	01 06 07 08	10 17 18	present		
MANGROVE PITTA Pitta megarhyncha	MA					14			Ind.

SPECIES	HABITAT	N	SW	NE	SE	PEN.	C	THREATS	STATUS
GARNET PITTA Pitta granatina	TR, level lowlands	present				present		1	T U
HOODED PITTA Pitta sordida	MD SE TR SG, plains - 700 m	present	07 09	08	04 06 08	04 (05) 10 13 16 17			T U
BAR-BELLIED PITTA Pitta elliotti	SE, lowlands or lower hills				probably present			1	T U
BLUE PITTA Pitta cyanea	MD SE BO, plains - 1500 m	02 (04) 06 14	07 09	03 (04) 08 13	02 (04) 07 08	04			
BANDED PITTA Pitta guajana	TR plains, - 600 m					(05) 10 13 15 17 18		3	
GURNEY'S PITTA Pitta gurneyi	TR SG, plains					present		1,3	E U
EARED PITTA Pitta phayrei	MD SE BO SG, plains - 1800 m	(04)	07	03 08	08 (04)				
SINGING BUSHLARK Mirafra javanica	O, plains	present	06	present	present		present	None	
RUFOUS-WINGED BUSHLARK Mirafra assamica	O, plains	present	06	present	present		present	None	
ORIENTAL SKYLARK Alauda gulgula	O, plains	present	06	present	present	present	present	None	

SPECIES	HABITAT	DISTRIBUTION						THREATS	STATUS
		N	SW	NE	SE	PEN.	C		
PLAIN MARTIN Riparia paludicola	O, along lowland rivers	present		present					U
DUSKY CRAG-MARTIN Hirundo concolor	Cliffs up to 1800 m	02 03 14 18	06	02 08		04 13		None	
BARN SWALLOW Hirundo rustica	O, above 1200 m	present	migrant only	migrant only	migrant only	migrant only	migrant only		U
PACIFIC SWALLOW Hirundo tahitica	O, seacoasts		present	present	present 14				
WIRE-TAILED SWALLOW Hirundo smithii	O, lowland rivers	13		present					
RED-RUMPED SWALLOW Hirundo daurica	Cliffs	13 14	present	migrant only	migrant only	migrant only	migrant only		
BAR-WINGED FLYCATCHER-SHRIKE Hemipus picatus	DD MD SE TR HE SG BO, plains- 1800 m	02 03 04 06 13 14 16 18	03 05 07 09	02 03(04) 08 13	04 06 07 08	04 10 11 13 15 16 18 19	present		
BLACK-WINGED FLYCATCHER- SHRIKE Hemipus hirundinaceus	TR MA SG, plains - 300 m					present			Ind. U
LARGE WOOD-SHRIKE Tephrodornis virgatus	DD MD SE TR HE, SG, plains - 1200 m	02 03 13 14 16 18	07 09	03 08 15	08	04 (05) 10 13 15 18 19			

SPECIES	HABITAT	DISTRIBUTION						THREATS	STATUS
		N	SW	NE	SE	PEN.	C		
COMMON WOOD-SHRIKE *Tephrodornis pondicerianus*	DD MD SG, plains - 1100 m	02 03 13	present 03						
LARGE CUCKOO-SHRIKE *Coracina novaehollandiae*	DD MD SE HE SG, plains - 1800	02 03 08 13 14	03 05 07 09	02 03	(04)		present		
BAR-BELLIED CUCKOO-SHRIKE *Coracina striata*	TR SG MA, level lowlands					13		1	T
INDOCHINESE CUCKOO-SHRIKE *Coracina polioptera*	DD MD SE HE, foothills-1500 m	02 03 04 13 18	07 09	08					
BLACK-WINGED CUCKOO-SHRIKE *Coracina melaschista*	SE HE, foothills - 1700 m DD MD	02 03 (04)	07	possibly migrant only	migrant only	migrant only	migrant only		
LESSER CUCKOO-SHRIKE *Coracina fimbriata*	TR, plains - 900 m					04 (05) 10 13 15 17			
PIED TRILLER *Lalage nigra*	O SG, lowlands, lower hills					13 18			
SMALL MINIVET *Pericrocotus cinnamomeus*	DD MD SE SG O, plains - 1000 m	02 03	07	03 08 15			present		
FIERY MINIVET *Pericrocotus igneus*	TR SG O, plains					13			
GREY-CHINNED MINIVET *Pericrocotus solaris*	HE, 1000-1800 m	02 03 04 18	07	present					

SPECIES	HABITAT	DISTRIBUTION						THREATS	STATUS
		N	SW	NE	SB	PEN.	C		
SHORT-BILLED MINIVET Pericrocotus brevirostris	HE, 1000 - 2000 m	02 03 04 18							
LONG-TAILED MINIVET Pericrocotus ethologus	HE, 1000 - 1800 m	02 03 04 14		(02)					
SCARLET MINIVET Pericrocotus flammeus	DD MD SE TR HE, plains - 1700 m	02 03 04 08 13	05 07 09	02 03 (04) 08 13 15	02 06 08	04 05 10 11 13 15 16 17 18 19			
GREEN IORA Aegithina viridissima	TR, plains - 800 m					04 11 13 14 17 19			
COMMON IORA Aegithina tiphia	DD MD MA SG O, plains - 1000 m	02 03 04 06 13 16	03 04 05 06 07 09	03 08 15	04 06 07 08	04 15 16 17 18	present	None	Common
GREAT IORA Aegithina lafresnayei	MD SE TR, plains - 1000 m	14	07	03 08	04 06 08	04(05) (10)13 15 16 18 19			
LESSER GREEN LEAFBIRD Chloropsis cyanopogon	TR, plains - 700 m					(05) 10 11 13 15 16 18 19			
GREATER GREEN LEAFBIRD Chloropsis sonnerati	TR, plains - 900 m					04 10 11 13 15 16 17 18 19			
GOLDEN-FRONTED LEAFBIRD Chloropsis aurifrons	DD MD SG, plains - 1000 m	02 03 06 08 13 16	03 06 07 09	02 03 08 13 15	06 07 08		present		
BLUE-WINGED LEAFBIRD Chloropsis cochinchinensis	MD SE TR HE, plains - 1200 m	02 03 04 06 13 16	03 05 07 09	03 08 15	02 04 06 07 08	04 (05) (10)13 15 16 17 18 19			

SPECIES	HABITAT	DISTRIBUTION N	SW	NE	SE	PEN.	C	THREATS	STATUS
ORANGE-BELLIED LEAFBIRD Chloropsis hardwickii	SE HE, 600 - 2100 m	02 03 04	07	03 15					
CRESTED FINCHBILL Spizixos canifrons	SG O, above 1200 m	(14)							
STRAW-HEADED BULBUL Pycnonotus zeylanicus	TR SG, along riverbanks, plains - 250 m*					present		3, 1	T U
STRIATED BULBUL Pycnonotus striatus	HE SG, 1200 m - 2590 m	02 03 18	07	13					
BLACK-AND-WHITE BULBUL Pycnonotus melanoleucos	TR HE, lowlands - 1800 m*					present			U
BLACK-HEADED BULBUL Pycnonotus atriceps	MD SE TR SG, plains - 1600 m	02 03 06 08 16	05 07 09	08 11	02 04 06 07 08	02 04(05) 10 13 15 16 17 18 19			
BLACK-CRESTED BULBUL Pycnonotus melanicterus	MD SE TR HE SG, plains - 2500 m	02 03 04 06 08 13 14 16 18	03 04 07 09	02 03 04 08 11 13 15	02 04 (05) 06 07 08	04 (10) 11 13 15 16 17 18 19			
SCALY-BREASTED BULBUL Pycnonotus squamatus	TR, foothills - 1000 m*					04 (05) 13 18 19			
GREY-BELLIED BULBUL Pycnonotus cyaniventris	TR, plains - 1000 m					04 (10) 13 15 18			
RED-WHISKERED BULBUL Pycnonotus jocosus	O SG, plains - 1800 m	02 03 14	04 05 09	02 03 08 13 15	06	04 15 (18)	present	None	Common

SPECIES	HABITAT	DISTRIBUTION N	SW	NE	SE	PEN.	C	THREATS	STATUS
BROWN-BREASTED BULBUL Pycnonotus xanthorrhous	O SG, above 1200 m	present						None	U
SOOTY-HEADED BULBUL Pycnonotus aurigaster	O SG, plains - 1800 m	02 03 04 08 13 14 18	03 04 07 09	02 03 08 13 15	06		present	None	Common
PUFF-BACKED BULBUL Pycnonotus eutilotus	TR SG, plains, foothills					13		1	V
STRIPE-THROATED BULBUL Pycnonotus finlaysoni	MD SE TR SG O, plains - 900 m	06 08 13 16	03 04 07 09	(04) 08 11 13	01 02 06 07 08	03 04(10) 11 13 14 15 16 17 18 19		None	Common
FLAVESCENT BULBUL Pycnonotus flavescens	SG O, 900 - 2400 m	02 03 04 13 14 18	07	13 15					
YELLOW-VENTED BULBUL Pycnonotus goiavier	O lowlands				01 (05) 08	04 16 18	present	None	Common
OLIVE-WINGED BULBUL Pycnonotus plumosus	SG lowlands					13			
STREAK-EARED BULBUL Pycnonotus blanfordi	O SG MD, lowlands, 02 foothills	02	04 06 07 09	11	(05) 06 08	04	present	None	Common
CREAM-VENTED BULBUL Pycnonotus simplex	TR SG, plains - 700 m*					04 (10) 13 (18)			
RED-EYED BULBUL Pycnonotus brunneus	TR SG, plains - 900 m*					03 04 10 13 14 15 16 18 19			

SPECIES	HABITAT	DISTRIBUTION						THREATS	STATUS
		N	SW	NE	SE	PEN.	C		
SPECTACLED BULBUL Pycnonotus erythropthalmos	TR SG, plains – 800 m*					04 (05) 10 13 15 16 18 19			U
FINSCH'S BULBUL Criniger finschii	TR, foothills – 600 m*					present			
WHITE-THROATED BULBUL Criniger flaveolus	SE, foothills – 1400 m	present	07						
PUFF-THROATED BULBUL Criniger pallidus	SE HE, foothills – 1150 m	02 03 04 06 14 18		(02) 03 (04) 08 13 15					
OCHRACEOUS BULBUL Criniger ochraceus	SE TR, plains – 900 m*		present		02 04 (05) 06 07 08	04 (05) 10 13 15 16 17 18			
GREY-CHEEKED BULBUL Criniger bres	TR, plains – 900 m*					(05)(10) 13 18 19			
YELLOW-BELLIED BULBUL Criniger phaeocephalus	TR, plains – 900 m					(05) 13 15 16 18 19			
HAIRY-BACKED BULBUL Hypsipetes criniger	TR, plains – 900 m*					04(05)10 13 15 16 17 18 19			
OLIVE BULBUL Hypsipetes viridescens	SE, foothills – 900 m	present	03 05 07						
GREY-EYED BULBUL Hypsipetes propinquus	SE TR HE SG, plains – 1100 m	02 03 04 06 13 14	present	(02) 03 (04) 08 13 15	02 04 06 07 08	04 (05)			

SPECIES	HABITAT	DISTRIBUTION						THREATS	STATUS
		N	SW	NE	SB	PEN.	C		
BUFF-VENTED BULBUL Hypsipetes charlottae	TR SG plains - 750 m					04 10 13 15 16 17 18 19			
MOUNTAIN BULBUL Hypsipetes mcclellandii	HE, 800 - 2590 m	02 03 04 14 18	07	(02) 03 13 15		(05)			
STREAKED BULBUL Hypsipetes malaccensis	TR plains - 900 m*					13 15 16 18 19			
ASHY BULBUL Hypsipetes flavala	SE TR HE, 200 - 2100 m	02 03 (04) 13 14 18	07 09	(02) 03 08 13 15		(05) 13			
BLACK BULBUL Hypsipetes madagascariensis	SB HE SG, 800 - 2590 m	02 03 04 18	07	(02) 03 13 15		migrant only			
WHITE-HEADED BULBUL Hypsipetes thompsoni	HE SG, 900 - 2000 m	02 03 14 18							
BLACK DRONGO Dicrurus macrocercus	O, plains, lower hills	02	03 05 06	present	present	present migrant only	present	None	Common
ASHY DRONGO Dicrurus leucophaeus	DD MD SE MA SG O, plains-1700 m	02 03 04 13 14 16 18	03 04 05 06 07 09	03 08 13 15	02 (04) (05) 07 08	present			
CROW-BILLED DRONGO Dicrurus annectans	MD, plains, foothills	present	07	probably migrant only	probably migrant only	migrant only	migrant only		
BRONZED DRONGO Dicrurus aeneus	MD SE TR HE SG, plains - 1700 m	02 03 04 08 13 14 18	03 05 06 07 09	02 03 08 13 15	(04) 07 08	10 11 13			

SPECIES	HABITAT	DISTRIBUTION						THREATS	STATUS
		N	SW	NE	SE	PEN.	C		
LESSER RACKET-TAILED DRONGO Dicrurus remifer	SE HE, 800 - 2590 m	02 03 04 13 14 18	07 09	02 03 (04) 08 13 15	(04) 08	present			
SPANGLED DRONGO Dicrurus hottentottus	MD SE HE SG, plains - 1800 m	02 03 04 06 14 16	03 05 07 09	02 03 08 15	02		present		
GREATER RACKET-TAILED DRONGO Dicrurus paradiseus	DD MD SE TR SG O, plains - 900 m	02 03 04 08 13 14 16 18	03 05 06 07 09	02 03 08 11 15	02 04 (05) 06 07 08	02 03 04 (05) 11 13 14	present		
DARK-THROATED ORIOLE Oriolus xanthonotus	TR, plains - 300 m					(05) 13 17 (18)		1	V
BLACK-HOODED ORIOLE Oriolus xanthornus	DD MD SG, plains - 900 m	02 03 08 13 16	03 04 (06) 07 09	present	(08)	status uncertain	present		
MAROON ORIOLE Oriolus traillii	SE HE, 800 - 2100 m	02 03 (04) (14) 18	migrant only	(02) 13	migrant only				
ASIAN FAIRY BLUEBIRD Irena puella	MD SE TR HE, plains - 1300 m	02 03 04 08 06 14 18	03 05 07 09	02 03 08 13 15	02 (04) (05) 06 07 08	02 04(05) 10 11 13 14 15 16 17 18 19			
CRESTED JAY Platylophus galericulatus	TR, plains - 750 m					10 16 19			
EURASIAN JAY Garrulus glandarius	DD MD HE PE, plains - 1800 m	02 03 04 13 16 18	07 09	02 03 (04)					
SHORT-TAILED MAGPIE Cissa thalassina	SE HE, foothills-1500 m				02 (04) 07 08				Rare

SPECIES	HABITAT	DISTRIBUTION						THREATS	STATUS
		N	SW	NE	SE	PEN.	C		
GREEN MAGPIE Cissa chinensis	MD SE HE, plains – 1800 m	02 03 04 13 14 18	03 05 07 09	03 08 13 15					
BLUE MAGPIE Urocissa erythrorhyncha	DD MD, plains – 1200 m	02 03 13 16	04 07 09	03	present				
RUFOUS TREEPIE Dendrocitta vagabunda	DD MD SG, plains – 500 m	(02) 03 18	07 09	03 13	present				
GREY TREEPIE Dendrocitta formosae	HE, 900 – 1800 m	02 03 (04) 13 (14) 18	07	(02) 03 13 15					
RACKET-TAILED TREEPIE Crypsirina temia	MD MA SG O, plains – 900 m	present	03 06 07 09	(08)	06 07 08	present	present	None	
BLACK MAGPIE Platysmurus leucopterus	TR, plains, foothills					13 16 19		1	V
HOUSE CROW Corvus splendens	O, plains, coast		formerly present						X
LARGE-BILLED CROW Corvus macrorhynchos	O, plains – 1800 m	02 03 08 18	01 03 05 06 07 09	03 08 11	06	02 03 13 14 15 18	present	None	
BLACK-THROATED TIT Aegithalos concinnus	HE, 1600 – 2100 m	present							Rare U
GREAT TIT Parus major	HE PE, 900–1800m MA, seacoasts	02 03 13		(02)		present			

SPECIES	HABITAT	DISTRIBUTION						THREATS	STATUS
		N	SW	NE	SE	PEN.	C		
YELLOW-CHEEKED TIT Parus spilonotus	HE, 900 - 2200 m	02 03 18	07	(02) 13					
SULTAN TIT Melanochlora sultanea	MD SE TR HE, plains - 1000 m	(02)(04) 13 14	03 04 05 07 08 09	(02) 03 08 15	07 08	13 (10) 17 18			Rare
YELLOW-BROWED TIT Sylviparus modestus	HE, 1800 - 2590 m	03							
CHESTNUT-VENTED NUTHATCH Sitta nagaensis	HE, 1350 m - 2100 m	02 03							
CHESTNUT-BELLIED NUTHATCH Sitta castanea	DD MD, plains - 800 m	03 13 14	07 09	03					
VELVET-FRONTED NUTHATCH Sitta frontalis	DD MD SE TR HE, plains - 1600 m	02 03 04 06 13 14 16 18	03 07 09	(02) 03 (04) 08 13 15	08	(05) 10 11 15 18			
GIANT NUTHATCH Sitta magna	PE/HE, 1200 - 1800 m	(03) 04 13 14						1	V
BEAUTIFUL NUTHATCH Sitta formosa	HE above 2000 m	present						1	V U
BROWN-THROATED TREECREEPER Certhia discolor	HE, 1300 - 2000 m	03						1	V
BROWN DIPPER Cinclus pallasii	HE, wooded streams, 400 - 1000 m	(03)							Ind.

SPECIES	HABITAT	DISTRIBUTION						THREATS	STATUS
		N	SW	NE	SE	PEN.	C		
PUFF-THROATED BABBLER Pellorneum ruficeps	MD SE TR BO HE SG,plains-1800 m	02 03 04 06 08 13 14 16 18	03 04 05 06 07 09	02 03 08 11 13 15	(04)(05) 06 07 08	04 10 11 13 15 16 17 18 19	present	None	Common
BLACK-CAPPED BABBLER Pellorneum capistratum	TR, plains - 750 m*					04 05 10 11 15 16 17 18 19			
SPOT-THROATED BABBLER Pellorneum albiventre	HE BO SG O, 1500 - 2100 m	02 03							
BUFF-BREASTED BABBLER Trichastoma tickelli	MD SE TR HE BO SG,plains-1500 m	02 03 04 06 14	07	(02) 03 13 15		(05) 10 18			
SHORT-TAILED BABBLER Trichastoma malaccense	TR SG, plains - 900 m*					04 (05) 13 15 18 19			
WHITE-CHESTED BABBLER Trichastoma rostratum	TR MA SG, plains - 200 m*					13 15			v
FERRUGINOUS BABBLER Trichastoma bicolor	TR, plains - 200 m					(05) 15 18 19		1	v
HORSFIELD'S BABBLER Trichastoma sepiarium	TR, foothills - 700 m					present			
ABBOTT'S BABBLER Trichastoma abbotti	SE TR SG, plains - 900 m		04 05	08 11	02 (04) 06 07 08	02 04(05) 10 13 14 15 16 17 18 19	formerly present		U
MOUSTACHED BABBLER Malacopteron magnirostre	TR, plains - 900 m					04(05)10 15 16 17 18 19			

SPECIES	HABITAT	DISTRIBUTION N	SW	NE	SE	PEN.	C	THREATS	STATUS
SOOTY-CAPPED BABBLER Malacopteron affine	TR, plains, foothills					present		1	T U
SCALY-CROWNED BABBLER Malacopteron cinereum	SE TR, plains - 800 m			08	08	05 10 13 15 16 18 19			
RUFOUS-CROWNED BABBLER Malacopteron magnum	TR, plains - 200 m					15		1	T
LARGE SCIMITAR-BABBLER Pomatorhinus hypoleucos	MD SE, plains - 1000 m	03 (04) (14)	03 04 05 07 09	(02) 03 (04) 08 11 13 15	(04) 07 08				
RUSTY-CHEEKED SCIMITAR-BABBLER Pomatorhinus erythrogenys	HE SG O, 1300 - 2000 M	03 14						None	
WHITE-BROWED SCIMITAR-BABBLER Pomatorhinus schisticeps	MD SE HE, SG, BO, plains - 2000 m	02 03 (04) 14 18	03 05 07 09	02 03 (04) 08 13 15	02 07 08 (04)	04 (05) (10) 11		None	
RED-BILLED SCIMITAR-BABBLER Pomatorhinus ochraceiceps	SE HE BO, 800 m - 1400 m	02 03 (04) 18	07	03 13					
CORAL-BILLED SCIMITAR-BABBLER Pomatorhinus ferruginosus	HE SG, 1200 m - 2000 m	03	07						

SPECIES	HABITAT	DISTRIBUTION						THREATS	STATUS
		N	SW	NE	SE	PEN.	C		
STRIPED WREN-BABBLER Kenopia striata	TR, plains and extreme lower hill slopes, below 300 m					10		1	T
LARGE WREN-BABBLER Napothera macrodactyla	TR, plains - 200 m (once at 397 m.					(05)(18) 17		1	T
LIMESTONE WREN-BABBLER Napothera crispifrons	MD SE, steep crags, below 900 m	present	03	present					
STREAKED WREN-BABBLER Napothera brevicaudata	SE TR HE, foothills-1500 m	02 (03) 13 14	07	(02) 13	02 (04) 08	(05) 10 11 13(18)			
EYE-BROWED WREN-BABBLER Napothera epilepidota	HE, 1000 m - 2100 m (down to 300m in peninsula)	02 03 (14)	07	03		(05)(18)			
PYGMY WREN-BABBLER Pnoepyga pusilla	HE, 1300 - 2590 m	03 (14) 18				(05)			
DEIGNAN'S BABBLER Stachyris rodolphei	HE BO, 1000 m - 1650 m	(14)							Rare
RUFOUS-FRONTED BABBLER Stachyris rufifrons	MD SE TR HE BO SG O, plains - 2100 m	02 03 13 (14)	03 05 07	03		04 15 16		None	
GOLDEN BABBLER Stachyris chrysaea	HE, 900 m - 1900 m	02 03 (14) 18	07	(02)		(05)			
GREY-THROATED BABBLER Stachyris nigriceps	SE HE SG, plains - 1800 m	02 03 14	07	(02) 03 (04)		04 (05) 10 13 15 18 19			

SPECIES	HABITAT	DISTRIBUTION						THREATS	STATUS
		N	SW	NE	SE	PEN.	C		
GREY-HEADED BABBLER Stachyris poliocephala	TR, foothills - 700 m*					05 10 17 18 19			
SPOT-NECKED BABBLER Stachyris striolata	SE HE, foothills - 1500 m	present	07			05 (18)			
CHESTNUT-RUMPED BABBLER Stachyris maculata	TR, plains					present			T U
WHITE-NECKED BABBLER Stachyris leucotis	TR, plains-800 m* (mainly lowlands)					(18)			Ind.
BLACK-THROATED BABBLER Stachyris nigricollis	TR, plains					17			T
CHESTNUT-WINGED BABBLER Stachyris erythroptera	TR, plains - 800 m*	02 03 04 06 13 14 16	03 04 05 06 07 09	02 03 (04) 11 13	02 04 (05) 06 07 08	04 (05) 10 15 16			
STRIPED TIT-BABBLER Macronous gularis	MD SE TR HE SG O, plains - 1500 m					03 04 (05) 10 11 13 14 15 16	present	None	Common
FLUFFY-BACKED TIT-BABBLER Macronous ptilosus	SG BO TR, (edge), plains, foothills, below 200 m					17		1	V
CHESTNUT-CAPPED BABBLER Timalia pileata	O, plains - 1400 m	18	07	08 11	08		present	None	Common
YELLOW-EYED BABBLER Chrysomma sinense	O, plains - 1800 m	03 14	present	08	06		present	None	Common

SPECIES	HABITAT	DISTRIBUTION						THREATS	STATUS
		N	SW	NE	SE	PEN.	C		
WHITE-CRESTED LAUGHINGTHRUSH Garrulax leucolophus	MD SE HE BO SG, plains - 1200 m	02 03 (04) 06 08 13 (14) 16	03 05 06 07 09	(02) 03 (04) 08 11 13 15	(04) 06 07 08		present	3	
LESSER NECKLACED LAUGHING-THRUSH Garrulax monileger	MD SE HE, plains - 1200 m	02 03 (04) 13 14	07 09	02 03 08 11	06 08			3	
GREATER NECKLACED LAUGHING-THRUSH Garrulax pectoralis	MD SE HE BO, plains - 1200 m	02 03 (04) 13 14	03 04 05 07 09					3	
WHITE-NECKED LAUGHINGTHRUSH Garrulax strepitans	HE, 1000 - 1800 m	02 03 (04)(14)	07					3	
BLACK-THROATED LAUGHING-THRUSH Garrulax chinensis	MD SE HE, plains - 1400 m	02 03 (04) 14	07 09	03 08 13				3	
SPOT-BREASTED LAUGHINGTHRUSH Garrulax merulinus	HE SG, above 1000 m	present						3	Rare U
WHITE-BROWED LAUGHINGTHRUSH Garrulax sannio	O SG, above 1000 m	present						None	U
CHESTNUT-CROWNED LAUGHING-THRUSH Garrulax erythrocephalus	HE, 1300-2590 m (above 1000 m in peninsula)	03 (14) 18				(05)		3	
RED-TAILED LAUGHINGTHRUSH Garrulax milnei	HE SG, 1800 - 2200 m	present						3	Rare U
RED-FACED LIOCICHLA Liocichla phoenicea	HE SG, 1400 - 2200 m	present						3	U

SPECIES	HABITAT	DISTRIBUTION						THREATS	STATUS
		N	SW	NE	SE	PEN.	C		
SILVER-EARED MESIA Leiothrix argentauris	HE SG O, 1200 - 2000 m	02 03 14 18		13		(05)		3	
CUTIA Cutia nipalensis	HE, 1200 - 2100 m	02 03							
WHITE-BROWED SHRIKE-BABBLER Pteruthius flaviscapis	HE, 900 m - 2200 m	02 03 04 13 14 18	07	08 13 15	08	(05)			
BLACK-EARED SHRIKE-BABBLER Pteruthius melanotis	HE, 1600 - 2200 m	03							
CHESTNUT-FRONTED SHRIKE-BABBLER Pteruthius aenobarbus	HE, 900 - 1750 M	02 03 04 18	07 08	13					
WHITE-HOODED BABBLER Gampsorhynchus rufulus	SE HE BO, 800 - 1400 m	02 (04) 14	07	03 (04) 15					
SPECTACLED BARWING Actinodura ramsayi	HE SG, 1200 - 2100 m	03							
BLUE-WINGED MINLA Minla cyanouroptera	HE, 900 - 2000 m	02 03 14 18	07	(02) 13		(05)			
CHESTNUT-TAILED MINLA Minla strigula	HE, 1800 - 2590 m	03							Rare
RUFOUS-WINGED FULVETTA Alcippe castaneceps	HE, 1200 - 2590 m	02 03 18	07						

SPECIES	HABITAT	DISTRIBUTION						THREATS	STATUS
		N	SW	NE	SE	PEN.	C		
RUFOUS-THROATED FULVETTA Alcippe rufogularis	SE, foothills - 900 m	present		03 (04)	(04)(08)				Ind.
BROWN FULVETTA Alcippe brunneicauda	TR, plains - 900 m					(05) 10 13 18 19			
BROWN-CHEEKED FULVETTA Alcippe poioicephala	MD SE TR HE BO, plains - 1200 m	02 03 04 13 14	04 05 07 09	(02) 03 (04) 13 15		04 (05) 15 16 18			
MOUNTAIN FULVETTA Alcippe peracensis	SE HE, foothills-1200 m				(04) 08				Rare
GREY-CHEEKED FULVETTA Alcippe morrisonia	HE, 900 - 2590 m	02 03 (04) 18	07	13					
RUFOUS-HEADED SIBIA Heterophasia annectens	HE, 1000 - 1800 m	02 03 18	07						
BLACK-HEADED SIBIA Heterophasia melanoleuca	HE, 1200 - 2590 m	02 03 (14) 18	07						
LONG-TAILED SIBIA Heterophasia picaoides	HE, 900 - 1800 m	02 03	07						
STRIATED YUHINA Yuhina castaniceps	HE SG, 1000 - 1800 m	02 03 04 14 18	07						
WHISKERED YUHINA Yuhina flavicollis	HE, 1200 - 2200 m	present							Rare U

SPECIES	HABITAT	DISTRIBUTION						THREATS	STATUS
		N	SW	NE	SE	PEN.	C		
BURMESE YUHINA Yuhina humilis	HE, 1800 M	18							Rare
WHITE-BELLIED YUHINA Yuhina zantholeuca	MD SE TR HE, plains - 1800 m	02 03 04 06 14 16	05 07 09	(02) 03 (04) 08 13 15	02 04 06 07 08	(05) 13 16 18 19			
MALAYSIAN RAIL BABBLER Eupetes macrocerus	TR, plains - 1000 m*					10 15 17 18			
SPOT-BREASTED PARROTBILL Paradoxornis guttaticollis	O SG, 1200 - 2100 m	present							U
BLACK-THROATED PARROTBILL Paradoxornis nipalensis	HE SG BO, 1200 - 2000 m	02 03		13					
SHORT-TAILED PARROTBILL Paradoxornis davidianus	SG BO O, 600 - 1000 m	present							
LESSER RUFOUS-HEADED PARROTBILL Paradoxornis atrosuperciliaris	SG BO, 1200 - 1900 m	present		(04)					Rare U
GREY-HEADED PARROTBILL Paradoxornis gularis	HE SG, 1200 - 1800 m	02 03 (04) 18							
LESSER SHORTWING Brachypteryx leucophrys	HE, 900 - 2100 m	02 03 (14) 18	07		(08)	(05)			
WHITE-BROWED SHORTWING Brachypteryx montana	HE, 1500 - 2590 m	03 (14)							Rare

SPECIES	HABITAT	DISTRIBUTION						THREATS	STATUS
		N	SW	NE	SE	PBN.	C		
MAGPIE ROBIN Copsychus saularis	MD SG O, plains - 1800 m	02 03 13 14 18	03 05 06 07 09	11 13 15	01 (05) 06 07	04 13 14 15 18 19	present	None	Common
WHITE-RUMPED SHAMA Copsychus malabaricus	MD SE TR HE BO SG, plains-1500 m	02 03 04 06 08 13 14 16	03 05 06 07 09	02 03 (04) 08 11 13	06 07 08	02 03 04 05 10 11 13 14 15 16 18 19	present	3	
PLUMBEOUS REDSTART Rhyacornis fuliginosus	wooded stream, above 600 m	03							
WHITE-TAILED ROBIN Cinclidium leucurum	HE, 900 - 2200 m	02 03 (04)	07	(02) 03 13	(08)				Rare U
BLUE-FRONTED ROBIN Cinclidium frontale	HE, above 2000 m	present							
CHESTNUT-NAPED FORKTAIL Enicurus ruficapillus	TR, (streams), foothills-900 m					04 05(10) 13 15 16 17 18 19			
BLACK-BACKED FORKTAIL Enicurus immaculatus	MD SE, (streams) foothills-750 m	02 03							
SLATY-BACKED FORKTAIL Enicurus schistaceus	MD SE HE, (streams), foot-hills - 1800 m	02 03 (04) 13	07	(02) 03 08 13	08	(05)			
WHITE-CROWNED FORKTAIL Enicurus leschenaulti	SE TR HE, (streams), - 1700 m	02 03 04 13	05 07	(02) 03 (04) 08		present			
PURPLE COCHOA Cochoa purpurea	HE, 1000 - 1800 m	02 18						1	V

SPECIES	HABITAT	DISTRIBUTION						THREATS	STATUS
		N	SW	NE	SE	PEN.	C		
GREEN COCHOA Cochoa viridis	HE, 1200 - 2100 m	02 03 (04) 13 18	07 08		(08)				U
STONECHAT Saxicola torquata	O, 1300 - 1600 m	present	migrant only	migrant only	migrant only	migrant only	migrant only	None	
PIED BUSHCHAT Saxicola caprata	O, plains - 1600 m	03 (04) 13 14 18		present			present		
JERDON'S BUSHCHAT Saxicola jerdoni	O, tall riverine grassland of plains	present							T U
GREY BUSHCHAT Saxicola ferrea	O, 1500 - 2590 m	03	migrant only	migrant only			migrant only	None	
CHESTNUT-BELLIED ROCK-THRUSH Monticola rufiventris	HE SE O, 2000 - 2590 m	03		migrant only					
BLUE ROCK THRUSH Monticola solitarius	O, cliffs, limestone outcrops	migrant only	migrant only	migrant only	migrant only	14	migrant only	None	
BLUE WHISTLING THRUSH Myophonus caeruleus	MD SE TR HE SG, plains - 2590 m	02 03 04 06 13 14 18	03 04 06 07 09	(02) 03 08 13	02 (04) (05) 08	04 (05) 14	present		
CHESTNUT-CAPPED THRUSH Zoothera interpres	TR, foothills - 750 m					(18)			Ind.
ORANGE-HEADED THRUSH Zoothera citrina	HE, 1000 - 1800 m	02 (04)	07	possibly migrant only	migrant only	migrant only			

SPECIES	HABITAT	DISTRIBUTION						THREATS	STATUS
		N	SW	NB	SB	PEN.	C		
SCALY THRUSH Zoothera dauma	SE HE, 600 – 2590 m	02 03 (04) 14	07	(04)	migrant only	(05)(18)			
DARK-SIDED THRUSH Zoothera marginata	SE HE, foothills–2590 m	02 03	07		(04) 08				
FLYEATER Gerygone sulphurea	MA SG SE TR, lowlands		06		present	present 17 19	present		
CHESTNUT-CROWNED WARBLER Seicercus castaniceps	HE, 900 – 2200 m	02 03 18	07			(05)			
YELLOW-BELLIED WARBLER Abroscopus superciliaris	MD SE TR BO, plains – 1000 m	02 03 04 06	03 04 05 07 09	08 13		04 05 (10) 15			
RUFOUS-FACED WARBLER Abroscopus albogularis	HE, 800–1350 m	(02(03						1	Ind.
ASHY-THROATED WARBLER Phylloscopus maculipennis	HE, 2000 – 2590 m	03							Rare
WHITE-TAILED WARBLER Phylloscopus davisoni	HE, 900 – 2590 m	02 03 (14) 18	07	(02) 08 13 15	08				
STRIATED WARBLER Megalurus palustris	O, (marshes) plains	present					present		U
LARGE GRASS WARBLER Graminicola bengalensis	O, (marshes) plains						formerly present		X U
COMMON TAILORBIRD Orthotomus sutorius	MD SE SG MA O, plains – 1500 m	02 03 04 06 08 13 14 16	03 04 05 06 07 09	03 08 11	01 02 04 06 07 08	04 10 13 15 18 19	present	None	Common

SPECIES	HABITAT	DISTRIBUTION						THREATS	STATUS
		N	SW	NE	SE	PEN.	C		
DARK-NECKED TAILORBIRD Orthotomus atrogularis	MD SE TR MA SG, plains – 1500 m	02 03 (04) 06 08 13 14	03 04 05 06 07 09	03 08 11	04 06 07 08	04 (05) 10 11 13 15 16 17 18 19 18	present	None	Common
ASHY TAILORBIRD Orthotomus ruficeps	MA SG, lowlands								
RUFOUS-TAILED TAILORBIRD Orthotomus sericeus	TR MA SG, plains – 400 m*					(10)13 17 18 19			
MOUNTAIN TAILORBIRD Orthotomus cuculatus	HE BO, 900 – 2000 m	03 18		13		(05)(18)			
GREY-BREASTED PRINIA Prinia hodgsoni	O, plains – 1500 m	02 03 (04) 14 18	05 06 09	02 13	07 08		present	None	Common
RUFESCENT PRINIA Prinia rufescens	DD MD SG O, plains – 1650 m	02 03 04 06 14 16 18	04 05 07 09	02 03 08	01 06	04 (05) 10 11 13 15 16 17	present	None	Common
PLAIN PRINIA Prinia inornata	O, plains – 800 m	present	05	08	present		present	None	Common
YELLOW-BELLIED PRINIA Prinia flaviventris	SG O, plains – 1200 m	08 14		08 13	08	04 10 15 16 19	present	None	Common
BROWN PRINIA Prinia polychroa	DD, foothills – 800 m	present		(02) 03					
HILL PRINIA Prinia atrogularis	SG, O 900 – 2590 m	02 03 (14) 18		13				None	

SPECIES	HABITAT	DISTRIBUTION						THREATS	STATUS
		N	SW	NE	SE	PEN.	C		
ZITTING CISTICOLA Cisticola juncidis	O, chiefly plains	present 06		present	present	present	present	None	Common
BRIGHT-CAPPED CISTICOLA Cisticola exilis	O, plains - 1200 m	present 04		08	01		present	None	
GREY-BELLIED TESIA Tesia cyaniventer	HE, above 1400 m	present							Ind. U
SLATY-BELLIED TESIA Tesia olivea	HE, 1200 - 2590 m	02 03 14 18							
CHESTNUT-HEADED TESIA Tesia castaneocoronata	HE, 1400 - 2590 m	02 03							
PALE-FOOTED BUSH-WARBLER Cettia pallidipes	SG O, 1300 m	03						None	
BROWN BUSH-WARBLER Bradypterus luteoventris	O, 1400 - 1600 m	present						None	U
FULVOUS-CHESTED FLYCATCHER Rhinomyias olivacea	TR, plains - 900 m					04 (05) 10 16 18 19			
GREY-CHESTED FLYCATCHER Rhinomyias umbratilis	TR, plains -900 m*					present			U
ASIAN BROWN FLYCATCHER Muscicapa latirostris	DD SE SG, (edge, clearings) foothills-900 m	03				04 (10) 18			

SPECIES	HABITAT	DISTRIBUTION						THREATS	STATUS
		N	SW	NE	SE	PEN.	C		
VERDITER FLYCATCHER Muscicapa thalassina	SE,TR,HE, plains - 2590 m	02 03 (04)(14) 18	05 07	(02) 03 (04 13 15	06 08	04 10 13 15 17 18 19	migrant only		
WHITE-GORGETTED FLYCATCHER Ficedula monileger	HE, 900 - 1900 m	02 03		13					
RUFOUS-BROWED FLYCATCHER Ficedula solitaria	SE TR HE, 400 - 1400 m		07			(05)(18)			
SNOWY-BROWED FLYCATCHER Ficedula hyperythra	HE, 900 - 2590 m	02 03 18		03 (13)					
RUFOUS-CHESTED FLYCATCHER Ficedula dumetoria	TR, plains 800 m*					(05)			
LITTLE PIED FLYCATCHER Ficedula westermanni	HE, 900 - 2590 m	02 03 18	07	(02) 03 13		(05)			
LARGE NILTAVA Niltava grandis	HE, 900 - 2590 m	03 18	07		(08)	(05)			
SMALL NILTAVA Niltava macgrigoriae	HE, 1300 - 1800 m	02 03 14	07						
WHITE-TAILED FLYCATCHER Cyornis concreta	TR HE, foothills-1000 m*					(18)			
HAINAN BLUE FLYCATCHER Cyornis hainana	MD SE BO, plains - 800 m	03 04 14	06 07 09	(04) 08	(04) 08				

SPECIES	HABITAT	DISTRIBUTION						THREATS	STATUS
		N	SW	NE	SE	PEN.	C		
PALE BLUE FLYCATCHER *Cyornis unicolor*	SE TR HE, plains - 1685 m	02 (03) (14)		(02) 13		(05) 17 18			
BLUE-THROATED FLYCATCHER *Cyornis rubeculoides*	MD HE BO, foothills-1400 m	03 (04) 16	07 09	present		migrant only			
HILL BLUE FLYCATCHER *Cyornis banyumas*	SE TR HE SG, 400 - 2100 m	02 03 04 06 13 14	07	(02) 03 (04) 08 13 15	(04) 08	(05)(10)			
TICKELL'S BLUE FLYCATCHER *Cyornis tickelliae*	MD SE TR SG BO, plains - 600 m	03 06 08	03 04 07 08	11	06 08	(05) 15 16 18	present		
GREY-HEADED FLYCATCHER *Culicicapa ceylonensis*	MD SE TR HE, plains - 2000 m	02 03 04 06 13 14 18	05 07 09	(02) 03 13 15	08	04(05)10 11 13 15 16 17 18	migrant only		
YELLOW-BELLIED FANTAIL *Rhipidura hypoxantha*	HE, 1600 - 2590 m	03 (14)							Rare
WHITE-THROATED FANTAIL *Rhipidura albicollis*	SE HE, 700 - 2100 m	02 03 04 14 18	07	(02) 03 (04) 13 15	(08)	(05)			
WHITE-BROWED FANTAIL *Rhipidura aureola*	DD MD, foothills-1000 m	13	07						
SPOTTED FANTAIL *Rhipidura perlata*	TR, plains - 750 m*					18			
PIED FANTAIL *Rhipidura javanica*	MA SG O, plains - 450 m		06 09		06	present	present	None	Common

SPECIES	HABITAT	N	SW	NE	SE	PEN.	C	THREATS	STATUS
BLACK-NAPED MONARCH Hypothymis azurea	MS SE TR HE MA, SG, plains – 1200 m	02 03 04 06 08 13 14 16 18	03 04 05 06 07 09	02 03 (04)08	02(04)06 (05)06 07 08	02 03 04 05 10 11 13 14 15 16 18 19	present		
MAROON-BREASTED FLYCATCHER Philentoma velatum	TR, plains – 1000 m					04 (05) (10) 13 17 18 19			
CHESTNUT-WINGED FLYCATCHER Philentoma pyrhopterum	TR, plains – 800 m*					04 (05) (10) 13 15 16 18			
ASIAN PARADISE FLYCATCHER Terpsiphone paradisi	MD SE TR HE MA, plains – 1500 m	02 03 04 14	04 05 07 09	(02) 03 (04) 08	(04)(05) 06 08	04 05 10 13 14 15 16 18 19	migrant only		
MANGROVE WHISTLER Pachycephala cinerea	MA MD SG, coastal areas		06		present	02	present		
RICHARD'S PIPIT Anthus novaeseelandiae	O, plains – 1800 m	03 13	05 06 07	02 03 (04) 08 11 13	06 08	(05) 15 18	present	None	Common
ASHY WOOD-SWALLOW Artamus fuscus	O, plains – 1500 m	02 03 18	09	02 08	06		present	None	Common
BURMESE SHRIKE Lanius collurioides	O, plains – 1300 m	03	migrant only	migrant only	present			None	
LONG-TAILED SHRIKE Lanius schach	O, plains – 2000 m	02 03 13 14	05	08	06		present	None	Common
PHILIPPINE GLOSSY STARLING Aplonis panayensis	O SG MA, lowlands					02 09 13 14 18 19		None	Common

SPECIES	HABITAT	DISTRIBUTION						THREATS	STATUS
		N	SW	NE	SE	PEN.	C		
CHESTNUT-TAILED STARLING Sturnus malabaricus	O SG MD, plains - 1200 m	02 (04)	migrant only	migrant only			migrant only		
ASIAN PIED STARLING Sturnus contra	O, chiefly lowlands	present 06	06	present	06		present	None	Common
BLACK-COLLARED STARLING Sturnus nigricollis	O, plains - 1500 m	(02) 03	04 05 09	03	present	present	present	None	Common
VINOUS-BREASTED STARLING Sturnus burmannicus	O, lowlands, lower hills		06	03	06 08	present	present	None	
COMMON MYNA Acridotheres tristis	O, plains - 1500 m	13	01 03 04 05 06 09	08 11	01 06 08	03 04 13 14 18	present	None	Common
JUNGLE MYNA Acridotheres fuscus	O MA, plains		06	present		present		None	
WHITE-VENTED MYNA Acridotheres javanicus	O, plains, foothills	08	04 06	08 11	01 06 08	present	present	None	Common
GOLDEN-CRESTED MYNA Ampeliceps coronatus	MD SE TR, foothills-800 m	08	07	08	06	present			
HILL MYNA Gracula religiosa	MD SE TR HE, plains-1350 m	02 03 (04) 08 13 14	03 05 07 09	03 08	(05) 06 07 08	02 03 04 13 14 15 16		3	
PLAIN SUNBIRD Anthreptes simplex	TR SG, plains - 900 m*					04 (05) 13 17 18			

SPECIES	HABITAT	DISTRIBUTION						THREATS	STATUS
		N	SW	NE	SE	PEN.	C		
BROWN-THROATED SUNBIRD Anthreptes malacensis	O SG MA, lowlands		present		(05)	02 03 09 14 15 16 18	present	None	Common
RED-THROATED SUNBIRD Anthreptes rhodolaema	TR, plains – 800 m					15 18			
RUBY-CHEEKED SUNBIRD Anthreptes singalensis	MD SE TR SG, plains – 1000 m	02 03 06 08 14 16	05 07	03 08 11 13	04 06 07 08	04 (05) (10) 13 15 16 18	present		
PURPLE-NAPED SUNBIRD Hypogramma hypogrammicum	SE TR, plains – 900 m	06 14		(04)		04 05 13 15 18 19			
PURPLE-THROATED SUNBIRD Nectarinia sperata	SE TR SG O, plains, foothills				03 (04)	14			
COPPER-THROATED SUNBIRD Nectarinia calcostetha	MA SG, lowlands				(04)	(14)			
OLIVE-BACKED SUNBIRD Nectarinia jugularis	DD MD MA SG O, plains – 900 m	02 03 06 08 13 16	03 05 06 07 09	02 08 11	(05)	02 03 11 14	present	None	Common
PURPLE SUNBIRD Nectarinia asiatica	DD MD SG O, plains – 400 m	02 03	06 07	present				None	
GREEN-TAILED SUNBIRD Aethopyga nipalensis	HE, 2000–2590 m (North);above 1000 m (Pen.).	03		(02) 03 08 13 15		(05)			Rare
BLACK-THROATED SUNBIRD Aethopyga saturata	SE HE, 600 – 2200 m	02 03 04 14	07	(02) 03 08 13 15	08	(05)(18)			

SPECIES	HABITAT	DISTRIBUTION						THREATS	STATUS
		N	SW	NE	SE	PEN.	C		
CRIMSON SUNBIRD Aethopyga siparaja	MD SE TR SG, plains - 1000 m	present	05 07	08	(04)(05) 06 08	02 (10) 16 14 15 16 17 19	present		
SCARLET SUNBIRD Aethopyga mystacalis	TR HE, plains - 1500 m*					(05)(18)			
LITTLE SPIDERHUNTER Arachnothera longirostra	MD SE TR SG, plains - 1500 m	02 04 06 08 14	03 05 07	03 (04) 08	02 04 06 07 08	04 (05) (10) 11 13 15 16 17 18 19			
THICK-BILLED SPIDERHUNTER Arachnothera crassirostris	TR SG, plains - 1200 m					04 13 15 (10)(18)			
LONG-BILLED SPIDERHUNTER Arachnothera robusta	TR HE, plains - 1260 m*					13 18			
SPECTACLED SPIDERHUNTER Arachnothera flavigaster	TR SG, plains - 600 m*					(10) 13 17 18 19			
YELLOW-EARED SPIDERHUNTER Arachnothera chrysogenys	TR HE, plains - 1600 m*					04 13 17 18 19			
GREY-BREASTED SPIDERHUNTER Arachnothera affinis	SE TR SG HE, plains - 1600 m		present			04 05 10 13 15 16 17 18 19			
STREAKED SPIDERHUNTER Arachnothera magna	SE HE SG, 600 - 2100 m	02 03 (04) 06 13 14 18	07	02 03 (04) 13					

| SPECIES | HABITAT | DISTRIBUTION | | | | | | THREATS | |
		N	SW	NE	SE	PEN.	C	STATUS	
SCARLET-BREASTED FLOWER-PECKER Prionochilus thoracicus	TR HE, plains - 1260 m					(18)			
YELLOW-BREASTED FLOWER-PECKER Prionochilus maculatus	TR HE SG, plains - 1600 m*					(05) 13 15 17 18			
CRIMSON-BREASTED FLOWER-PECKER Prionochilus percussus	TR SG, plains foothills					04 (05) (10) 18			
THICK-BILLED FLOWERPECKER Dicaeum agile	MD SE TR HE SG, plains - 1500 m	(04) 06 14 16	07	03 (04) 08	06 08	04 13 17			
YELLOW-VENTED FLOWERPECKER Dicaeum chrysorrheum	SE TR SG, plains - 1100 m	present	05 07 09	08	08	04 (10) (14) 15			
YELLOW-BELLIED FLOWERPECKER Dicaeum melanoxanthum	HE, 2500 m	03				18 19		Rare	
ORANGE-BELLIED FLOWERPECKER Dicaeum trigonostigma	SE TR SG, plains - 900 m		present			02 04 10 14 15 16 17 18 19			
PLAIN FLOWERPECKER Dicaeum concolor	DD MD SE HE SG, plains - 1685 m	02 03 (04) 14 18	03 07	02 (04) 08	08	02 04 09			
SCARLET-BACKED FLOWERPECKER Dicaeum cruentatum	DD MD SG O, plains - 1200 m	02 03 06 13 14 16	05 06 09	03 (04) 08 11	01 (04) (05) 06 08	02 04 09 14 15 16 18	present	None Common	
BUFF-BELLIED FLOWERPECKER Dicaeum ignipectus	SE HE, 600 - 2590 m	02 03 (04) 18	07	02 08 13	02 08	(18)			

SPECIES	HABITAT	DISTRIBUTION						THREATS	STATUS
		N	SW	NE	SE	PEN.	C		
ORIENTAL WHITE-EYE *Zosterops palpebrosa*	MD SE TR HB MA, SG,O, plains - 1800 m	02 03 14 18	07	08 13	04 06 08	04 15 18	present	None	
EVERETT'S WHITE-EYE *Zosterops everetti*	SE TR HE, foothills-1600 m				(08)	(05)			
EURASIAN TREE SPARROW *Passer montanus*	O, plains - 1800 m	02 03 13 14	03 04 05 06 07 09	08 11 13	01 06	04 18	present	None	Common
PLAIN-BACKED SPARROW *Passer flaveolus*	O, plains - 800 m	08	06	08	06	present	present	None	Common
HOUSE SPARROW *Passer domesticus*	O, plains	present						None	U
BAYA WEAVER *Ploceus philippinus*	O, plains foothills	08	present	present	present	04	present	3	
STREAKED WEAVER *Ploceus manyar*	O, plains	present	06		present	present	present	3	
ASIAN GOLDEN WEAVER *Ploceus hypoxanthus*	O, plains						present	3	U
RED AVADAVAT *Amandava amandava*	O, plains - 800 m	present					present	3	U
PIN-TAILED PARROTFINCH *Erythrura prasina*	SE TR BO SG, plains - 1500 m	(02)	08	03 (04) 08		10		3	

SPECIES	HABITAT	DISTRIBUTION						THREATS	STATUS
		N	SW	NE	SE	PEN.	C		
JAVA SPARROW Padda oryzivora	O, plains						present		U
WHITE-RUMPED MUNIA Lonchura striata	O SG, plains - 1700 m	02 03 06 08 13 14	04 07 09	02 03 13	08 06 08	04 10 13 15 16 17 18 19	present	None	
WHITE-BELLIED MUNIA Lonchura leucogastra	O,SG, plains -1500 m					04 13			
SCALY-BREASTED MUNIA Lonchura punctulata	O, plains - 1500 m	08 13	05 06 09	08 11 13	06	04	present	None	
CHESTNUT MUNIA Lonchura malacca	O, plains	present	06			present	present		
WHITE-HEADED MUNIA Lonchura maja	O,SG, plains - 300 m*					(18)			
SCARLET FINCH Haematospiza sipahi	HE SG, 1200 - 2100 m	(03)							
SPOT-WINGED GROSBEAK Coccothraustes melano-zanthos	HE SG, 1400 - 2100 m	02 03							

APPENDIX II

LIST OF NATIONAL PARKS AND WILDLIFE SANCTUARIES IN THAILAND

Code numbers for each region correspond with those used in the text and in Appendix I. Areas given in sq km. (C = island or coastal site)

Unnumbered sites are those established since 1983, not dealt with in this report.

	NATIONAL PARKS	Area	WILDLIFE SANCTUARIES	Area
i)	*Northern Region*			
	01 Namotok Surin	397	12 Salawin	875
	02 Doi Suthep-Pui	262	13 Lum Nam Pai	1,194
	03 Doi Inthanon	482	14 Doi Chiang Dao	521
	04 Doi Khun Tan	255	15 Doi Pha Chang	577
	05 Mae Ping	1,003	16 Doi Pha Muang	583
	06 Wiang Kosai	410	17 Mae Tuen	1,173
	07 Srisachanalai	213	18 Om Koi	1,224
	08 Ramkhamhaeng	341	Doi Luang	97
	09 Taksin Maharat	150	Khao Sanam Phriang	101
	10 Lan Sang	104	Mae Yuam Fang Khwa	292
	11 Khlong Larn	300		
	Mae Yom	455		
ii)	*Southern-western Region*			
	01 Srinagarind	1,532	07 Huai Kha Khaeng	2,575
	02 Chaloem Rattanakosin	59	08 Thung Yai	3,200
	03 Sai Yok	500	09 Salak Phra	859
	04 Erawan	550	10 Maenam Phachi	489
	05 Kaeng Krachan	2,915		
	06 Khao Sam Roi Yot	98 C		

NATIONAL PARKS	Area	WILDLIFE SANCTUARIES	Area

iii) *North-eastern Region*

	NATIONAL PARKS	Area		WILDLIFE SANCTUARIES	Area
01	Phu Rua	120	12	Phu Miang-Phu Thong	545
02	Phu Kradeung	348	13	Phu Luang	848
03	Nam Nao	962	14	Phu Wua	187
04	Thung Salaeng Luang	1,262	15	Phu Khieo	1,560
05	Tat Ton	218	16	Yot Dom	203
06	Phuphan	665	17	Phanom Dongrak	316
07	Kaeng Tana	80			
08	Khao Yai	2,168			
09	Tab Lan	2,240			
10	Pang Sida	844			
11	Sam Lan	44			
	Phu Hin Rong Kla	307			
	Phu Kao – Phu Phan Kham	322			

iv) *South-eastern Region*

	NATIONAL PARKS	Area		WILDLIFE SANCTUARIES	Area
01	Ko Samet	131 C	06	Khao Khieo	145
02	Khao Chamao	83	07	Khao Ang Ru Nai	108
03	Khao Kitchakut	58	08	Khao Soi Dao	745
04	Khao Sabap	134			
05	Mu Ko Chang	650 C			

v) *Peninsular Region*

	NATIONAL PARKS	Area		WILDLIFE SANCTUARIES	Area
01	Laem Son	315 C	15	Khlong Nakha	480
02	Mu Ko Surin	135 C	16	Khlong Saeng	1,155
03	Mu Ko Ang Thong	102 C	17	Khlong Phraya	95
04	Khao Sok	645	18	Khao Banthad	1,267
05	Khao Luang	570	19	Ton Nga Chang	182
06	Ao Phang-nga	400 C			
07	Mu Ko Similan	128 C			
08	Hat Nai Yang	90 C			
09	Mu Ko Phi Phi	390 C			
10	Khao Phanom Bencha	50			
11	Khao Pu	694			
12	Hat Chao Mai	231 C			
13	Thaleban	102			
14	Tarutao	1,490 C			
	Mu Ko Phetra	494 C			
	Khao Lam Pi – Hat Thai Muang	72			

APPENDIX III

WATERBIRDS WHICH BREED OR WHICH MAY HAVE FORMERLY BRED IN THAILAND, WHICH ARE NOT TREATED IN THIS REPORT

M = may no longer breed; thought to be represented only by seasonal migrants or by wandering, non-breeding individuals. x = recently recorded from Non-Hunting Area or nature reserve. Other symbols for species status as in Appendix I.

Common name	Scientific name	Present in Non-Hunting Area or nature reserve		
Little Grebe	*Tachybaptus ruficollis*	x		
Brown Booby	*Sula leucogaster*		X/E	M
Great Cormorant	*Phalacrocorax carbo*	x		M
Indian Shag	*P. fuscicollis*	x		
Little Cormorant	*P. niger*	x		
Grey Heron	*Ardea cinerea*	x		M
Purple Heron	*A. purpurea*	x		
Little Heron	*Butorides striatus*	x		
Javan Pond Heron	*Ardeola speciosa*	x		
Cattle Egret	*Bubulcus ibis*	x		
Pacific Reef-Egret	*Egretta sacra*	x		
Great Egret	*E. alba*	x		
Intermediate Egret	*E. intermedia*	x		
Little Egret	*E. garzetta*	x		
Black-crowned Night-Heron	*Nycticorax nycticorax*	x		
Yellow Bittern	*Ixobrychus sinensis*	x		
Cinnamon Bittern	*I. cinnamomeus*	x		
Black Bittern	*Dupetor flavicollis*	x		
Asian Openbill	*Anastomus oscitans*	x		
Lesser Whistling Duck	*Dendrocygna javanica*	x		
Cotton Pygmy Goose	*Nettapus coromandelianus*	x		
Slaty-breasted Rail	*Rallus striatus*	x		
Ruddy-breasted Crake	*Porzana fusca*	x		
White-browed Crake	*P. cinerea*	x		

Common name	Scientific name	Present in Non-Hunting Area or nature reserve	
White-breasted Waterhen	*Amaurornis phoenicurus*	x	
Watercock	*Gallicrex cinerea*	x	
Common Moorhen	*Gallinula chloropus*	x	
Purple Swamphen	*Porphyrio porphyrio*	x	
Pheasant-tailed Jacana	*Hydrophasianus chirurgus*	x	
Bronze-winged Jacana	*Metopidius indicus*	x	
Greater Painted Snipe	*Rostratula benghalensis*	x	
Red-wattled Lapwing	*Vanellus indicus*	x	
River Lapwing	*V. duvaucelii*	x	
Little Ringed Plover	*Charadrius dubius*		
Malaysian Plover	*C. peronii*	x	
Black-winged Stilt	*Himantopus himantopus*	x	
Stone Curlew	*Burhinus oedicnemus*		Ind.
Great Thick-knee	*Esacus recurvirostris*		Ind.
Beach Thick-knee	*E. magnirostris*	x	Rare
Oriental Pratincole	*Glareola maldivarum*	x	
Small Pratincole	*G. lactea*	x	
River Tern	*Sterna aurantia*		Ind.
Roseate Tern	*S. dougallii*	x	
Black-naped Tern	*S. sumatrana*	x	
Black-bellied Tern	*S. acuticauda*		Ind.
Bridled Tern	*S. anaethetus*	x	
Little Tern	*S. albifrons*	x	
Great Crested Tern	*S. bergii*	x	
Brown Noddy	*Anous stolidus*		Ind.

APPENDIX IV

MAPS

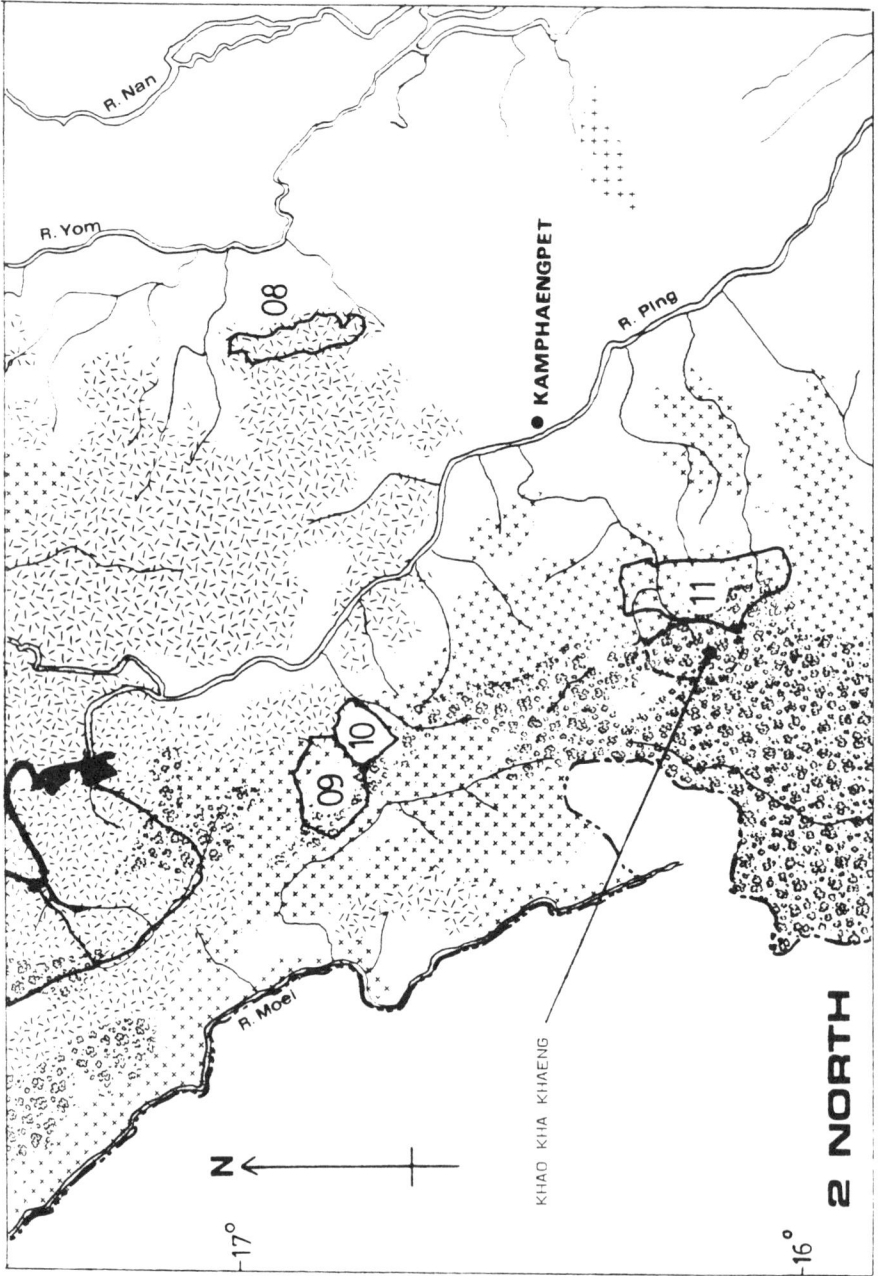

R. Nan

R. Yom

08

KAMPHAENGPET

R. Ping

11

10

09

R. Moei

KHAO KHA KHAENG

N

17°

16°

2 NORTH

BURMA

101°

3 NORTH

N
↑

20°

CHIANG
RAI

LAOS

DOI PHU KHA

15

19°

●NAN

04

NAN RIVER

R. Wang

LAOS

18°

06

R. Yom

07

R. Nan
●UTTARADIT

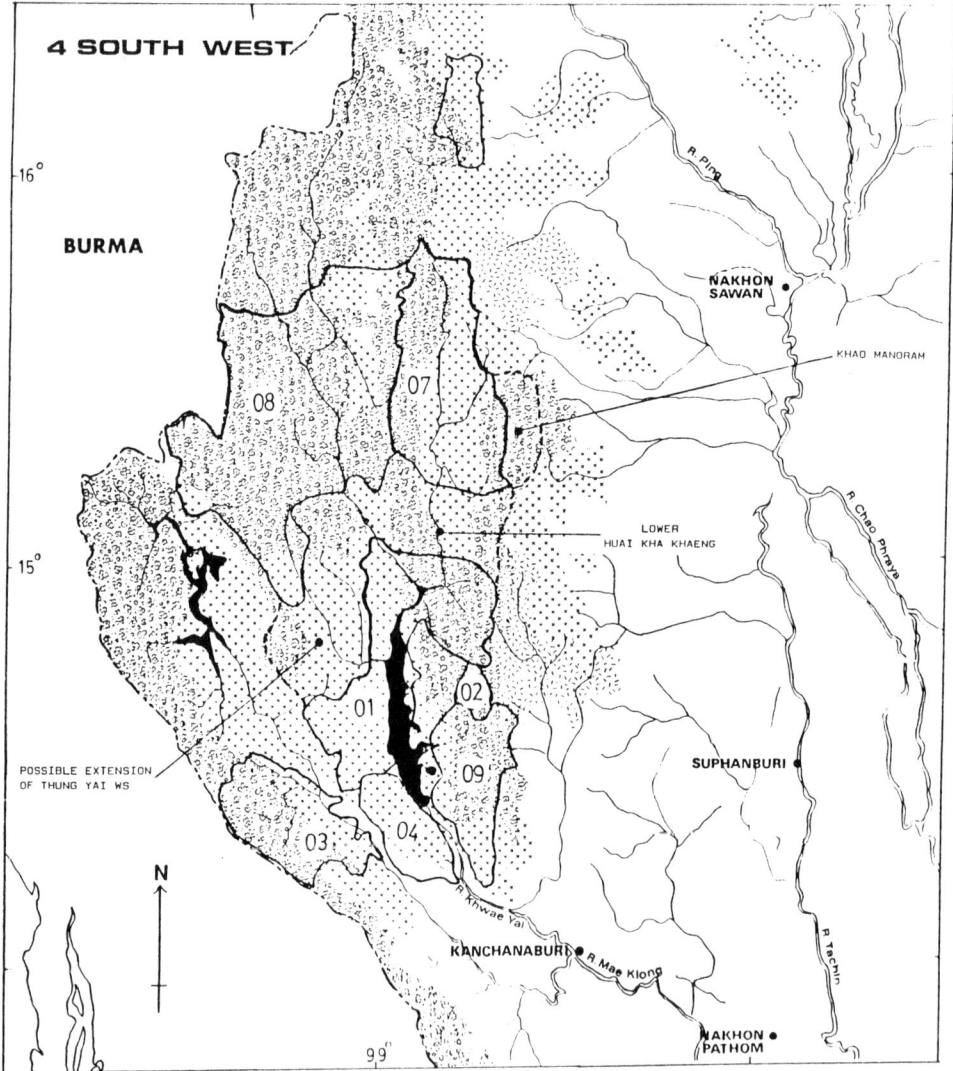

5 SOUTH WEST

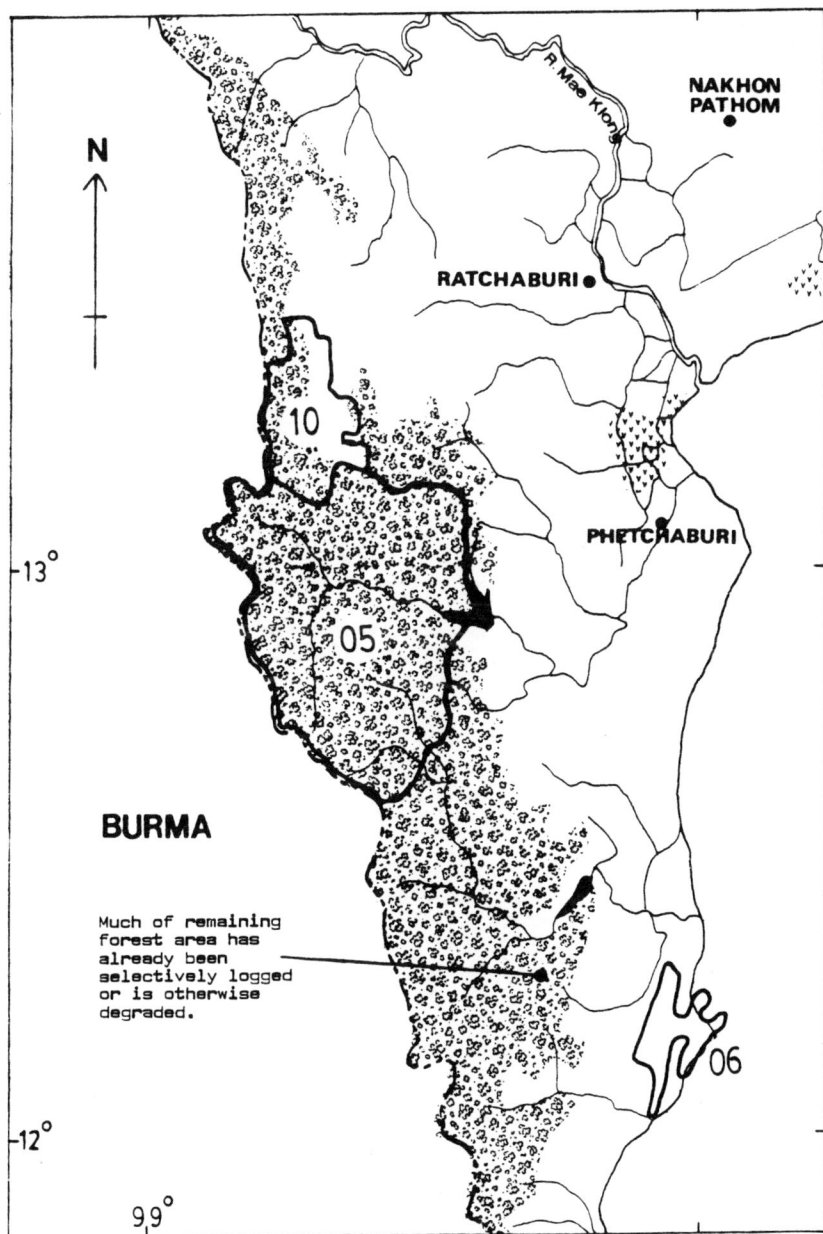

N

NAKHON
PATHOM

R Mae Klong

RATCHABURI

10

PHETCHABURI

-13°

05

BURMA

Much of remaining
forest area has
already been
selectively logged
or is otherwise
degraded.

06

-12°

9.9°

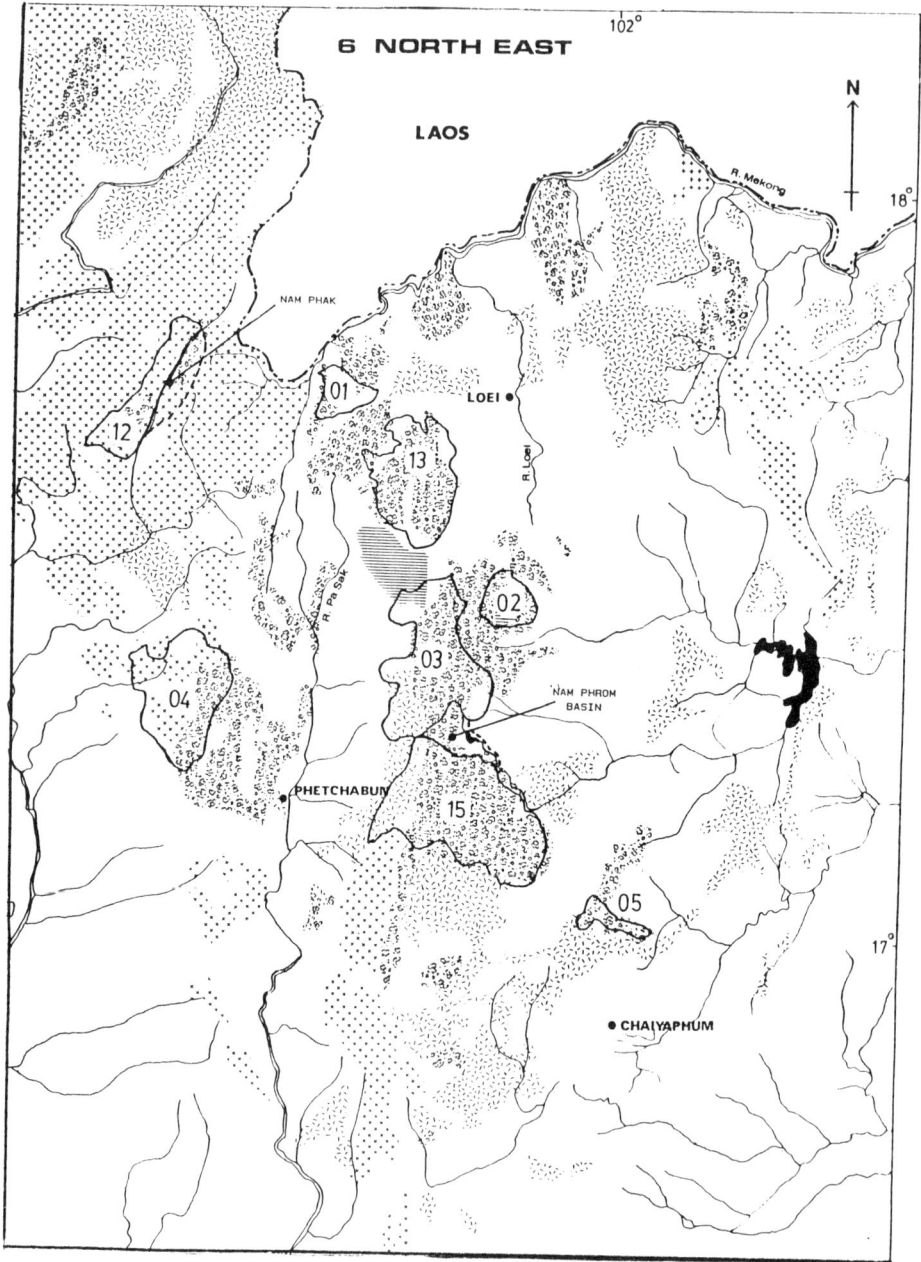

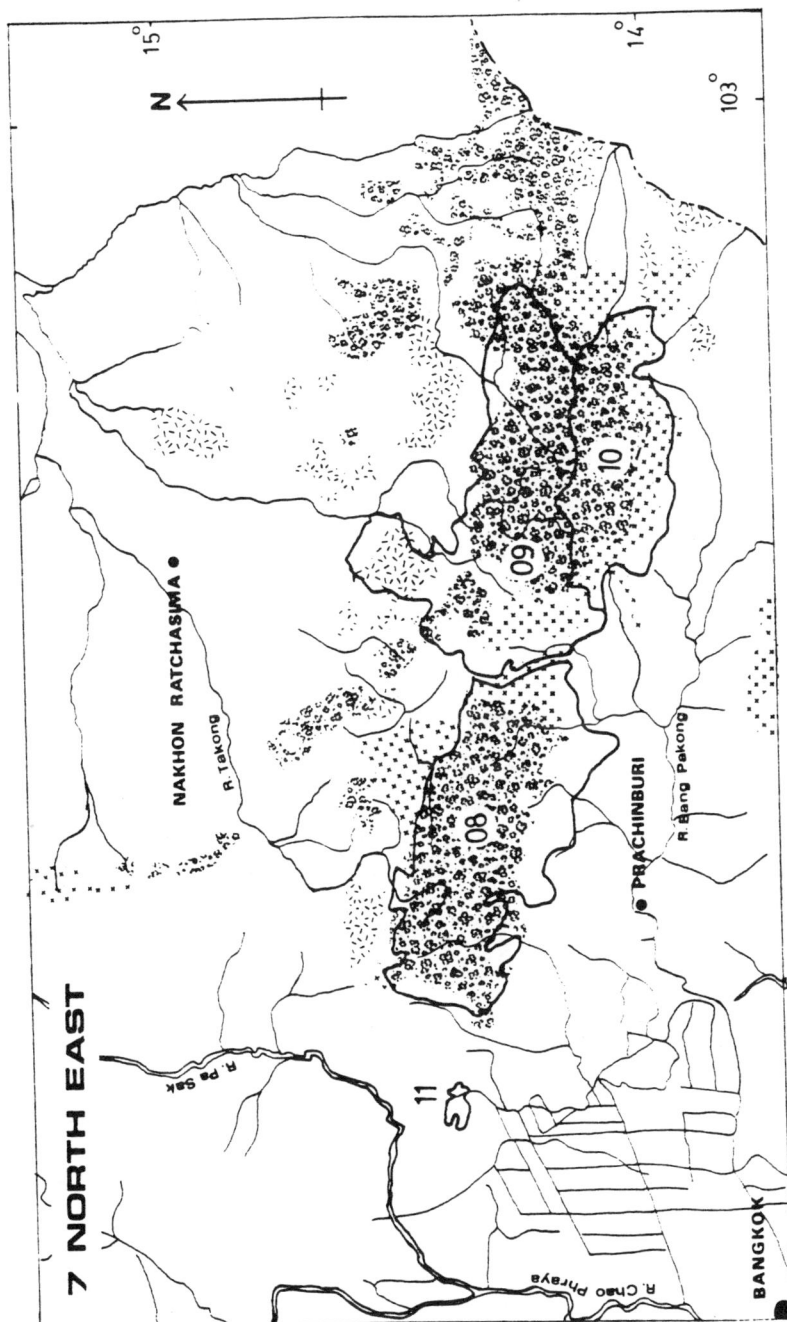

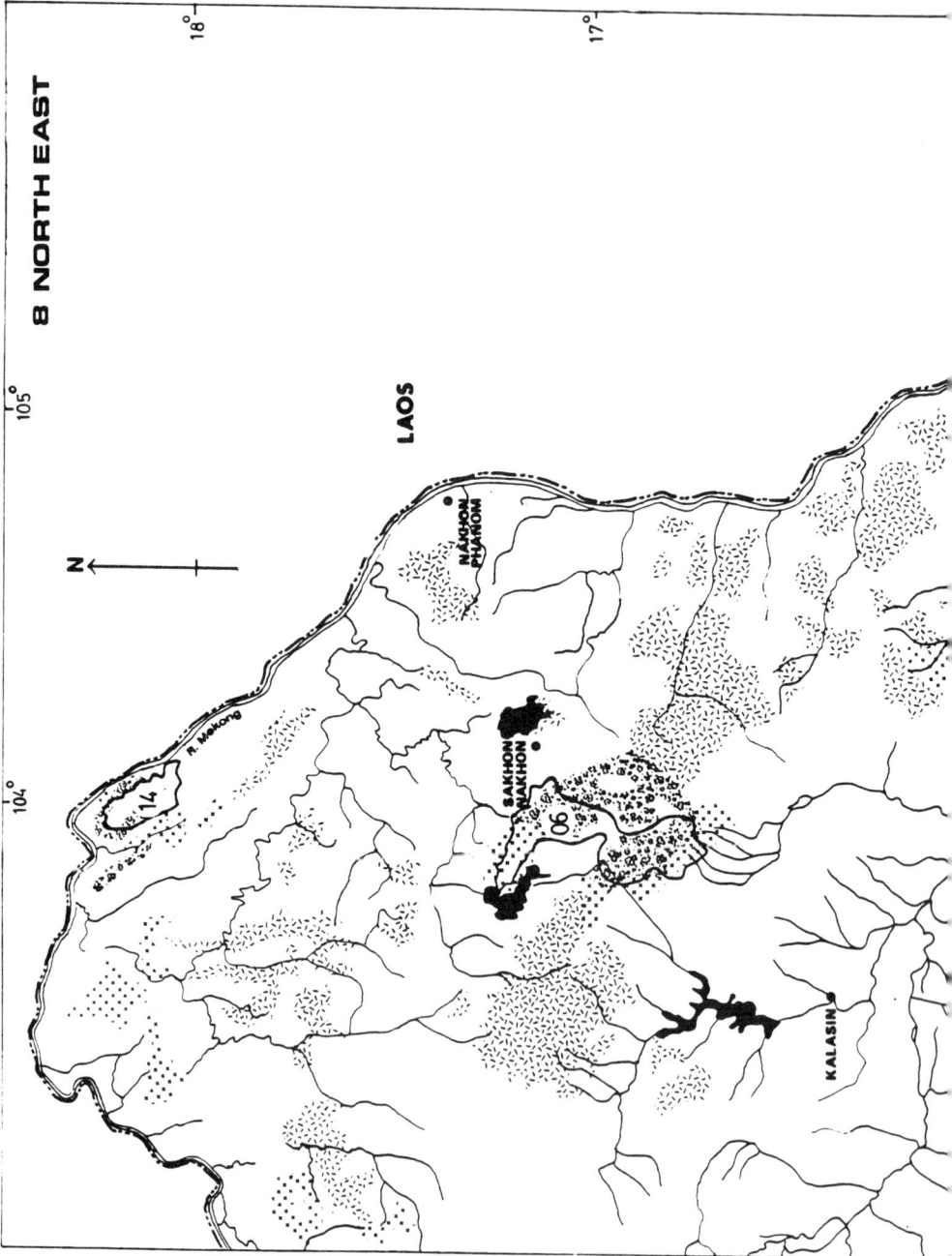

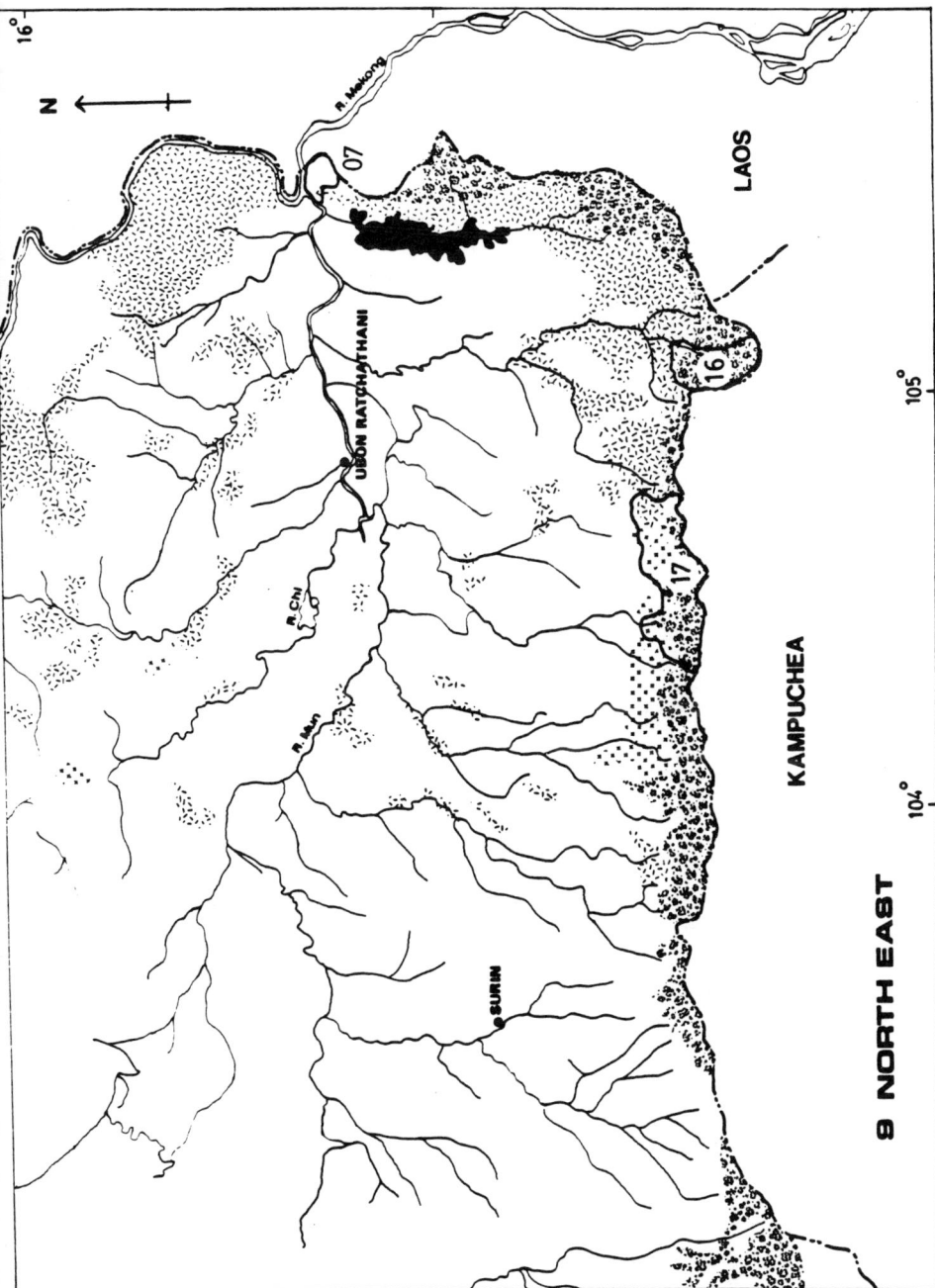

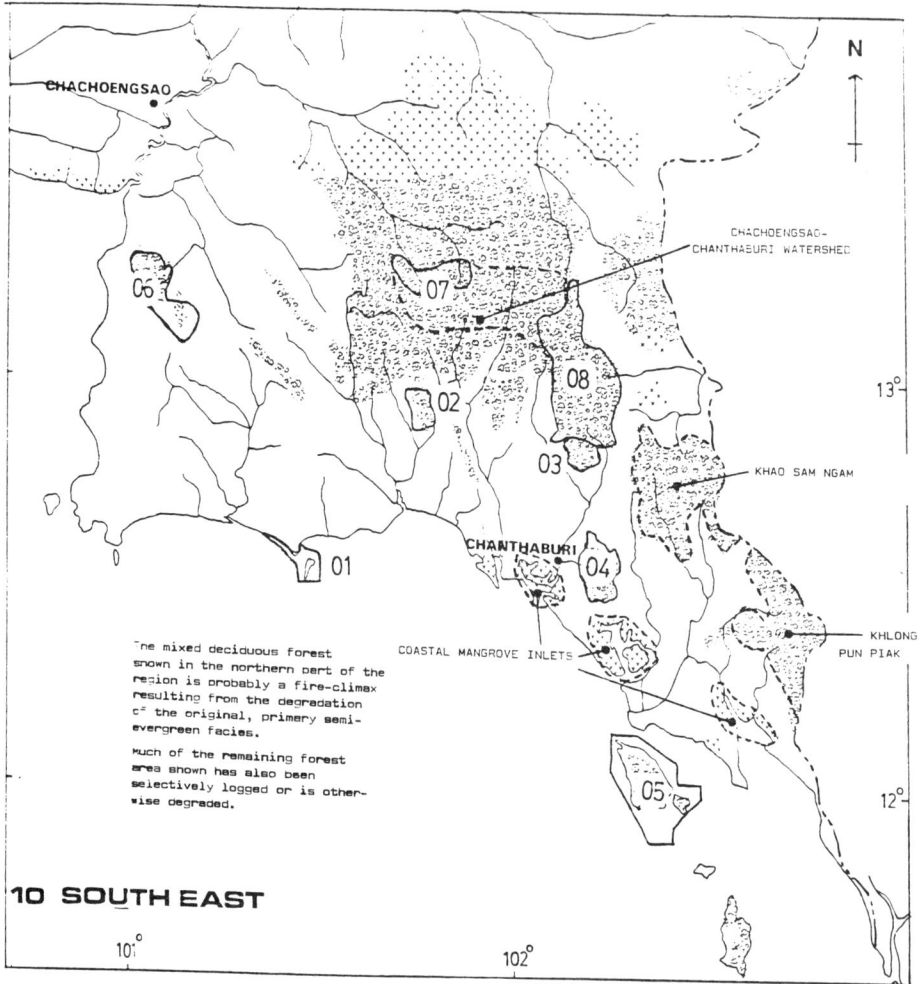

N

CHACHOENGSAO

CHACHOENGSAO–
CHANTHABURI WATERSHED

06

07

02

08

03

13°

KHAO SAM NGAM

CHANTHABURI

01

04

KHLONG
PUN PIAK

The mixed deciduous forest
shown in the northern part of the
region is probably a fire-climax
resulting from the degradation
of the original, primary semi-
evergreen facies.

Much of the remaining forest
area shown has also been
selectively logged or is otherwise degraded.

COASTAL MANGROVE INLETS

05

12°

10 SOUTH EAST

101°   102°

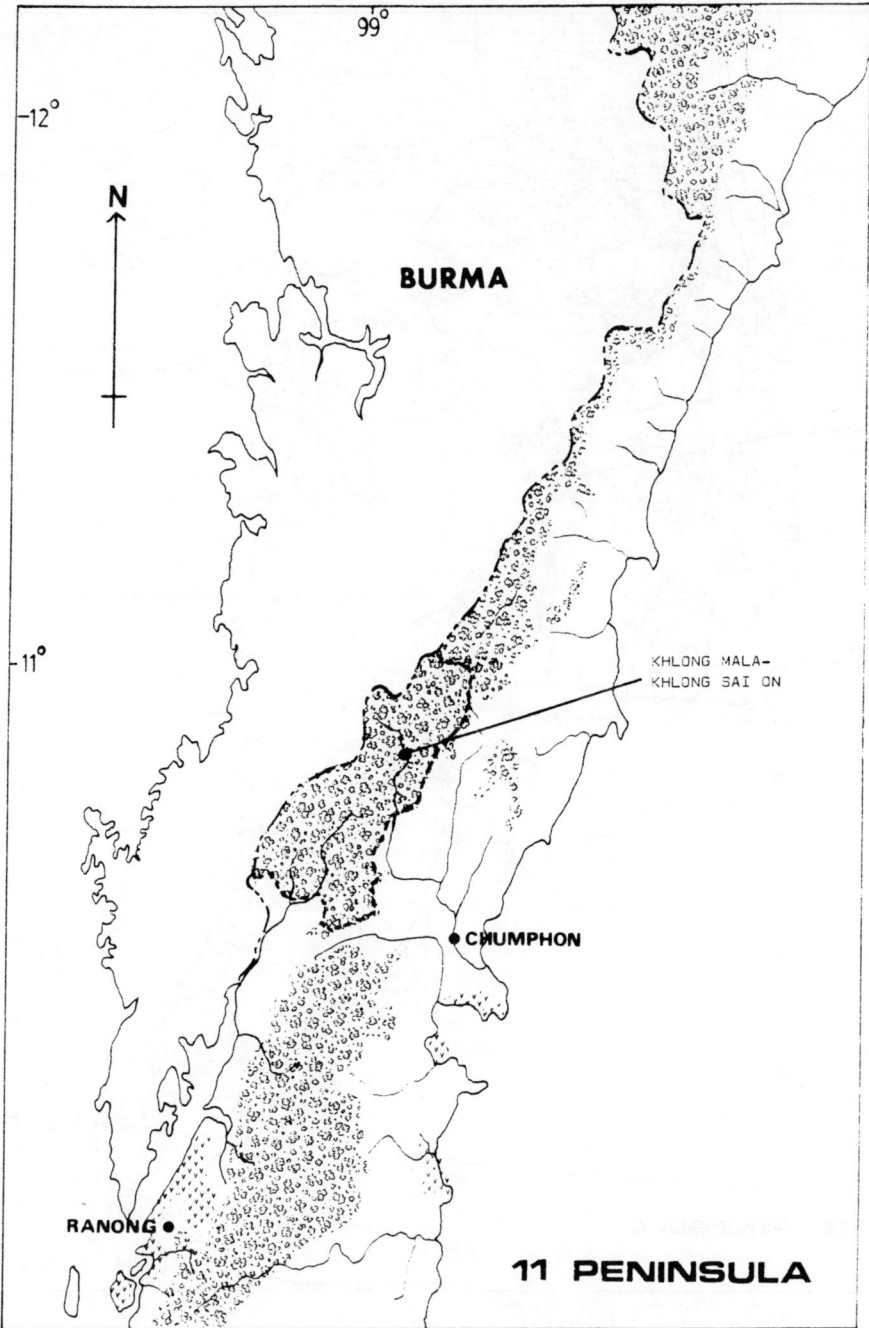

11 PENINSULA

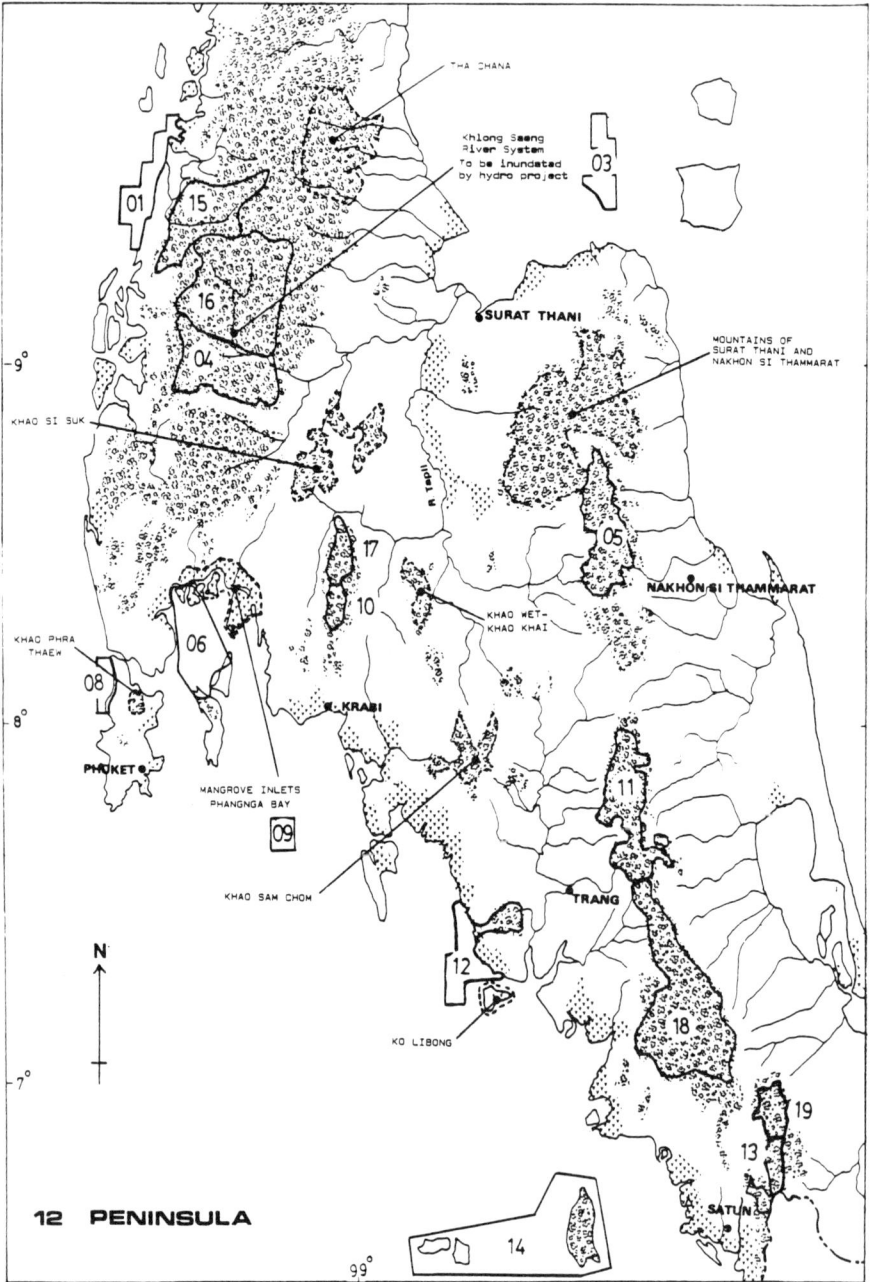

12 PENINSULA

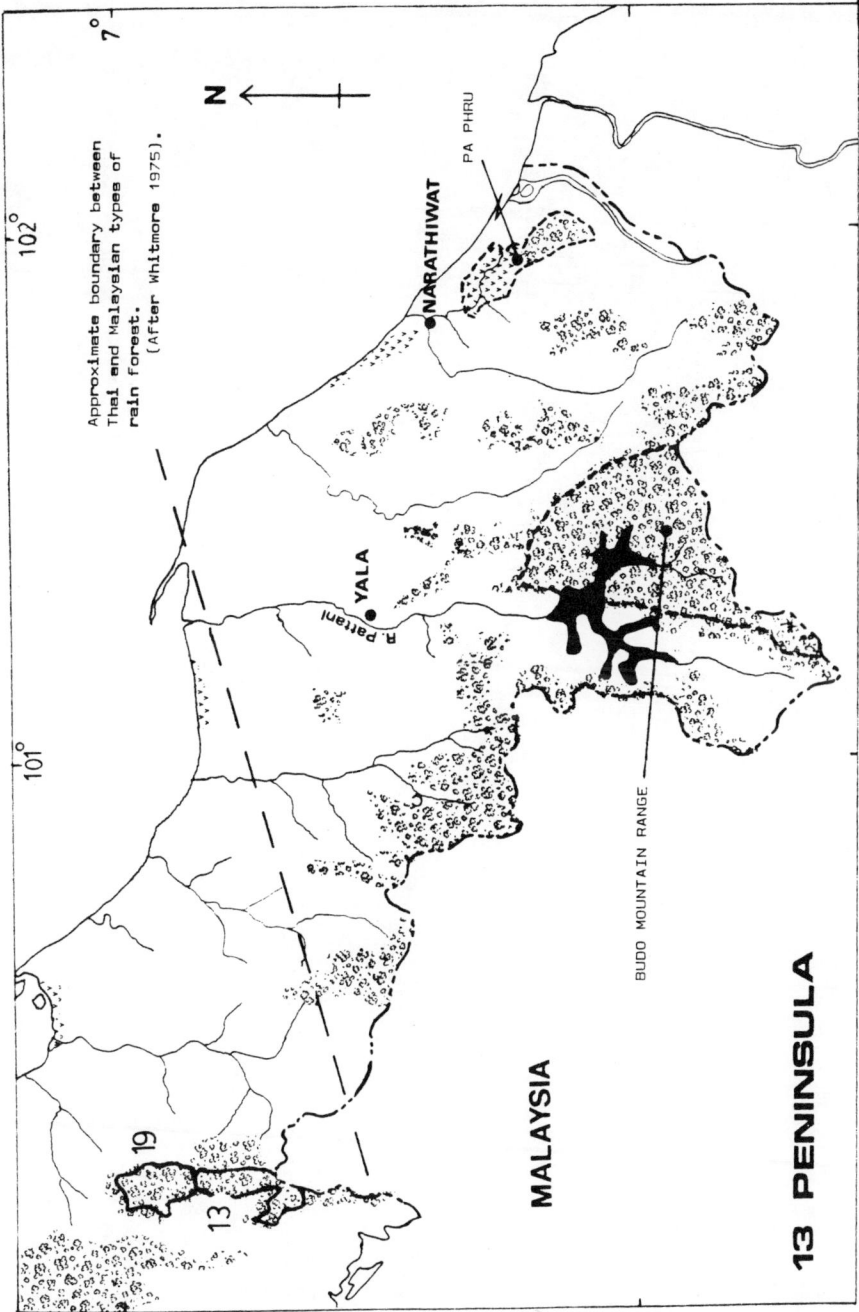

N ←——+——

Approximate boundary between
Thai and Malaysian types of
rain forest.
(After Whitmore 1975).

7°

102°

101°

PA PHRU

NARATHIWAT

R. Pattani

YALA

BUDO MOUNTAIN RANGE

MALAYSIA

19

13

13 PENINSULA